cmbook is warm.

You've been told that if you laugh, the world laughs with you. That laughter is the best medicine. If you're one of the lucky, funny few, you are a barrel of laughs. But when it comes to describing the laughter that will always stay with you, you're at a loss for words. The talented photographers in this collection have captured that emotion. Each chuckle. Every belly laugh. Explore these images and we're sure that you'll find something to laugh about. Something that clicks.

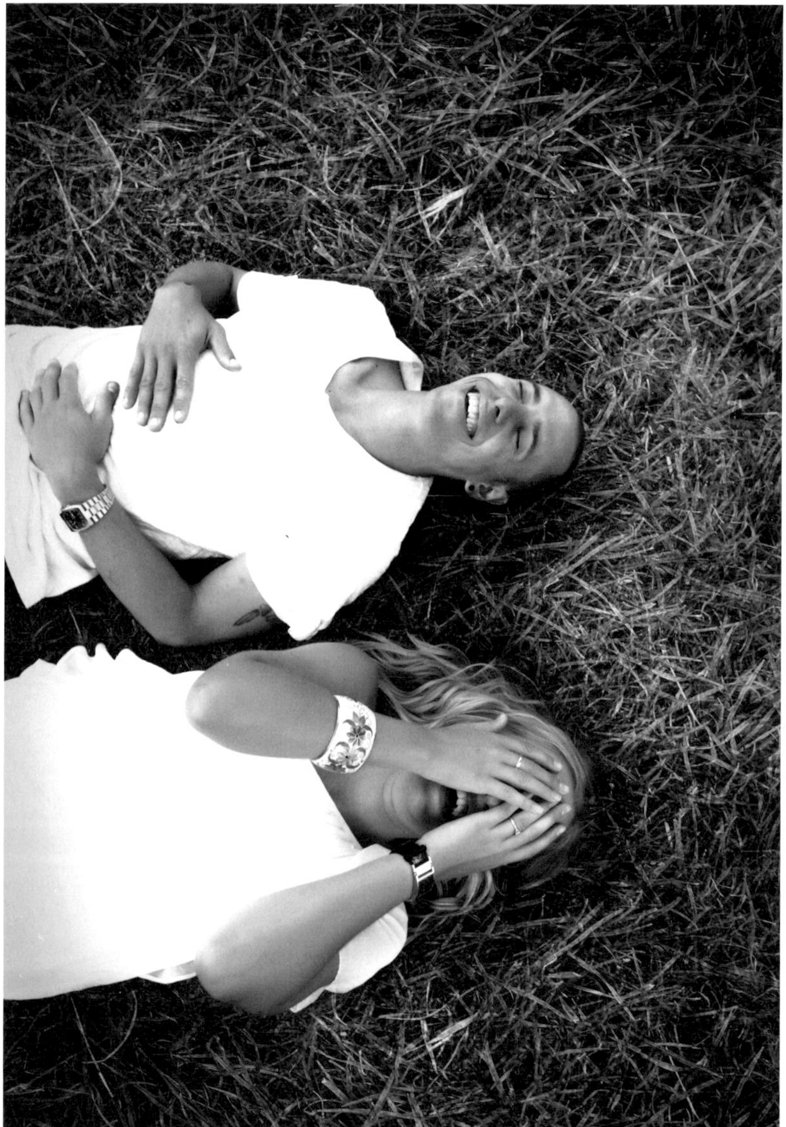

Deborah Arnold Butterfly Moments Photography

Perth Australia

butterflymomentsphotographyblog.com

Katie Baldi Photography

San Francisco, CA

katiebaldiphotography.com

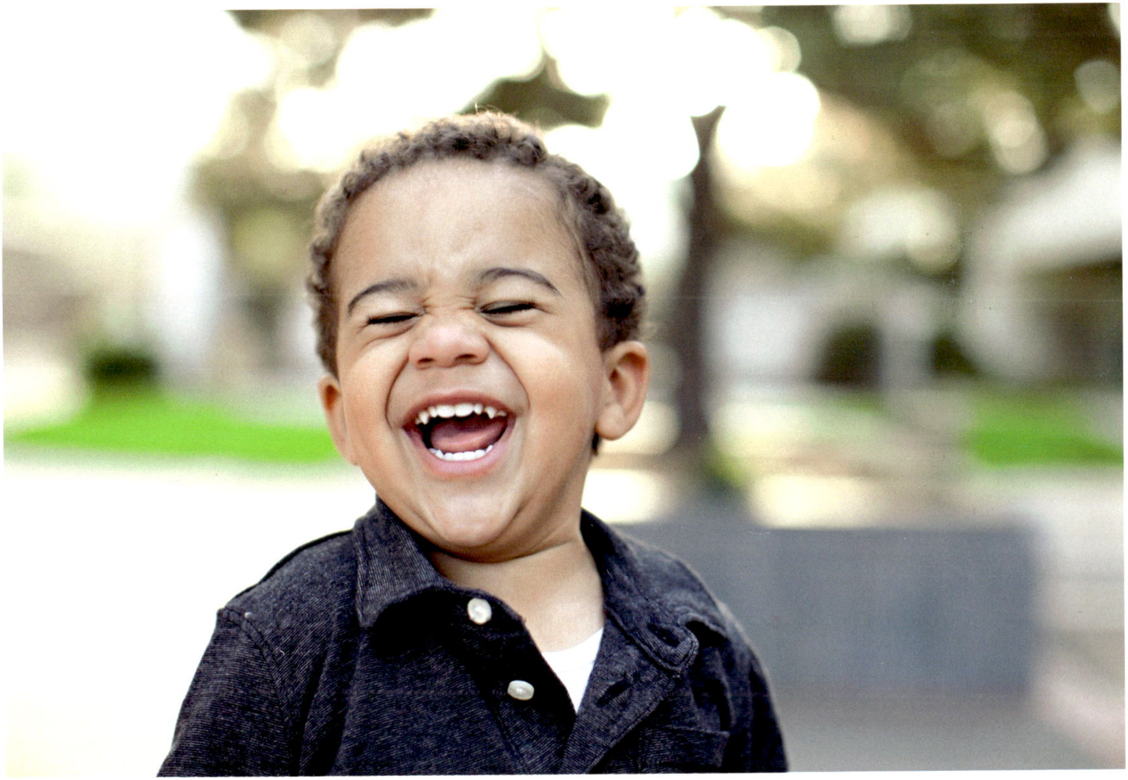

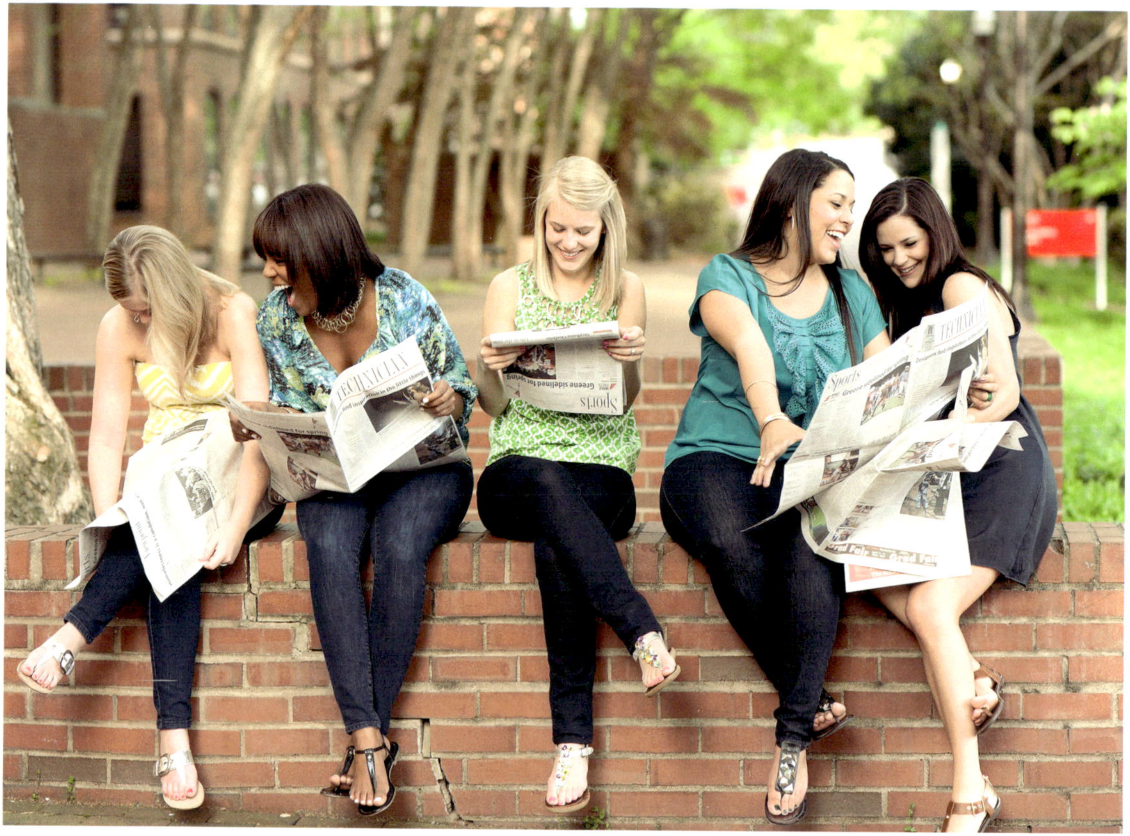

Amy Ames

Holly Springs, NC

amyamesphotography.com

Krystal Barr - KB Imagery

Ventura County, CA

kbimagery.com

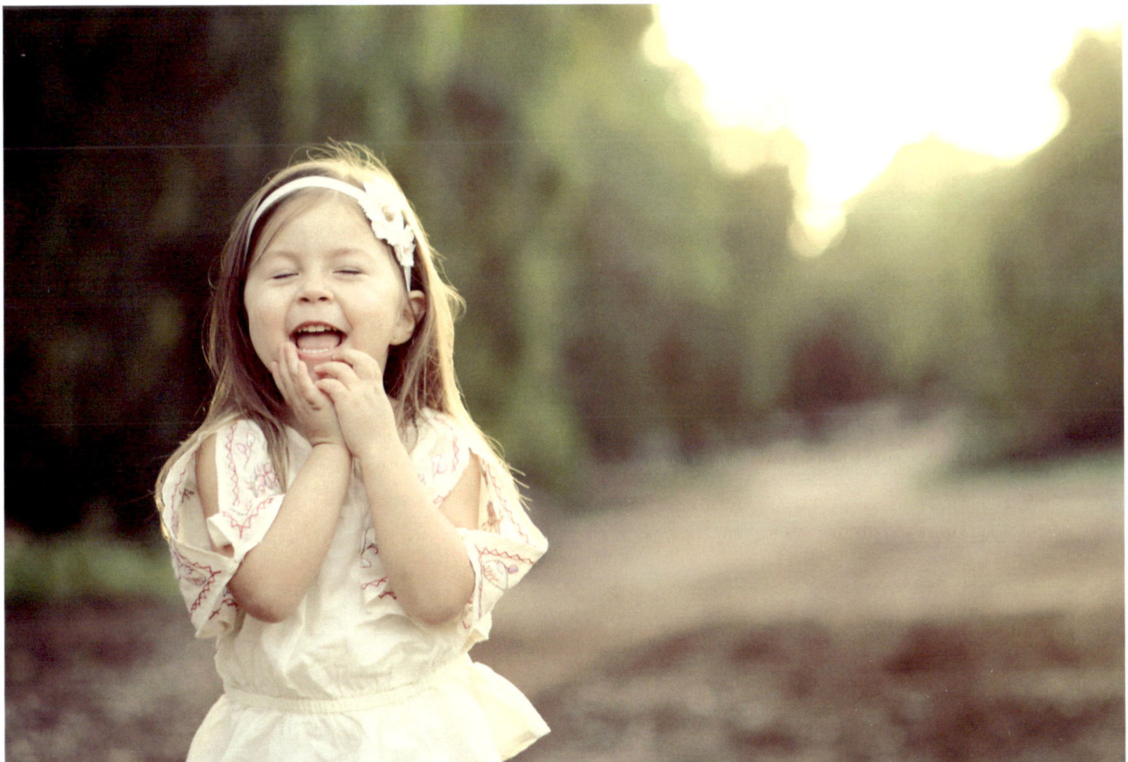

Kristin Rachelle Photography

San Diego, CA

kristinrachellephotography.com

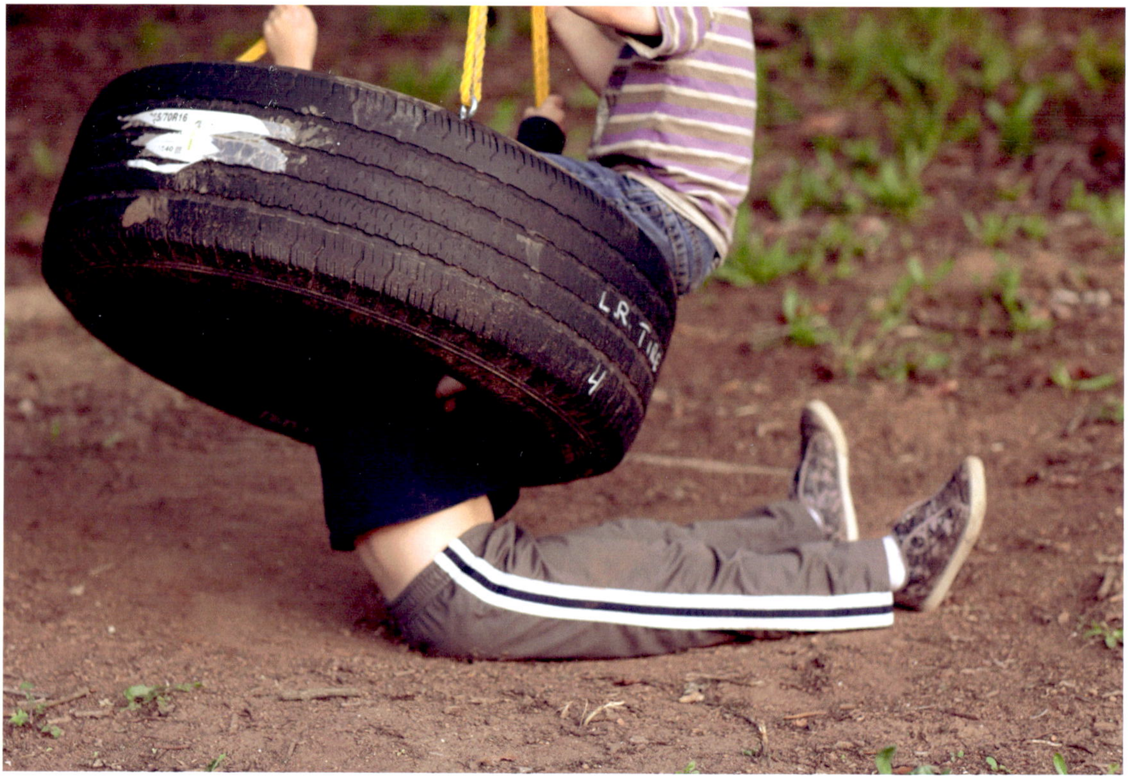

Carrie Novak Photography

Northern MI

carrienovakphotography.com

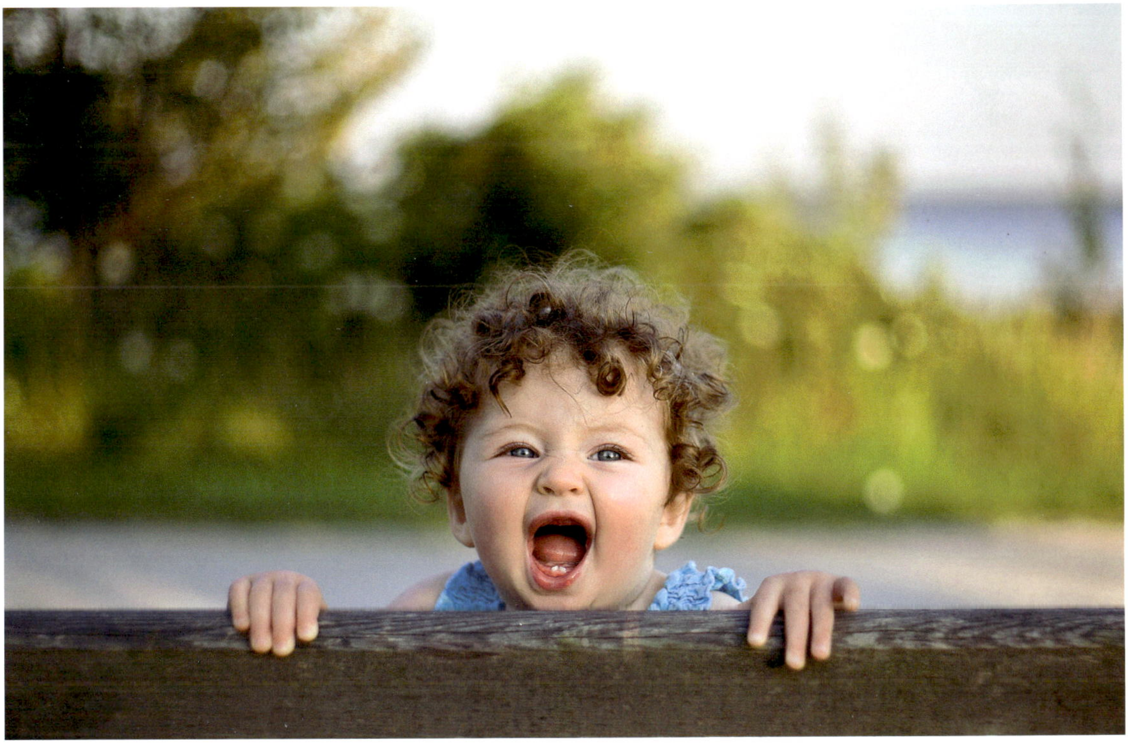

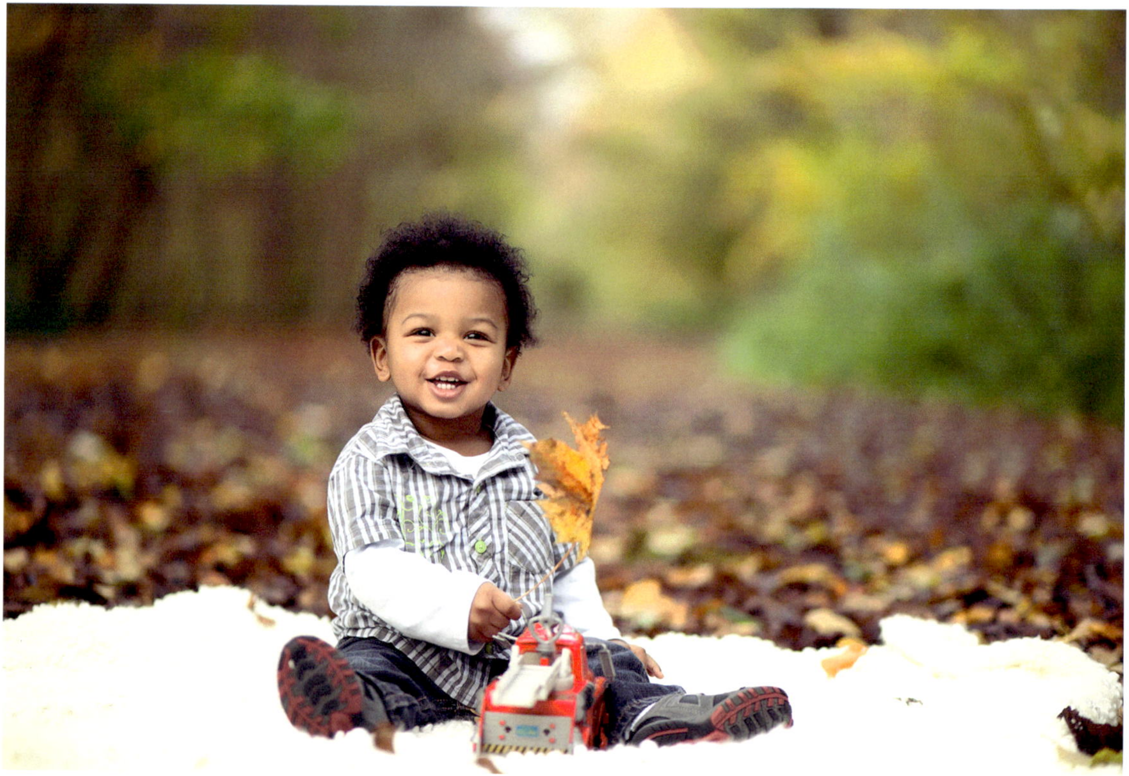

Sarah Cambio Photography

Cambridge, England

sarahcambio.com

Jodi Arego

Houston, TX

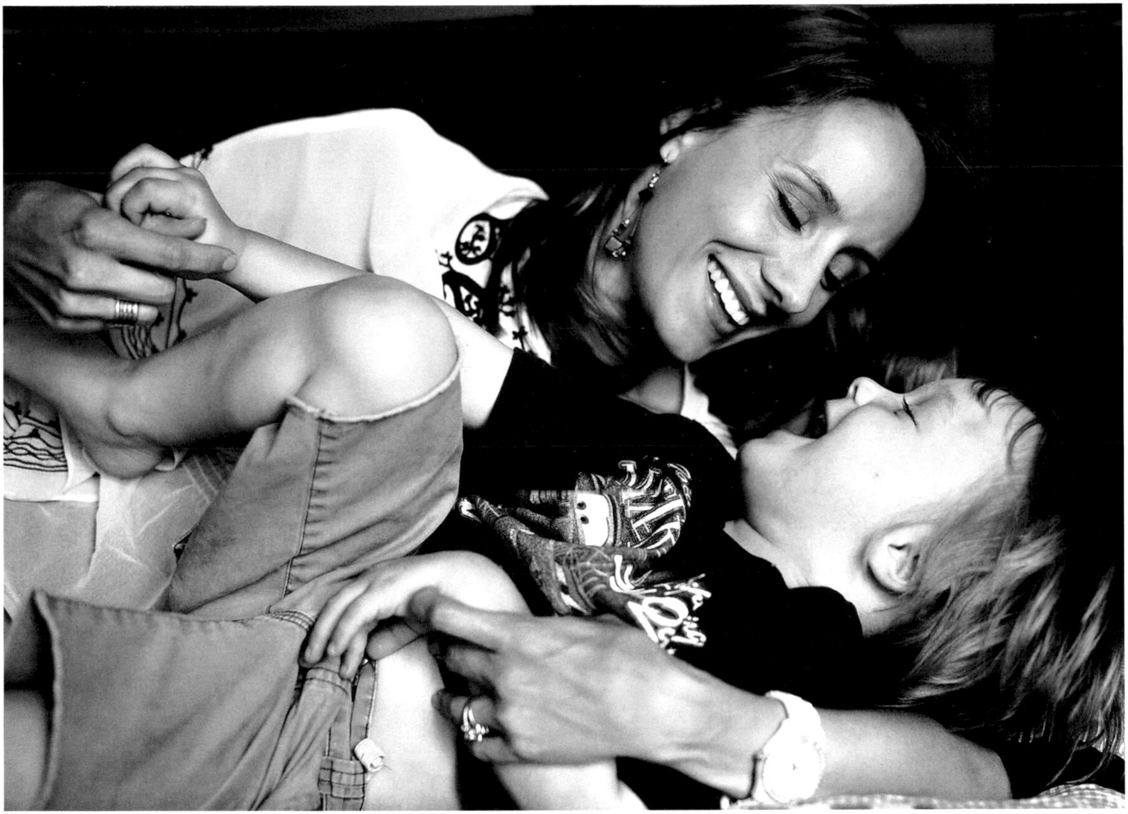

Krista Campbell Photography

Phoenix, AZ

kristacampbellphotography.com

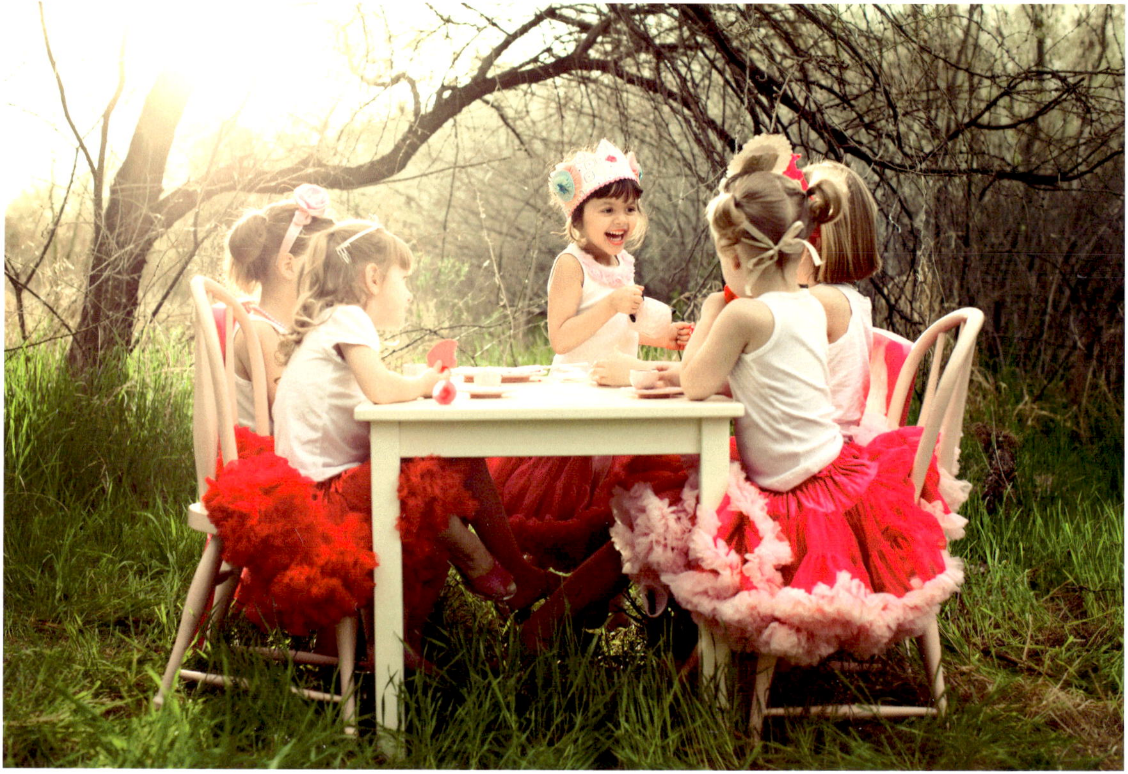

Krystal Barr - KB Imagery

Ventura County, CA

kbimagery.com

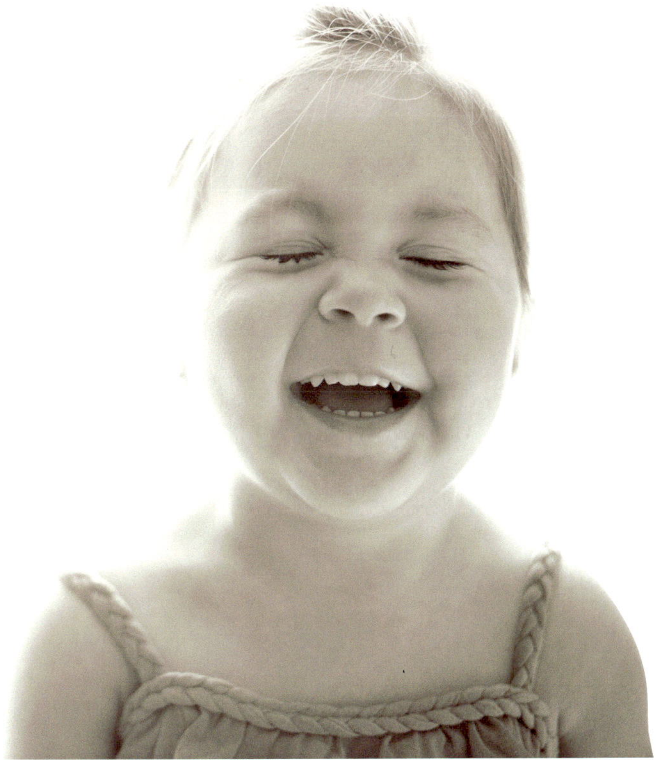

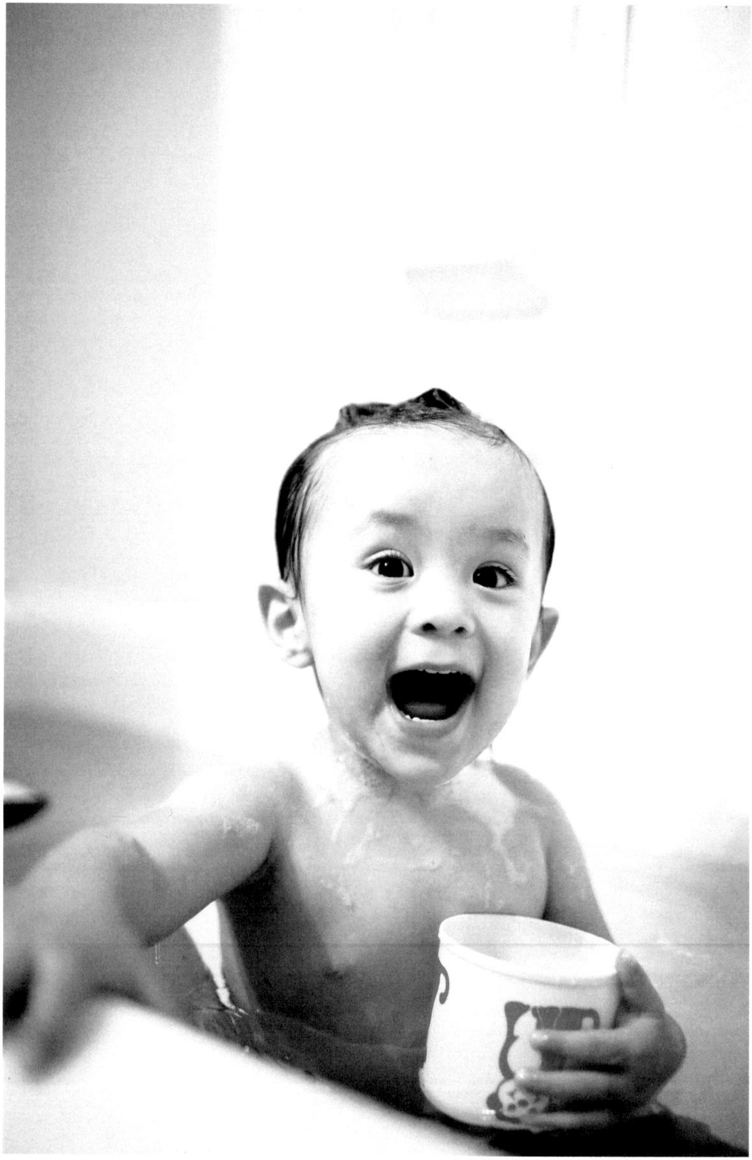

Casey Yu Photography

Tallahassee, FL

caseyyuphotography.com

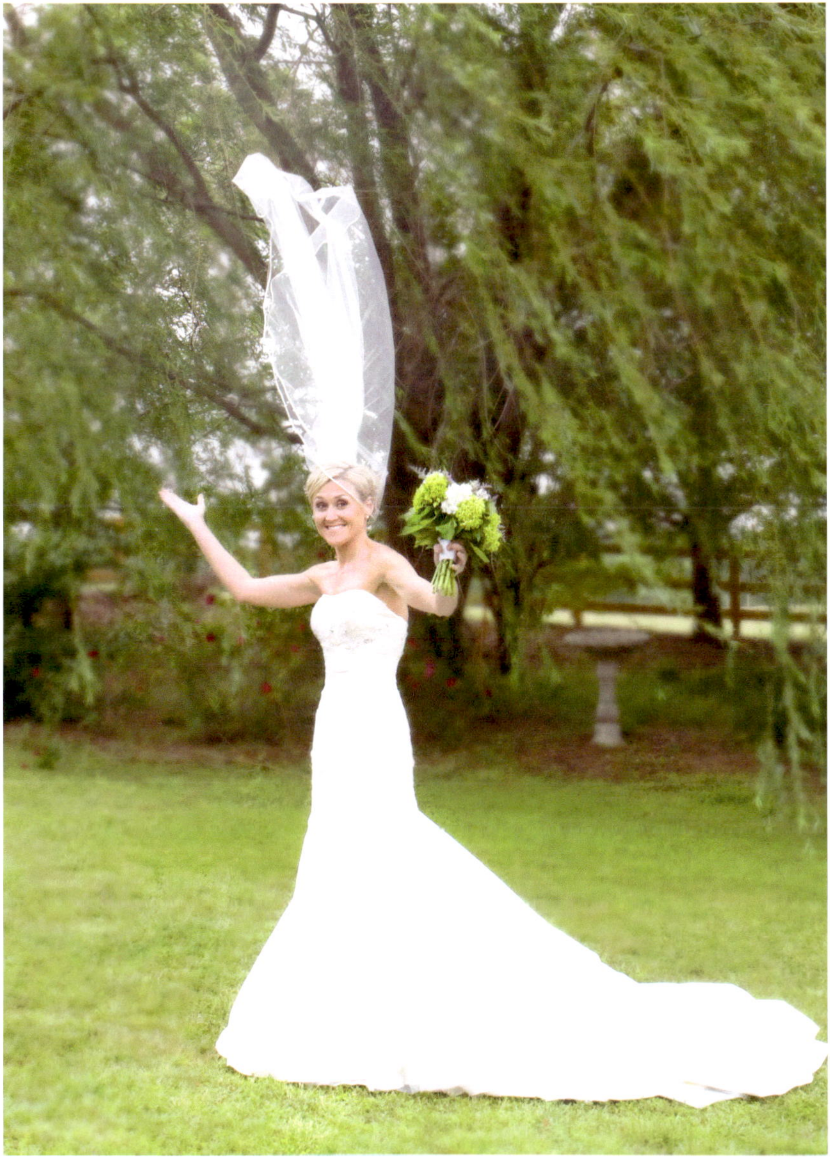

Jeannette Anthos Photography

Loganville, GA

artopiadream.com

Jessica Hamlin Photography

Seattle, WA

jessicahamlinphotography.com

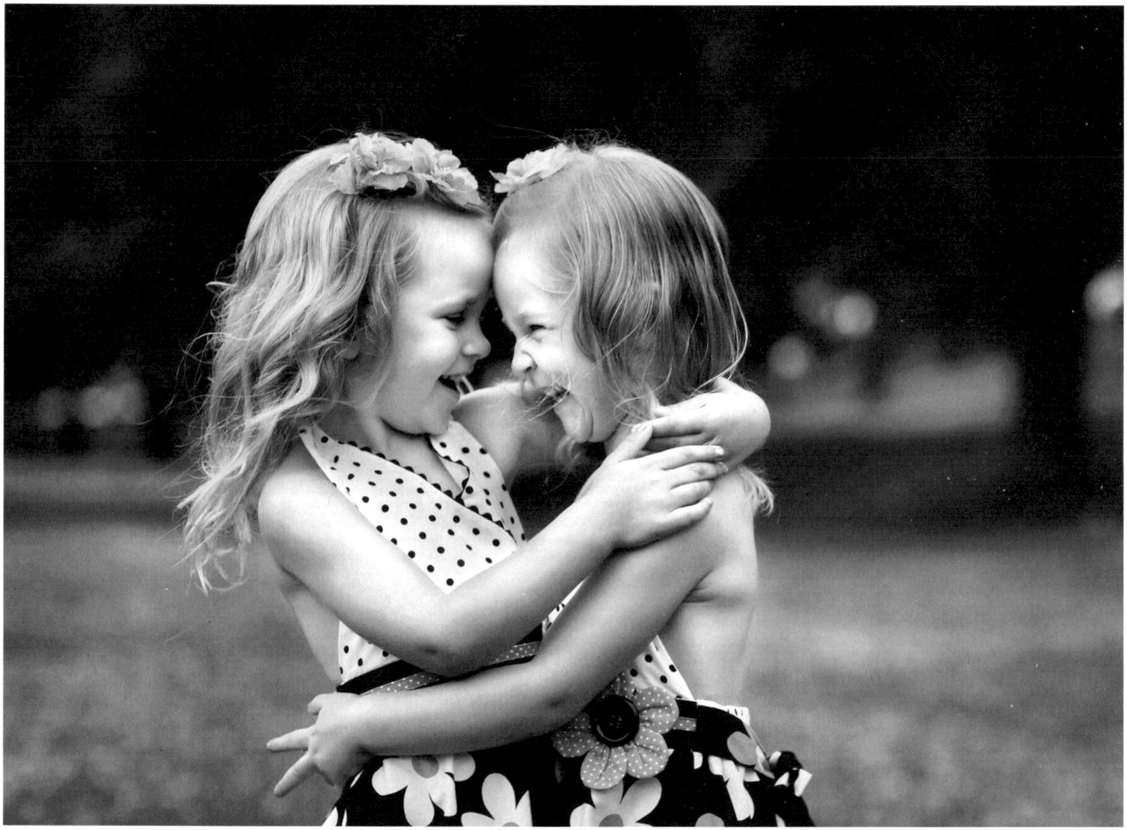

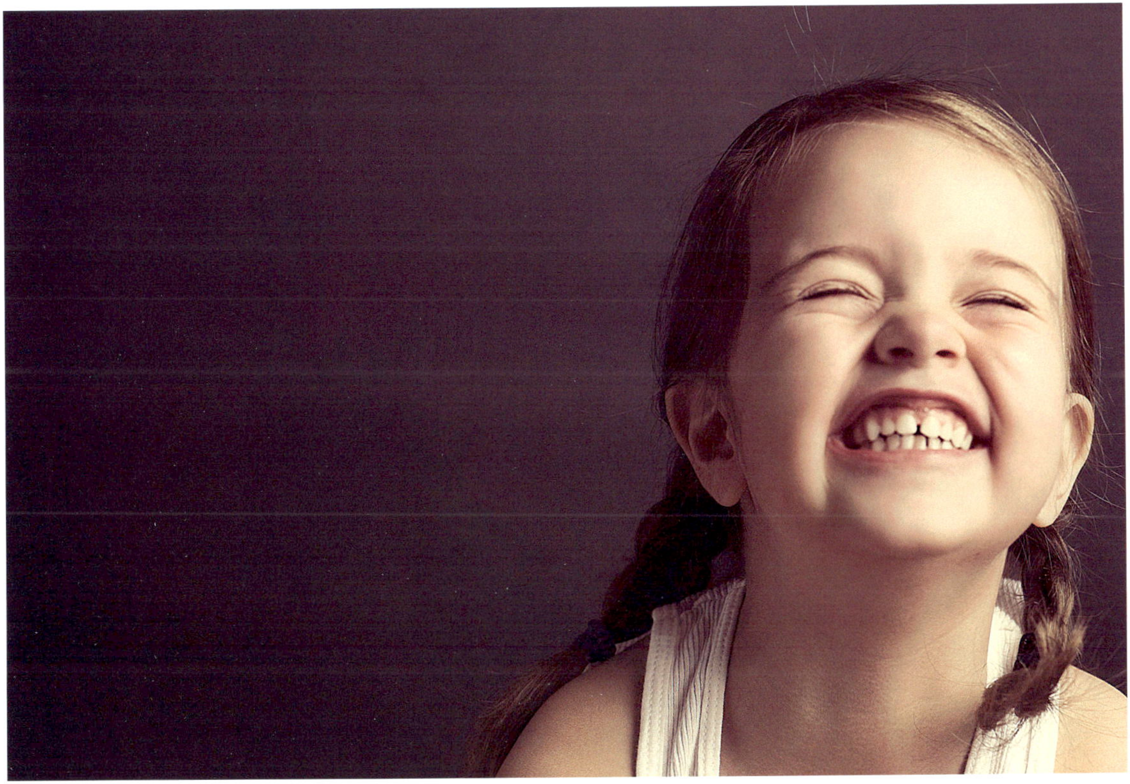

Lora Swinson

Denver, CO

lleephotography.com

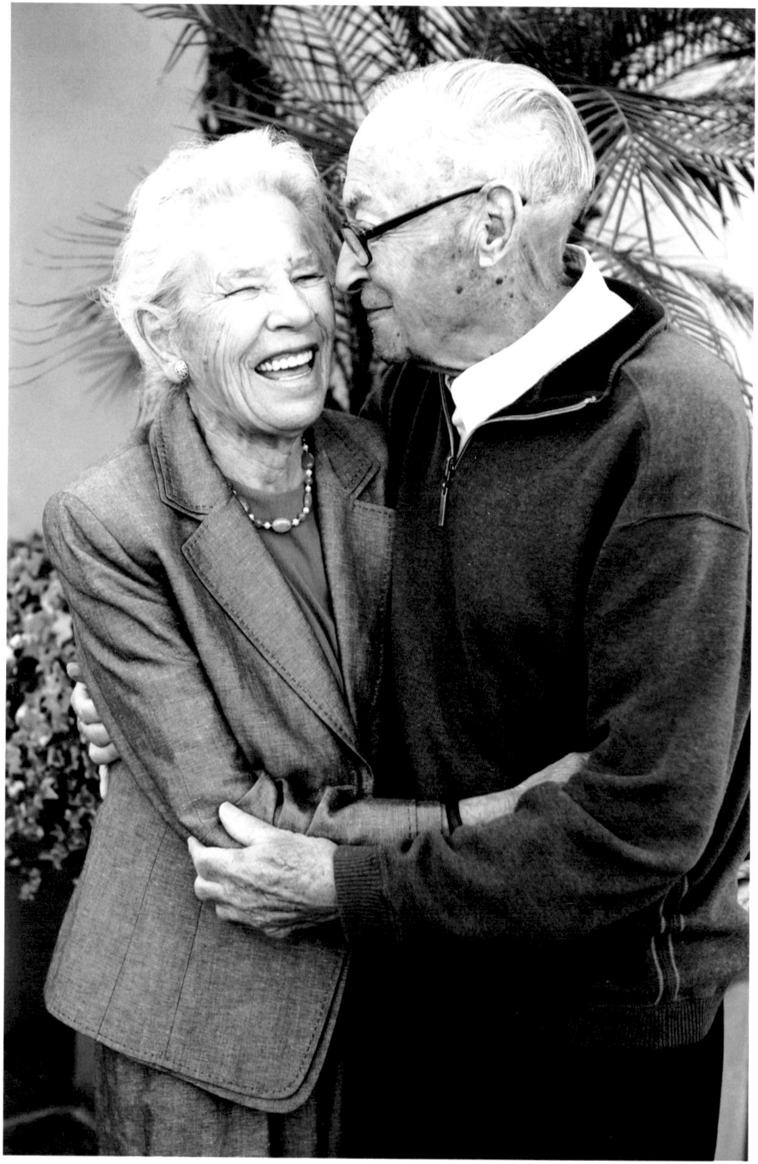

Kristen Bons Photography

San Diego, CA

kristenbons.com

Heather Starr Photography

San Diego, CA

heatherstarrphotography.com

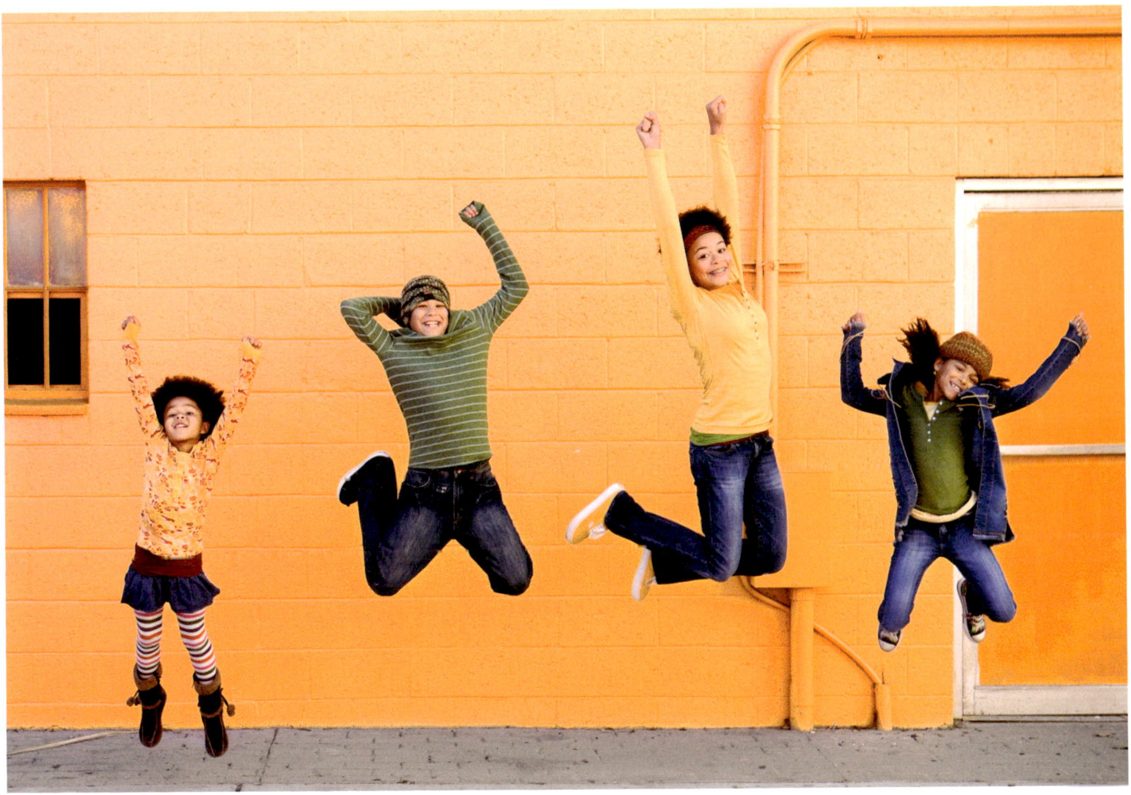

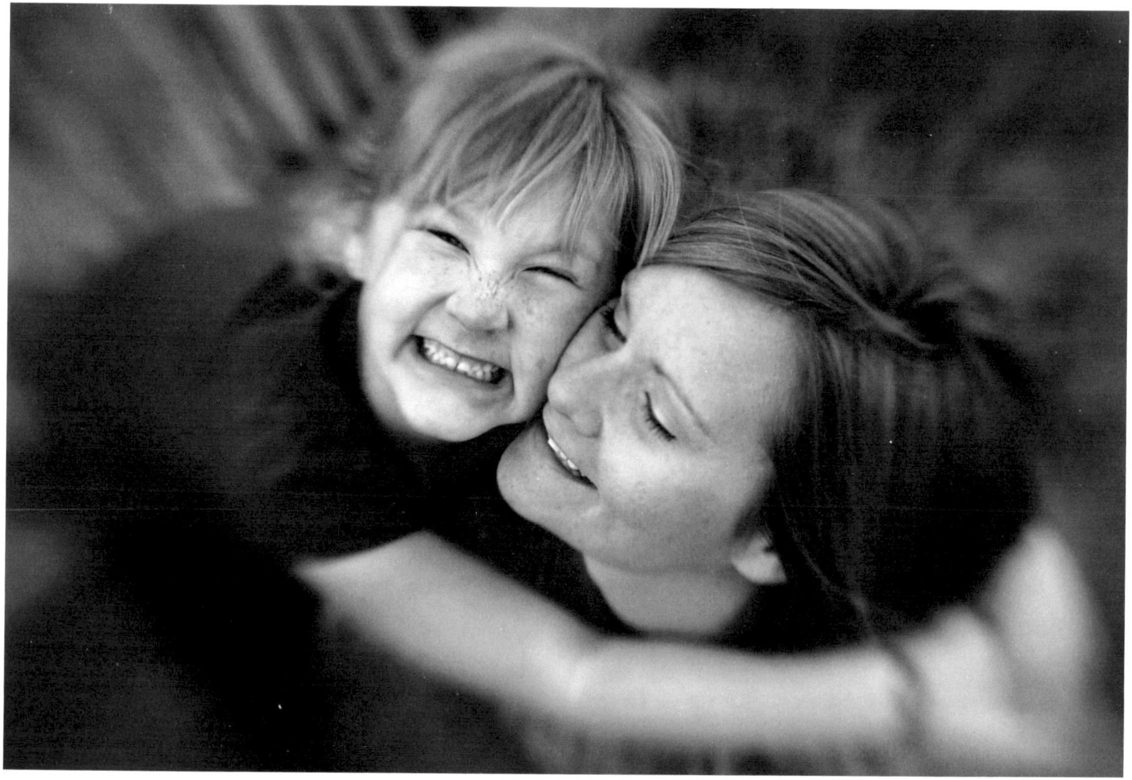

Stacey Bruce Photography

Springfield, MO

staceybruce.com

Meg Bitton Photography

Tenafly, NJ

megbitton.com

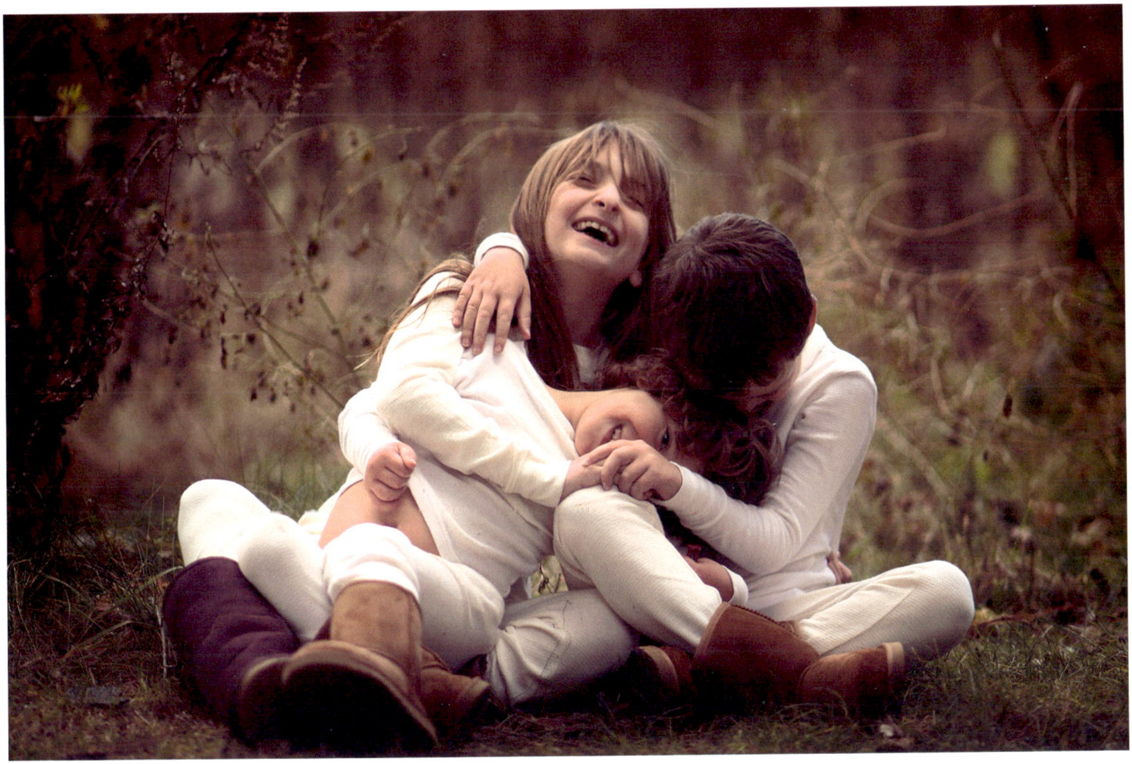

Sarah Cambio Photography

Cambridge, England

sarahcambio.com

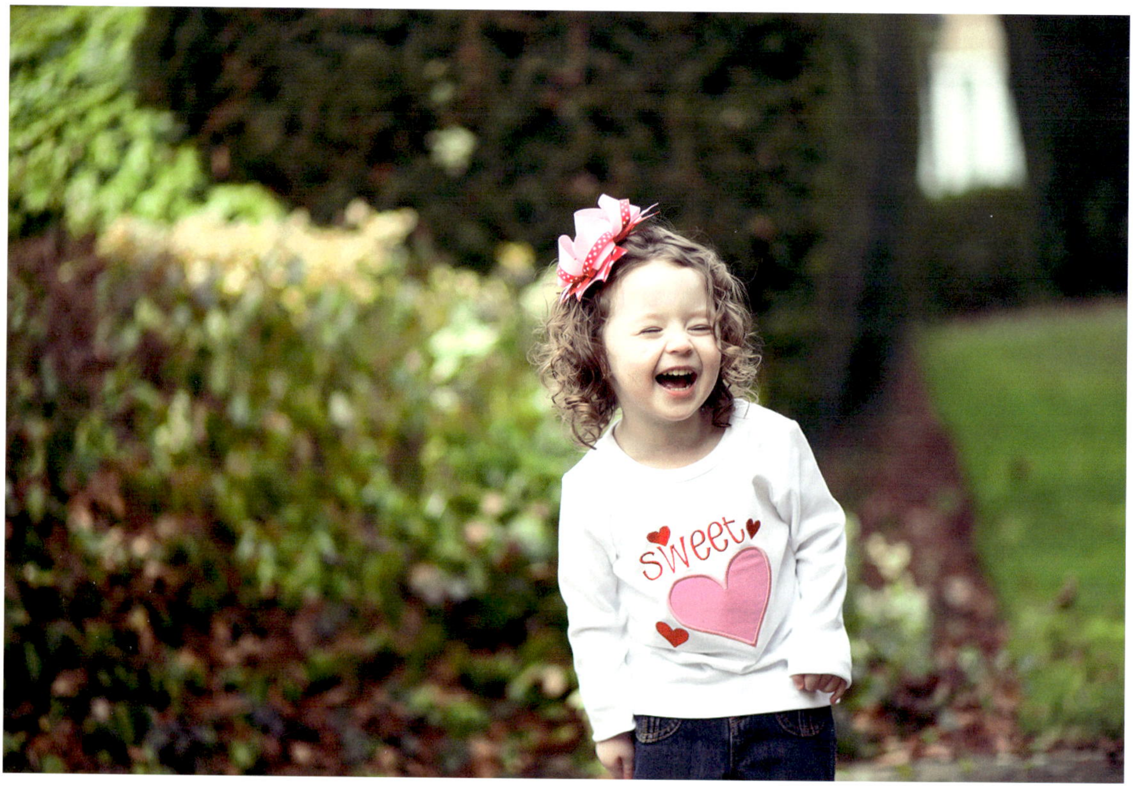

Emily Dawes Photography

Grand Forks, ND

emilydawesphotography.com

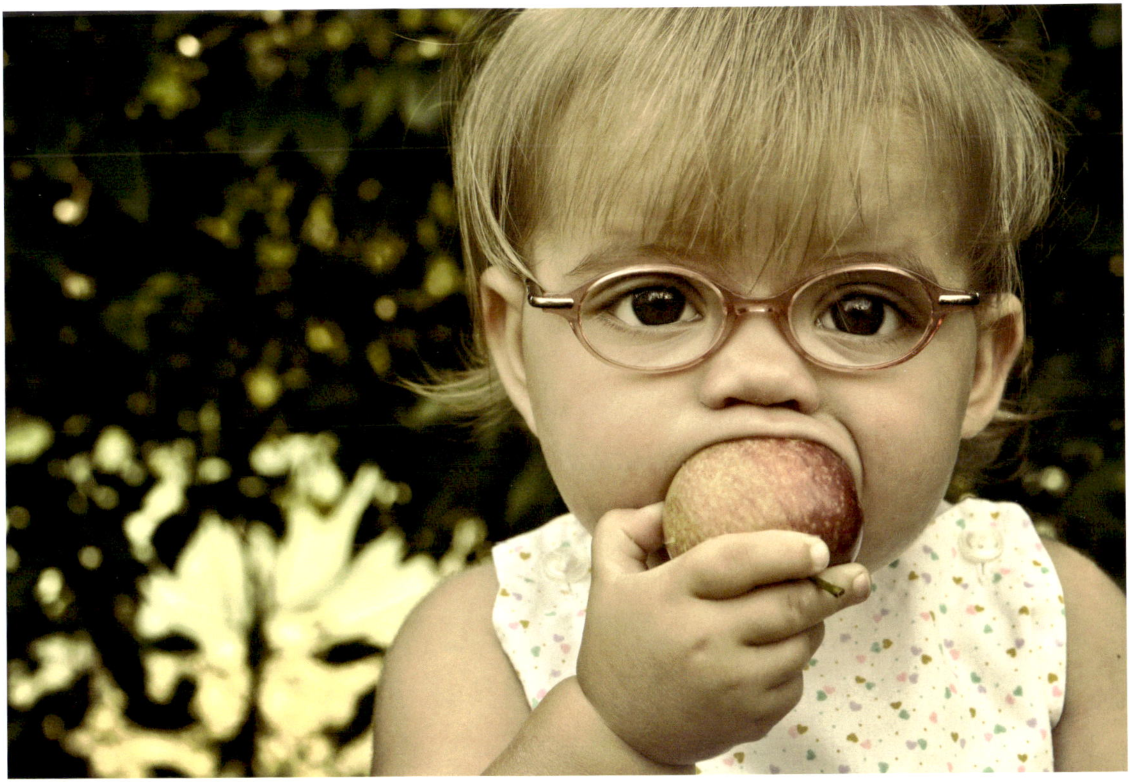

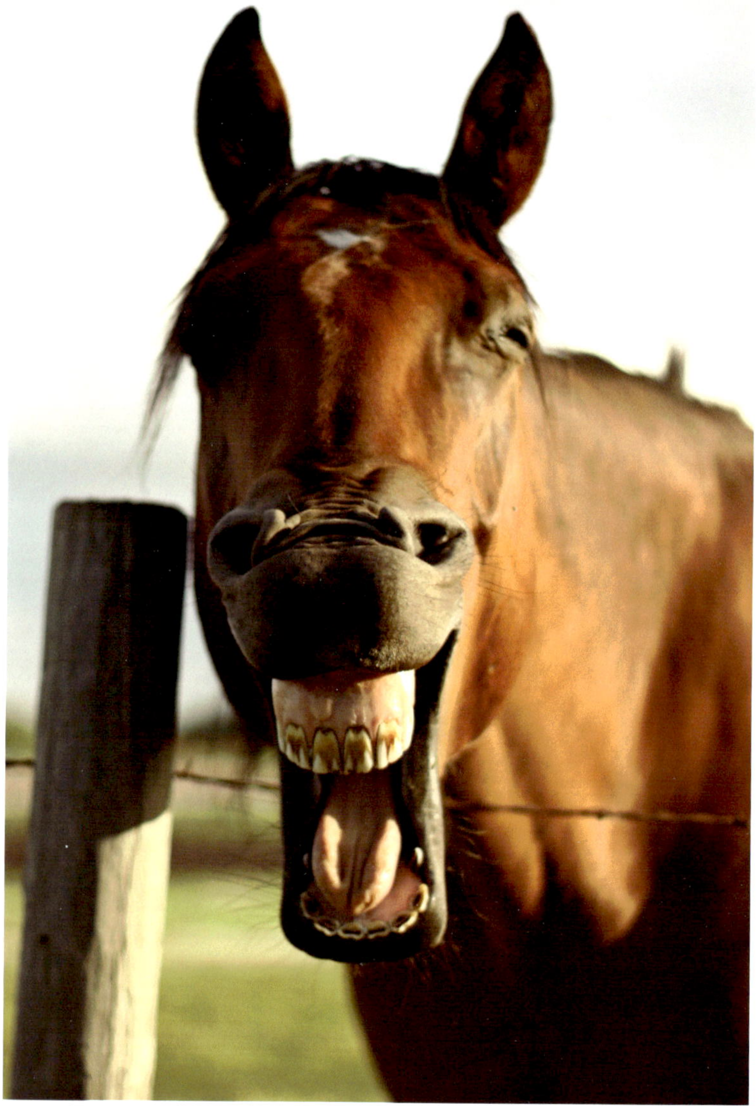

Photography by Jana Dee

Walhalla, ND

Erin Farrell Photography

Smyrna, DE

erinfarrellphotography.com

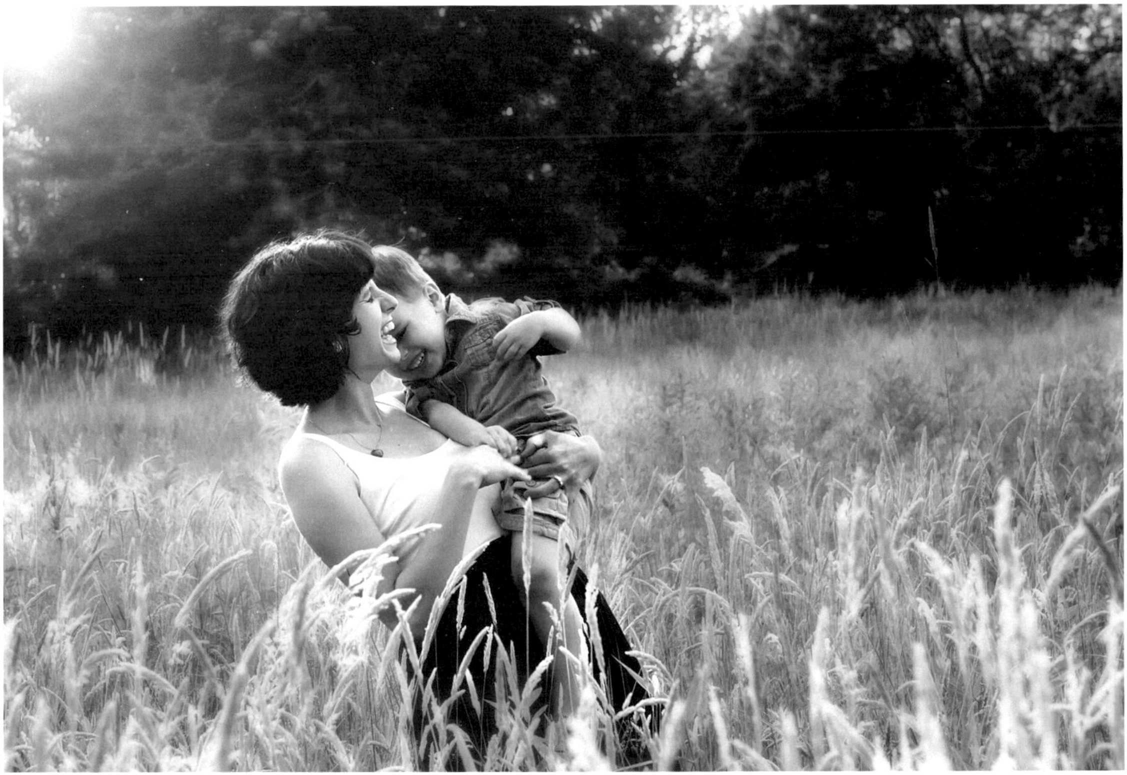

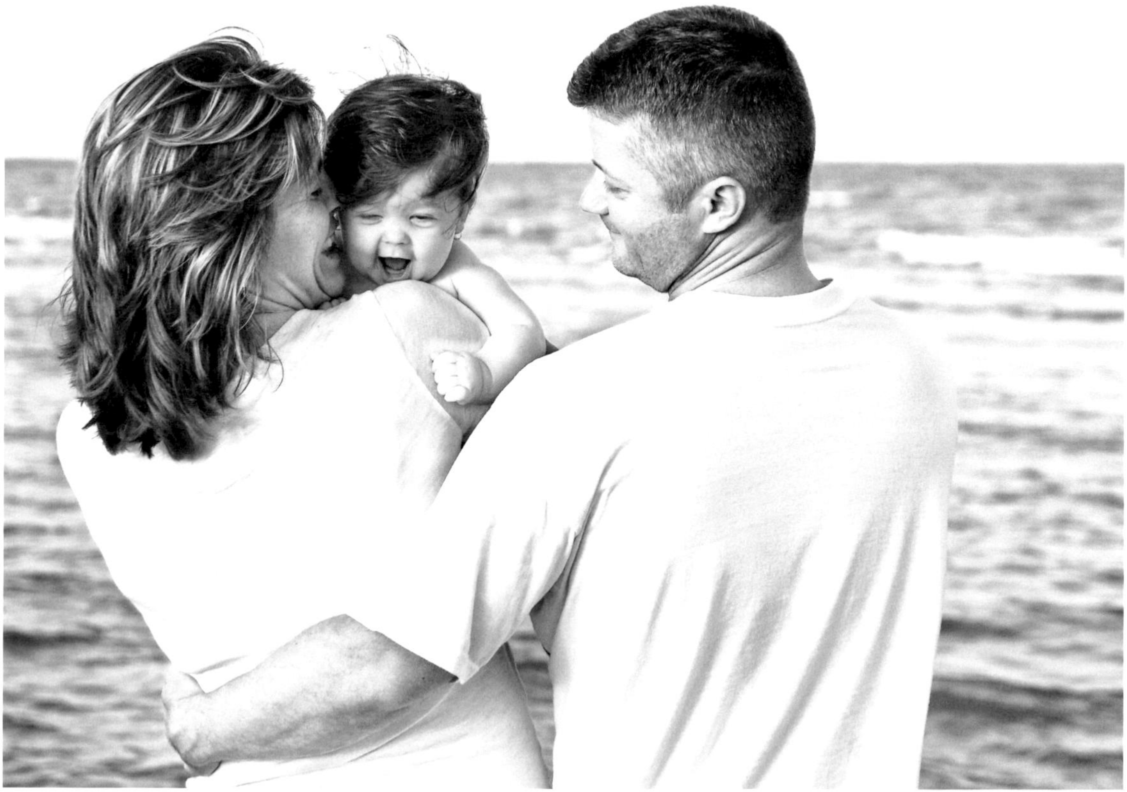

Life Imprints by Kim

Kendalia, TX

lifeimprintsbykim.com

Nicki Cermak - Nicki C Photography

Minneapolis, MN

nickicphotography.com

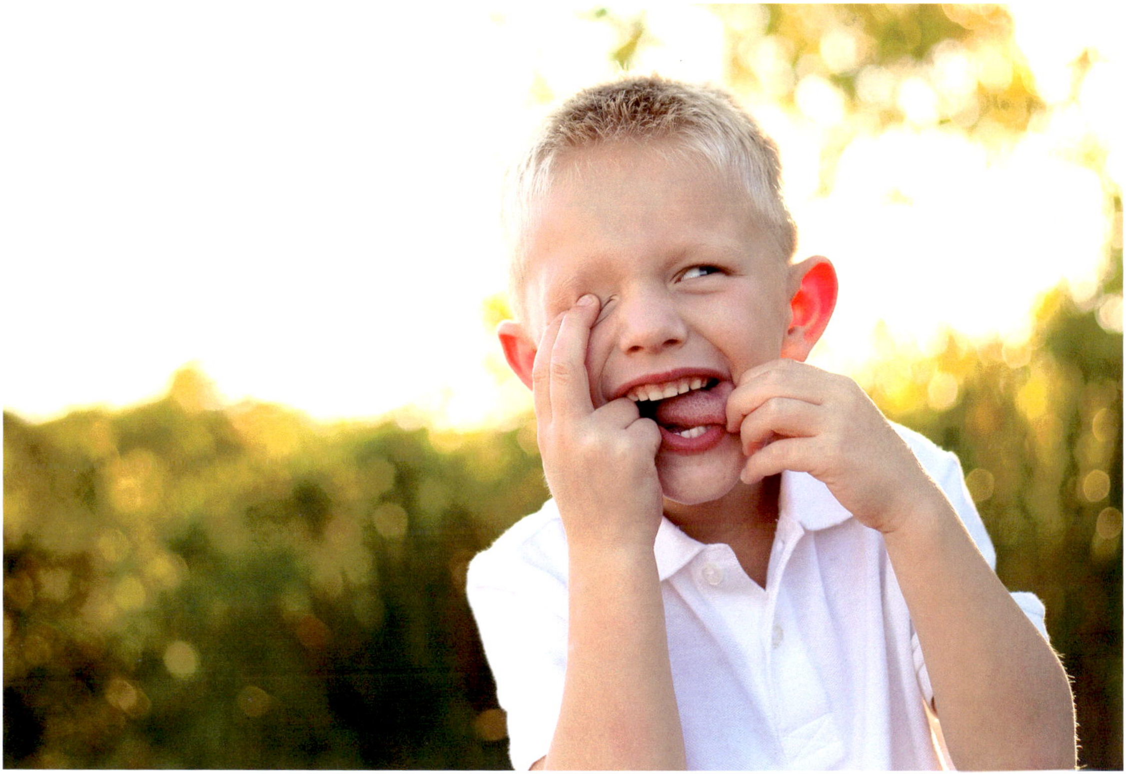

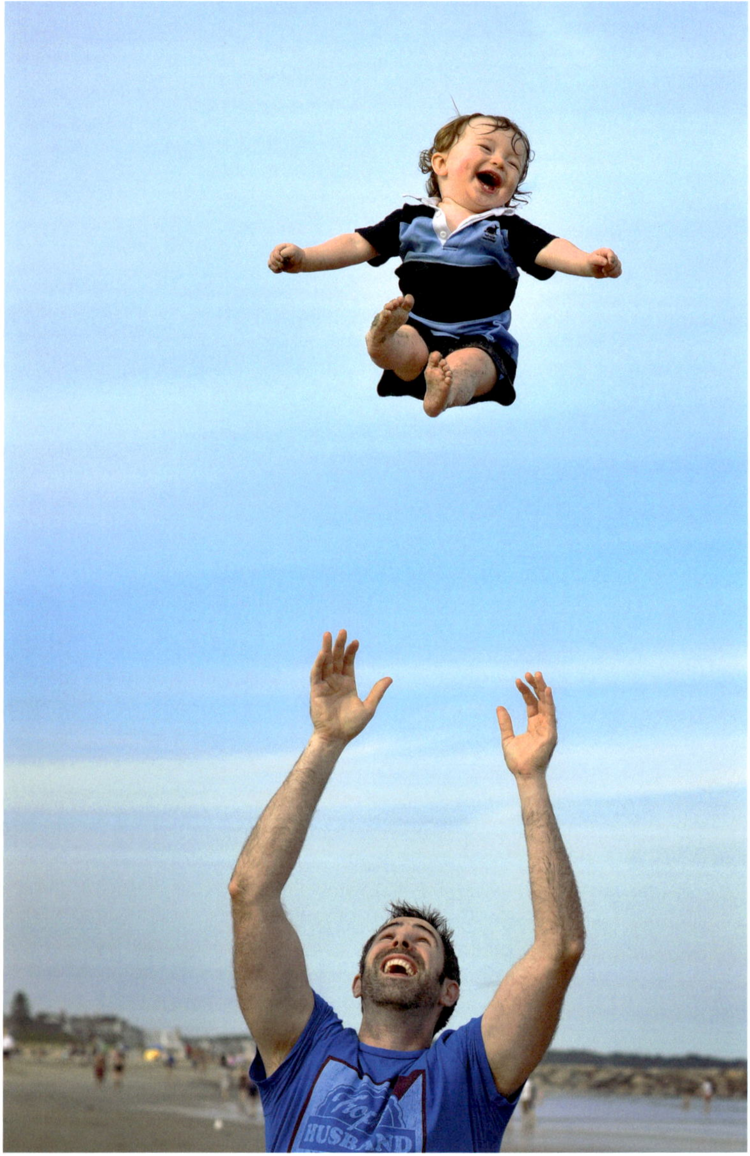

Kami Friday Photography

Nashua, NH

kamifridayphotography.com

Stacey Brown

Zachary, LA

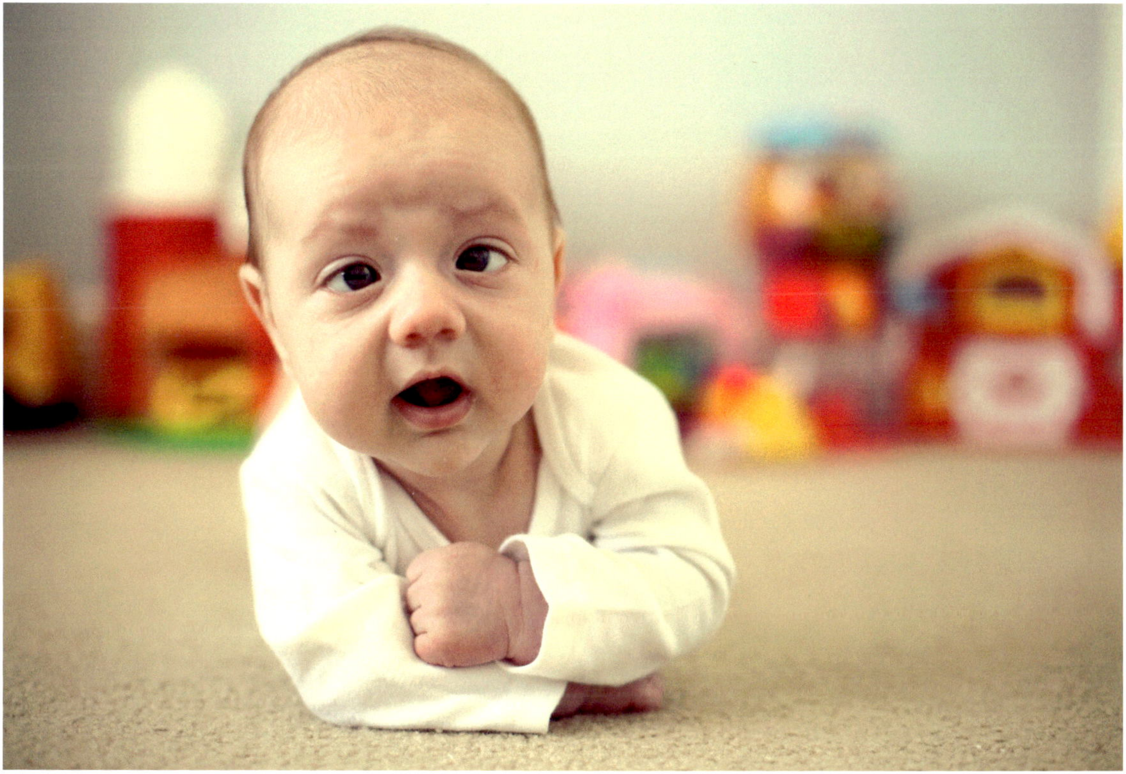

Megan Cieloha

Lincoln, CA

megancieloha.com

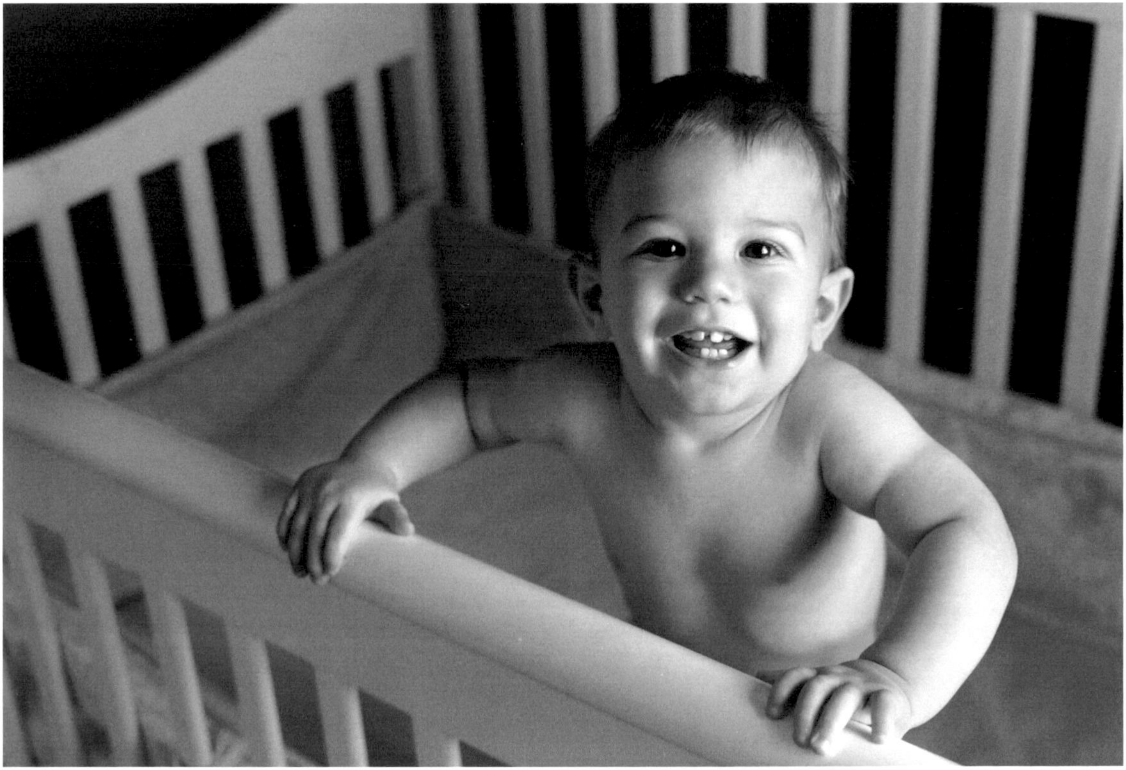

Kristi Clark Photography

Katy, TX

kristiclarkphotography.com

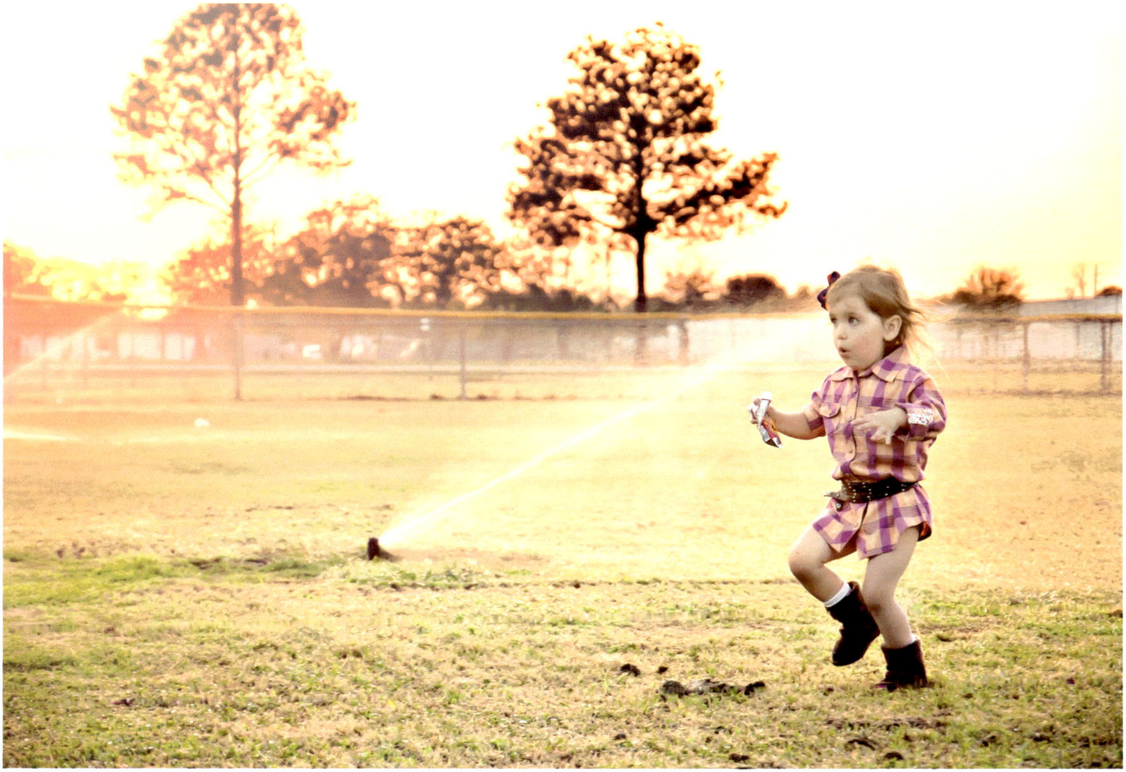

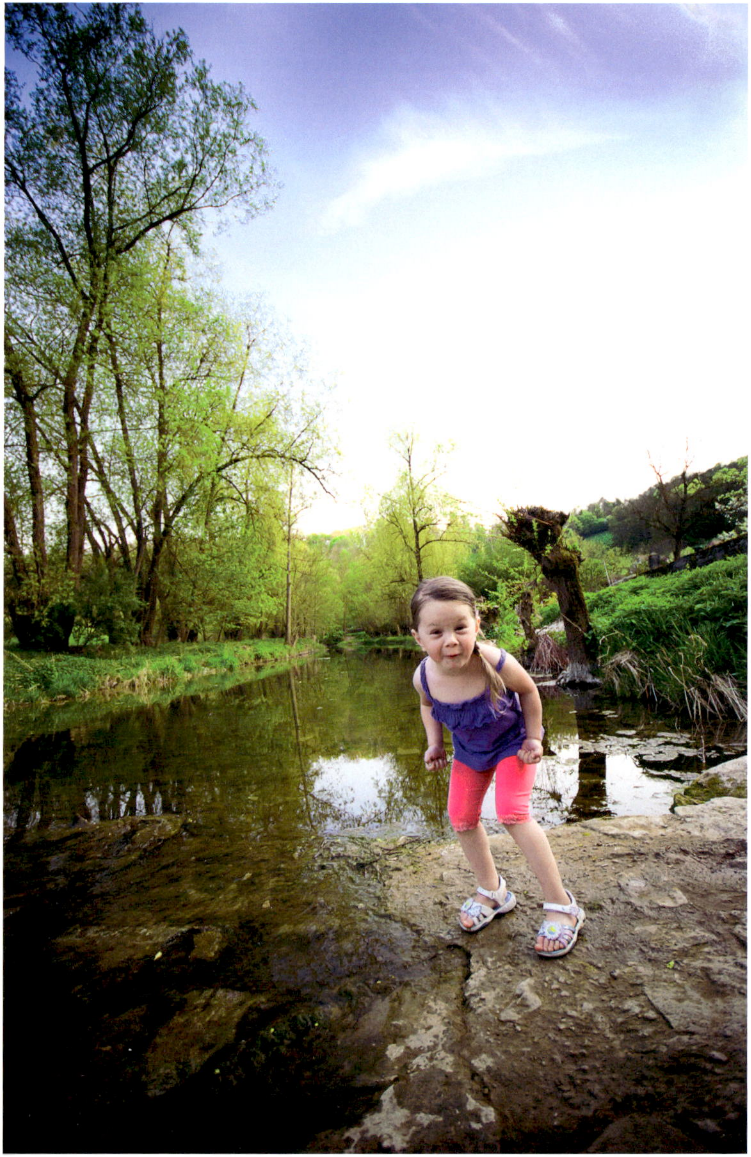

Sonia Boukaia Photography

Germany

soniaboukaia.com

Mona Kay · Mona K Photography

Omaha, NE

monakphotography.com

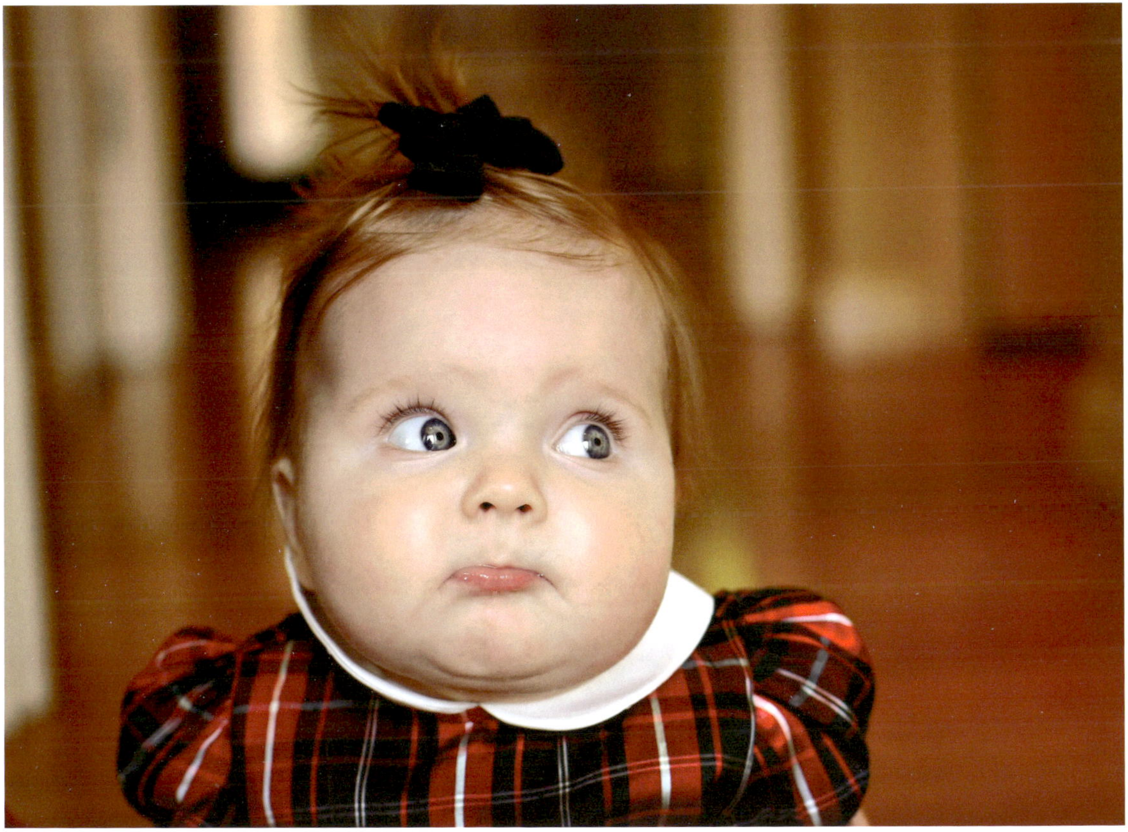

Lisa Clarke

Victoria, BC

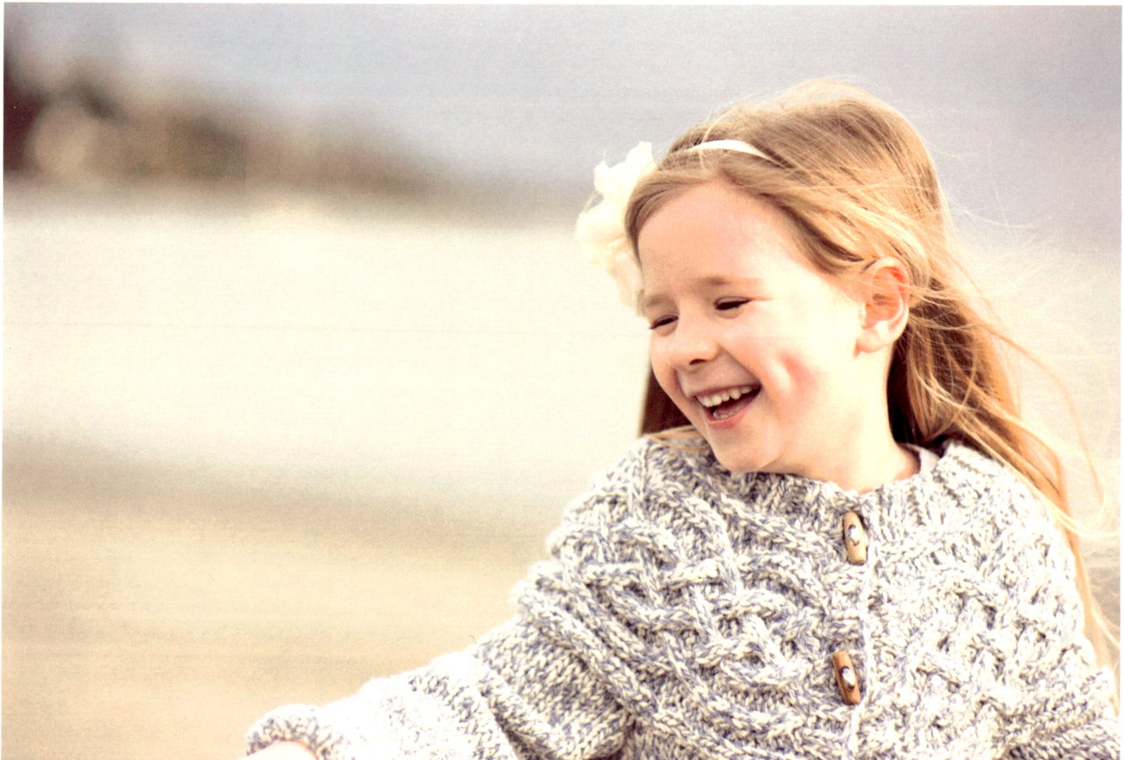

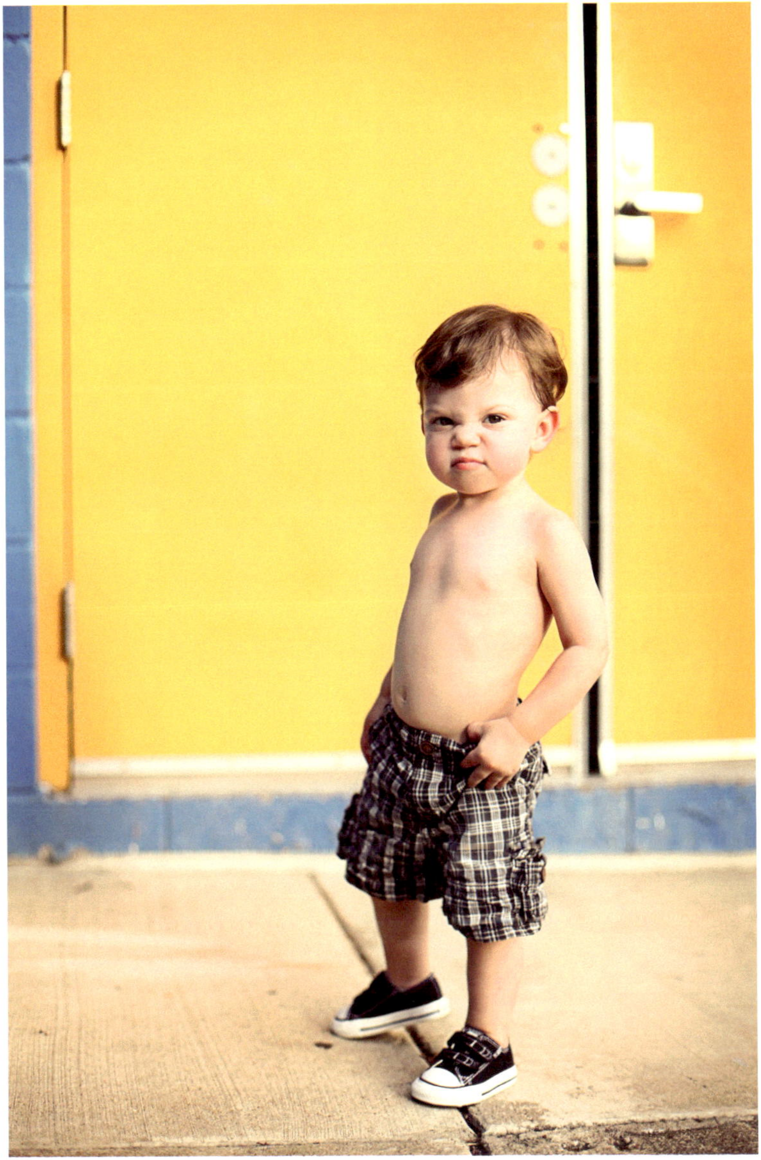

Leah Cook | Life's Little Images

Dallas, TX

lifeslittleimages.com

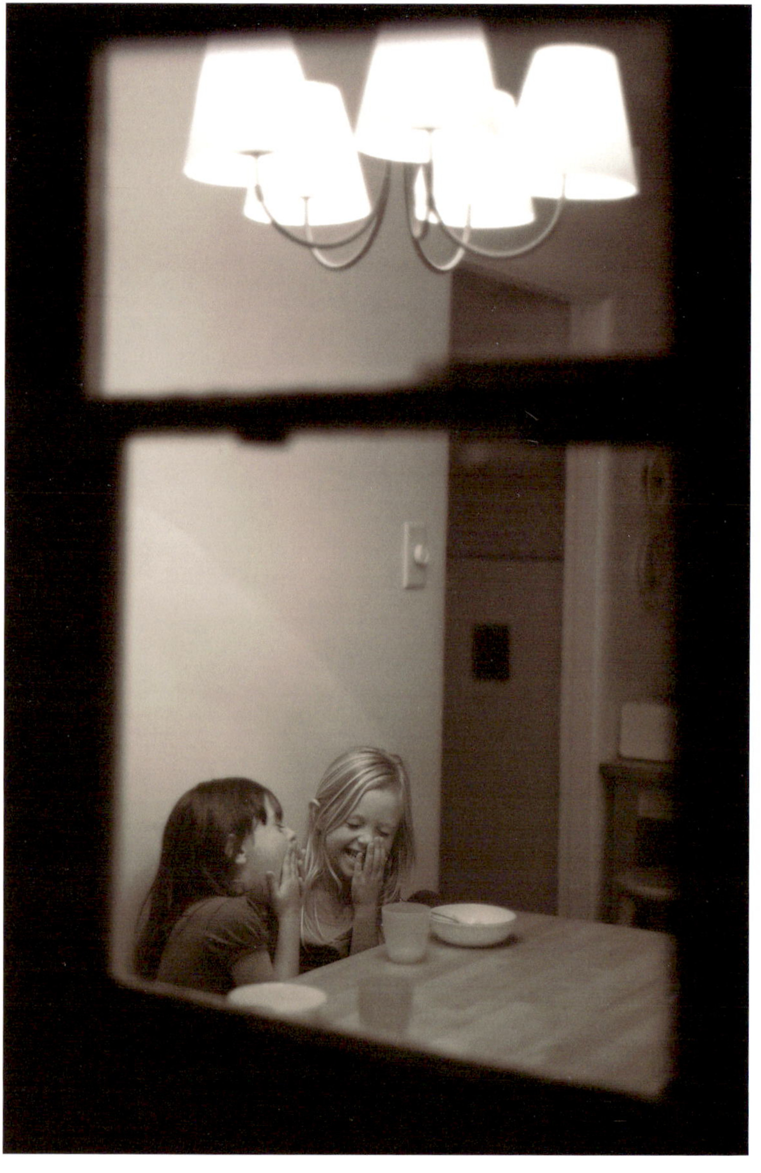

Allison Zercher - snippets from suburbia

Southern CA

snippetsfromsuburbia.com

CMC Photography

Wallingford, CT

cmcphoto.net

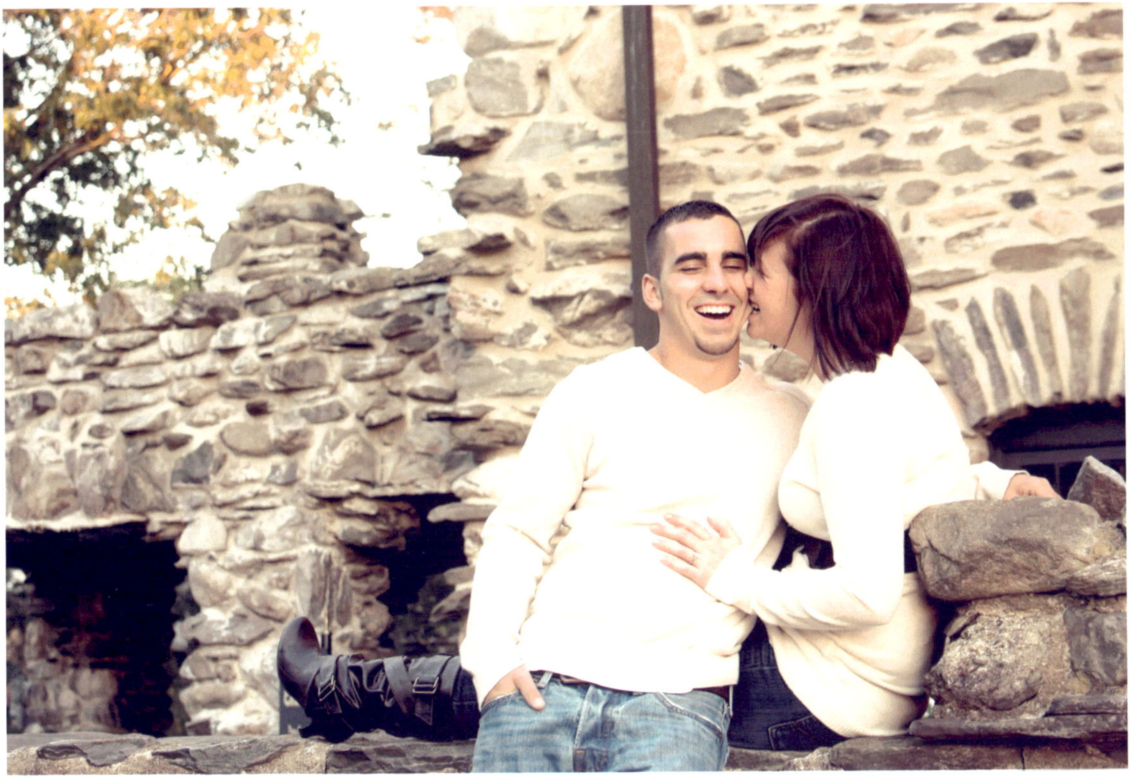

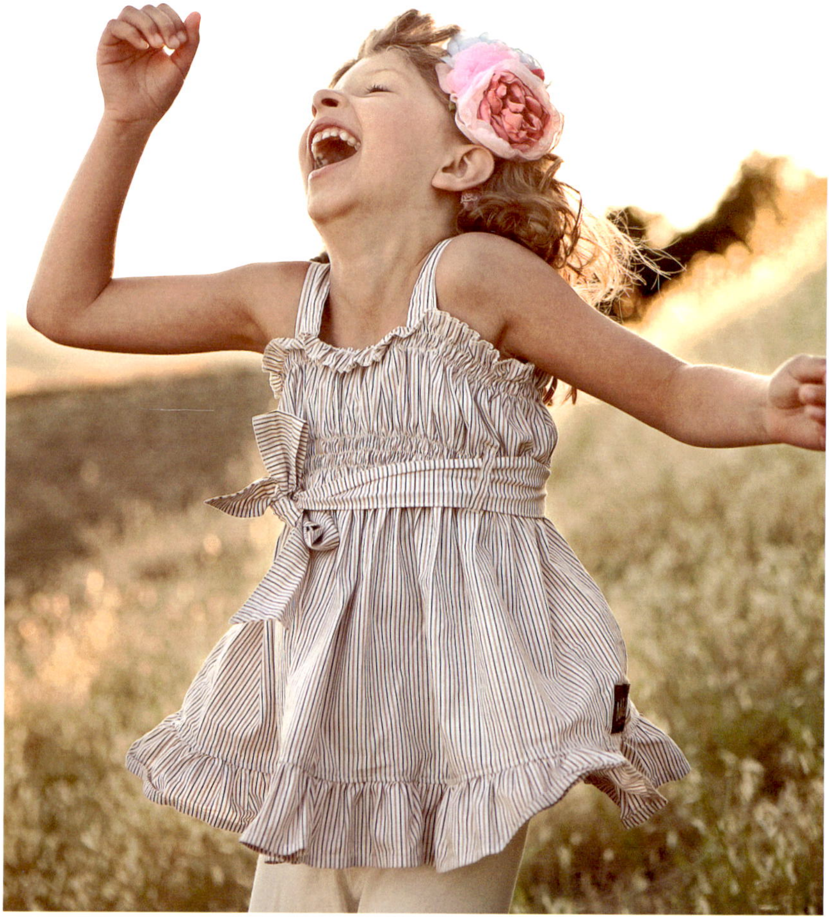

Alison Crane Photography

Lafayette, CA

alisoncranephotography.com

Leah Cook | Life's Little Images

Dallas, TX

lifeslittleimages.com

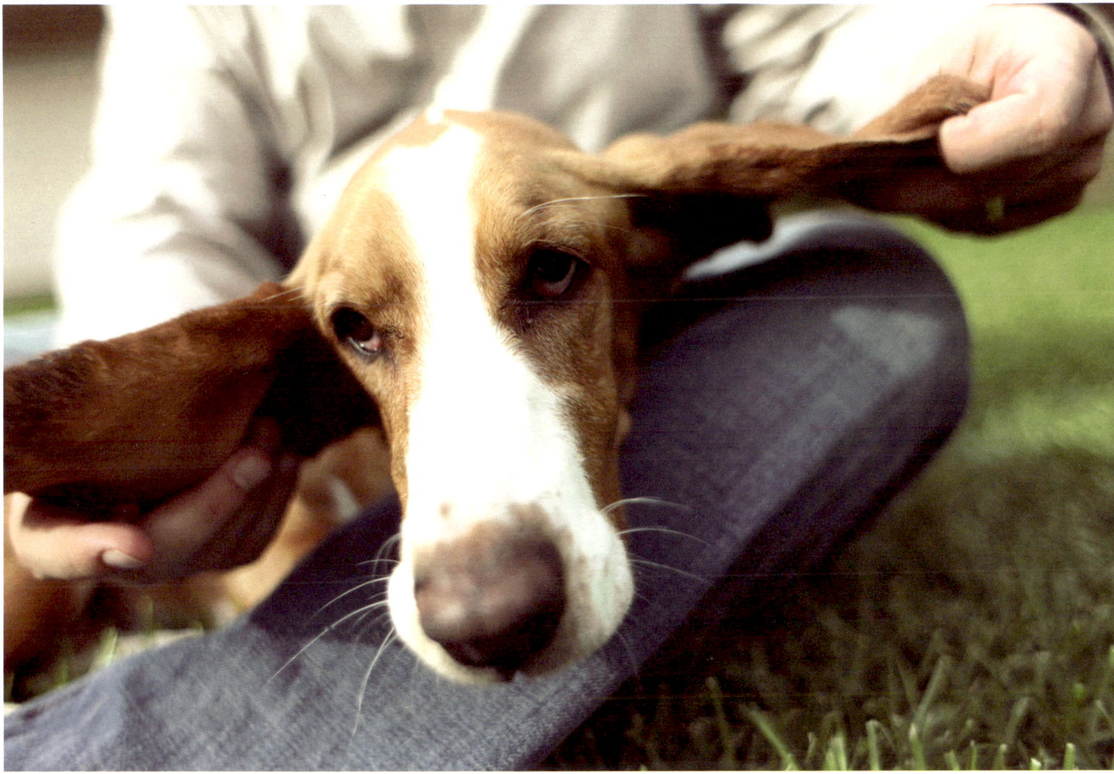

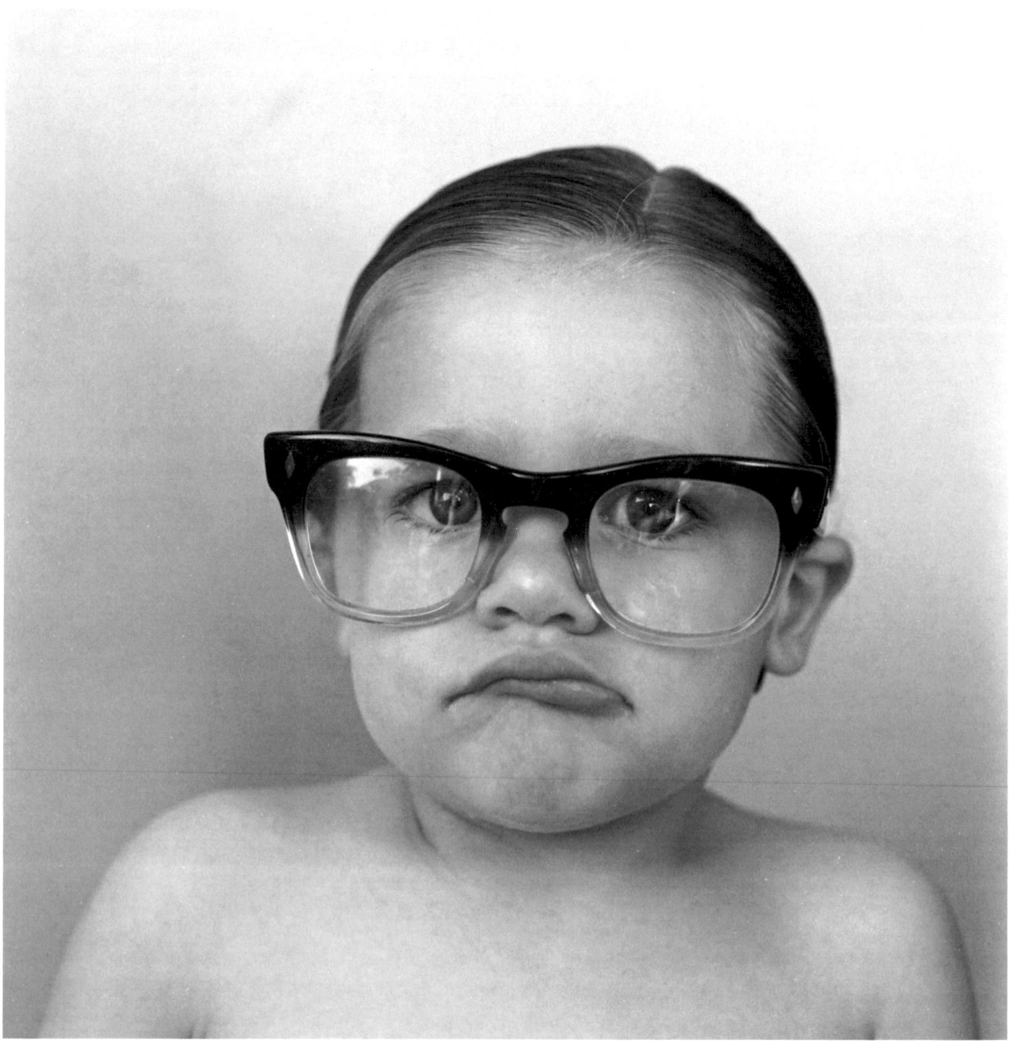

Michelle Dupont

Tasmania, Australia

michelledupont.com.au

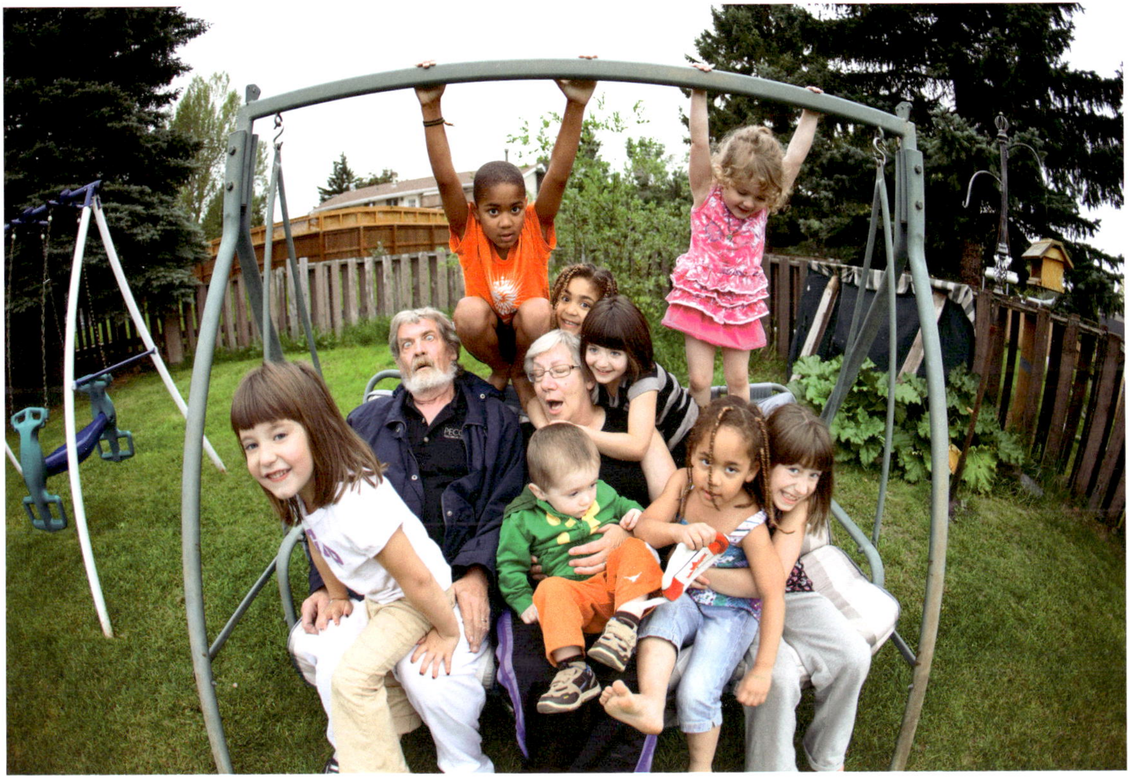

Jen Cooke Photography

Edmonton, AB, Canada

jencookephotography.com

Andie Freeman Photography

Athens, GA

andiefreemanphotography.com

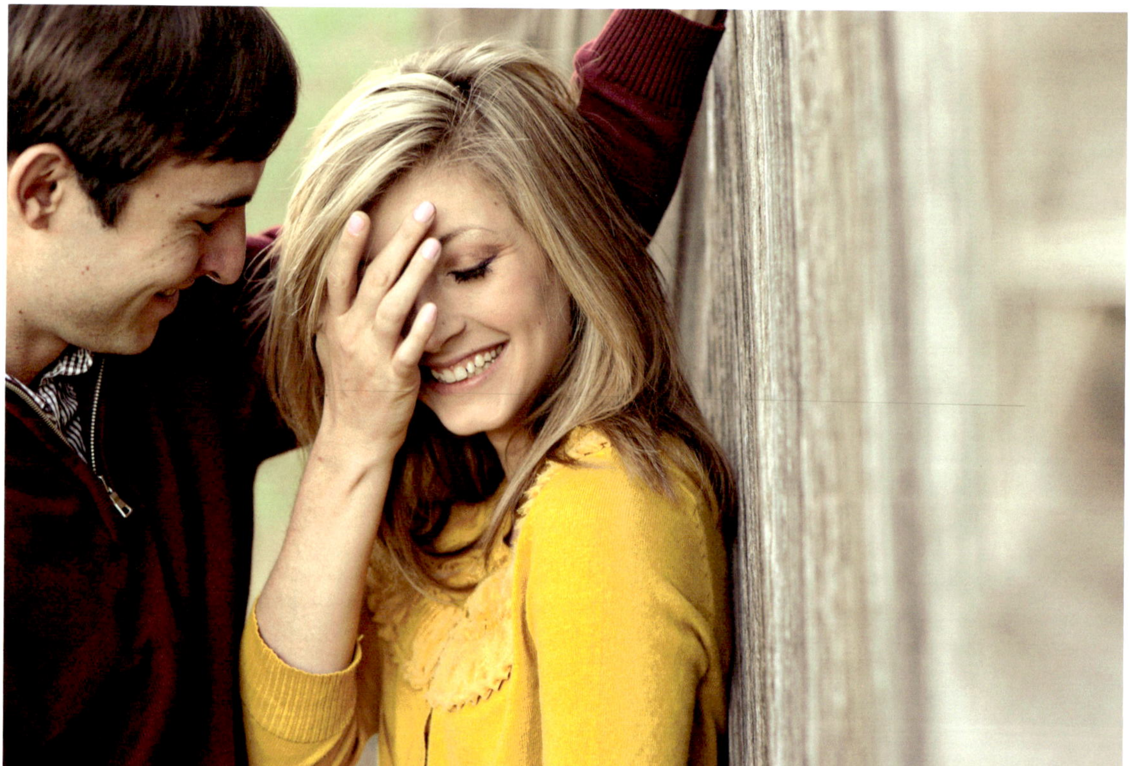

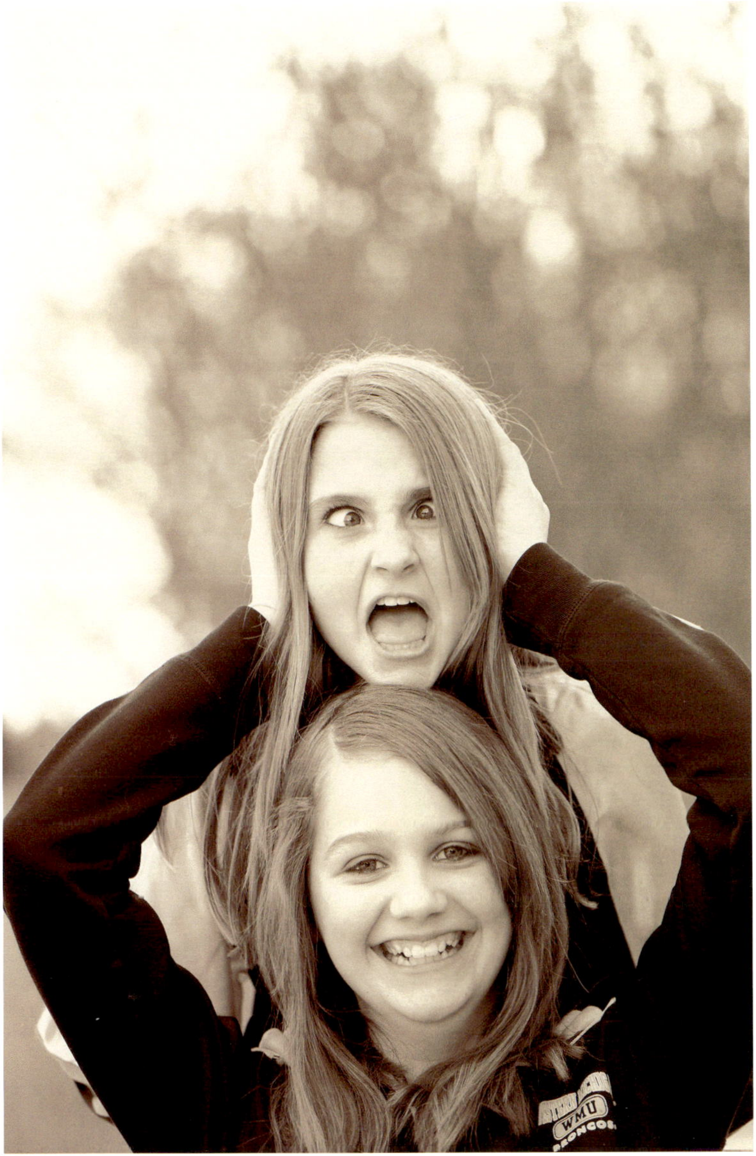

Julie Anders

julieandersphotography.com

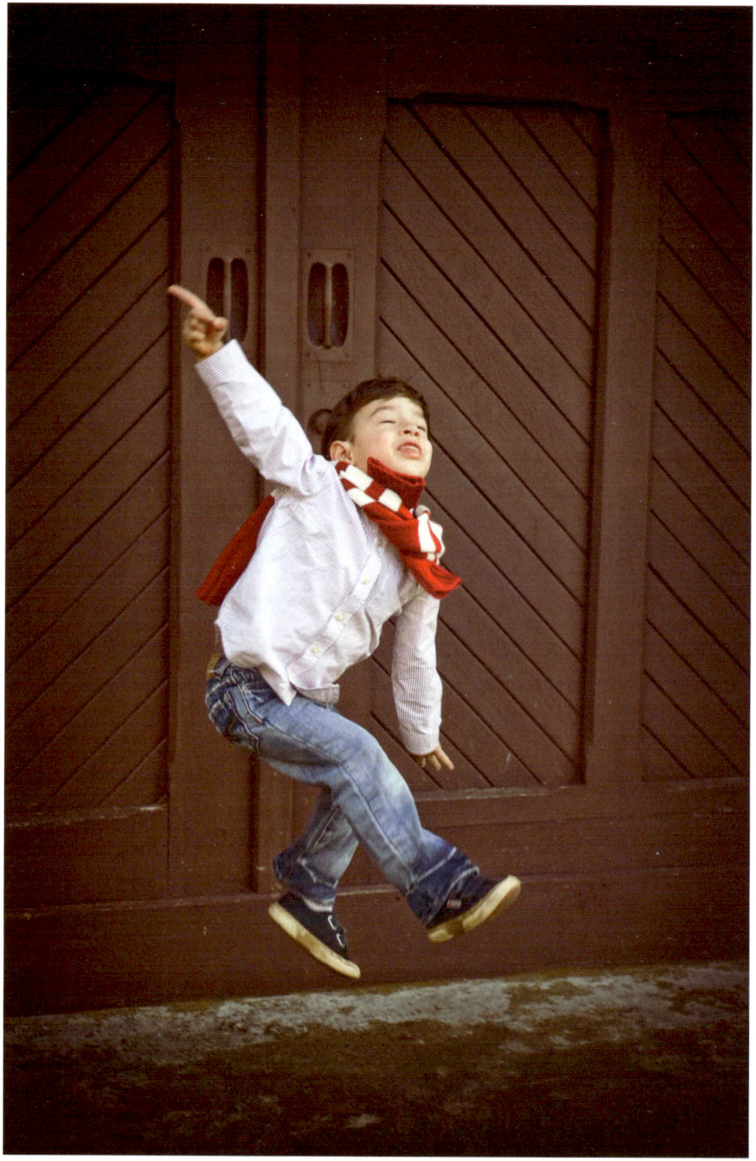

Amanda diMonda - diMonda Photography

Wantagh, NY

dimondaphotography.com

Kristin Ingalls

Kirkland, WA

kristiningalls.com

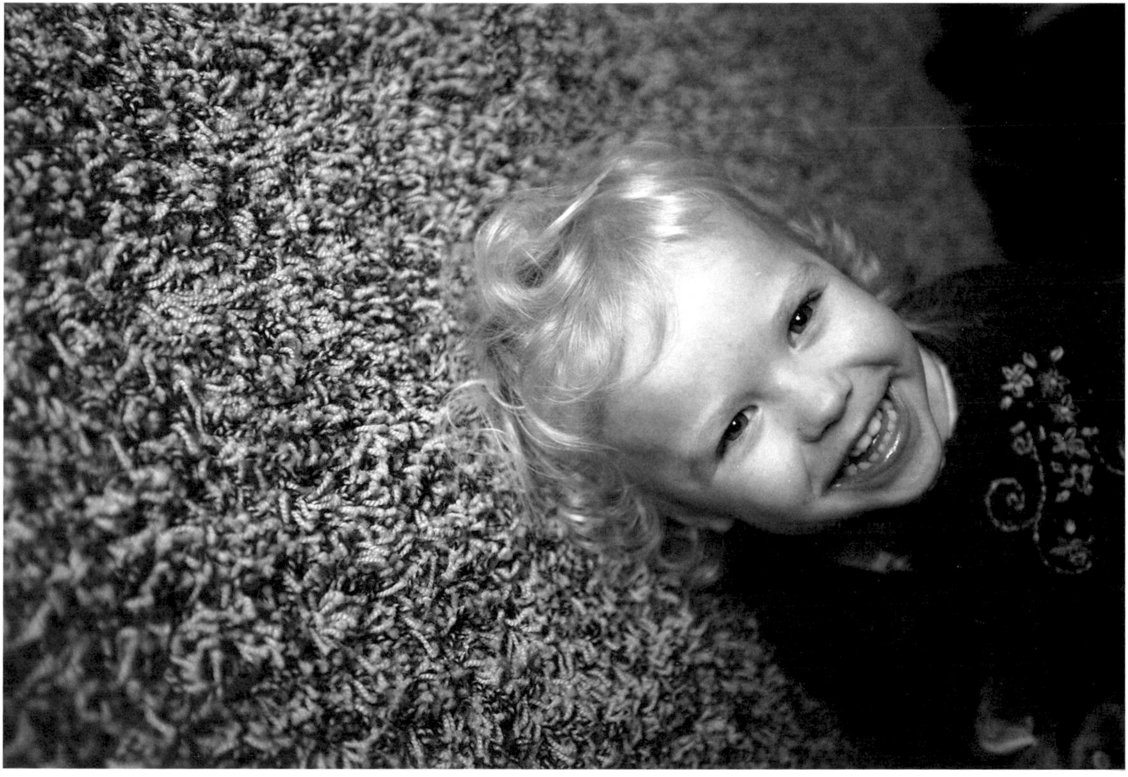

Sheryl Dagenais Photography

Escanaba, MI

sheryldagenaisphotography.com

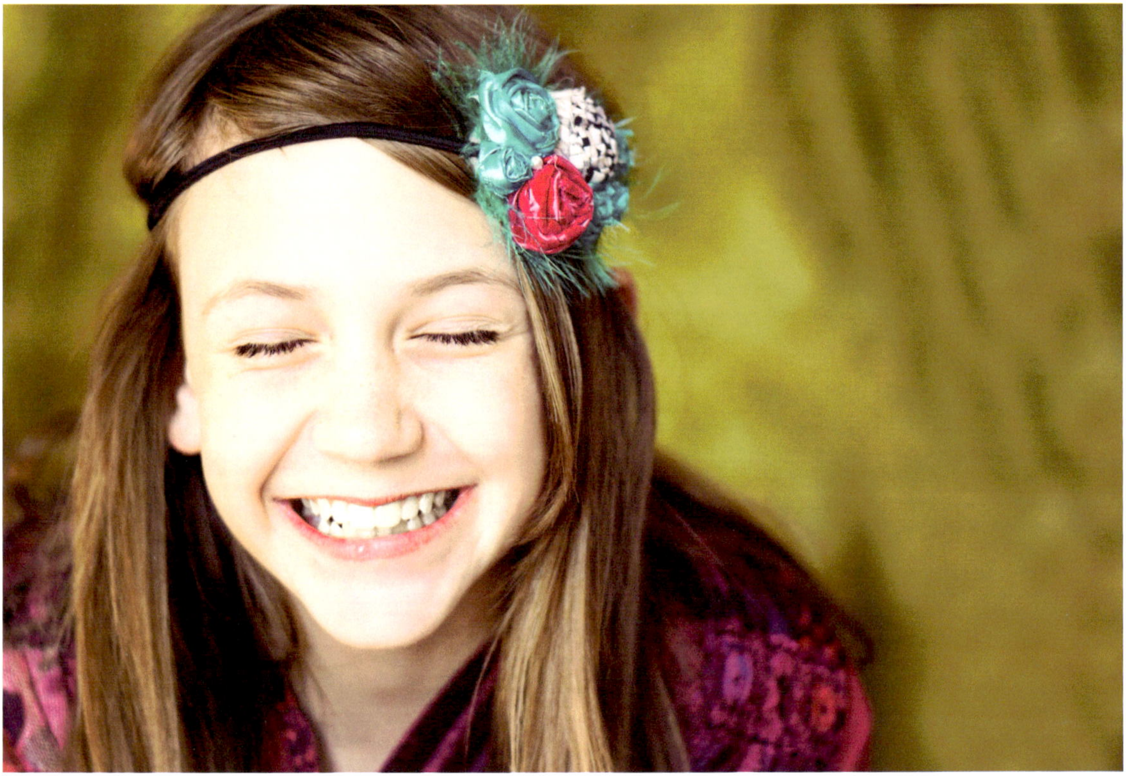

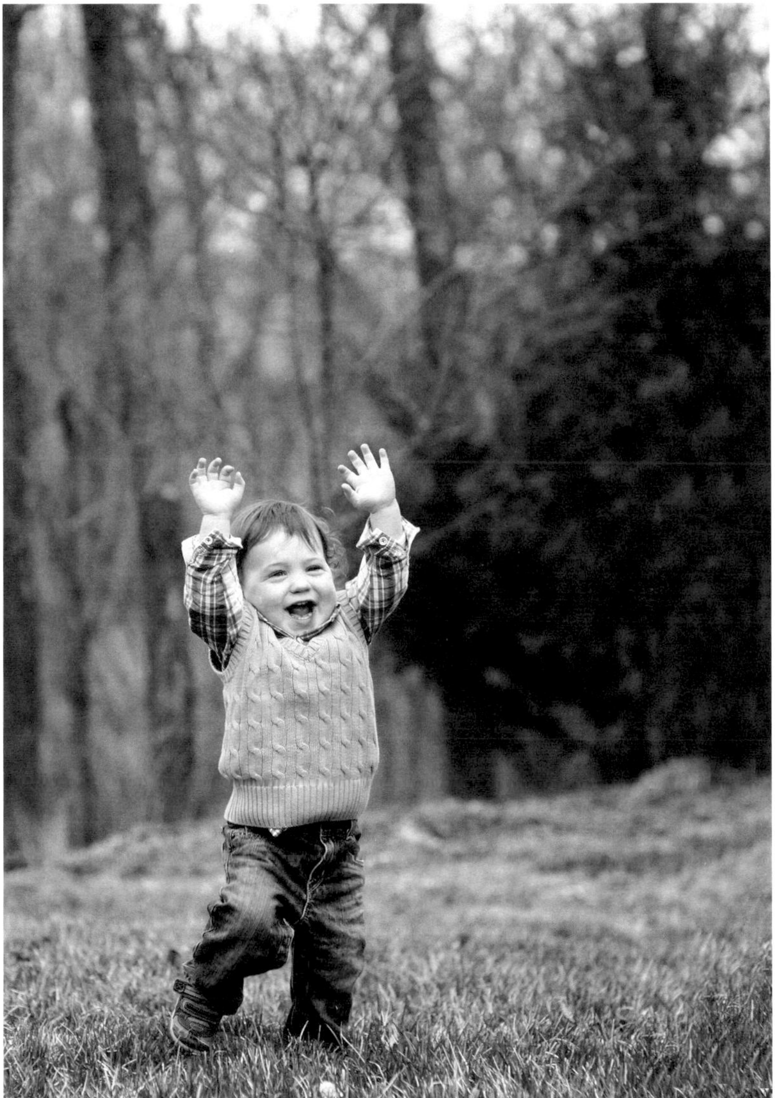

Nance Heidemann Photography

Overland Park, KS

nanceheidemannphotography.com

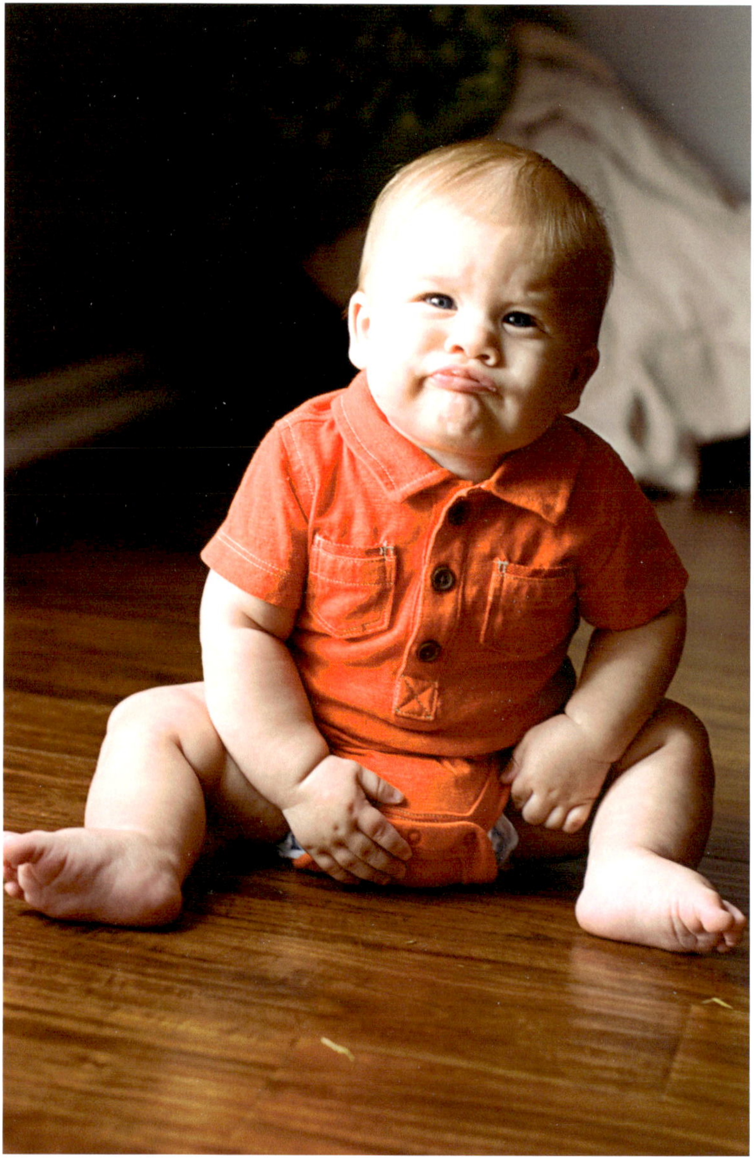

Lauren Everly Photography

Jacksonville, FL

laureneverly.com

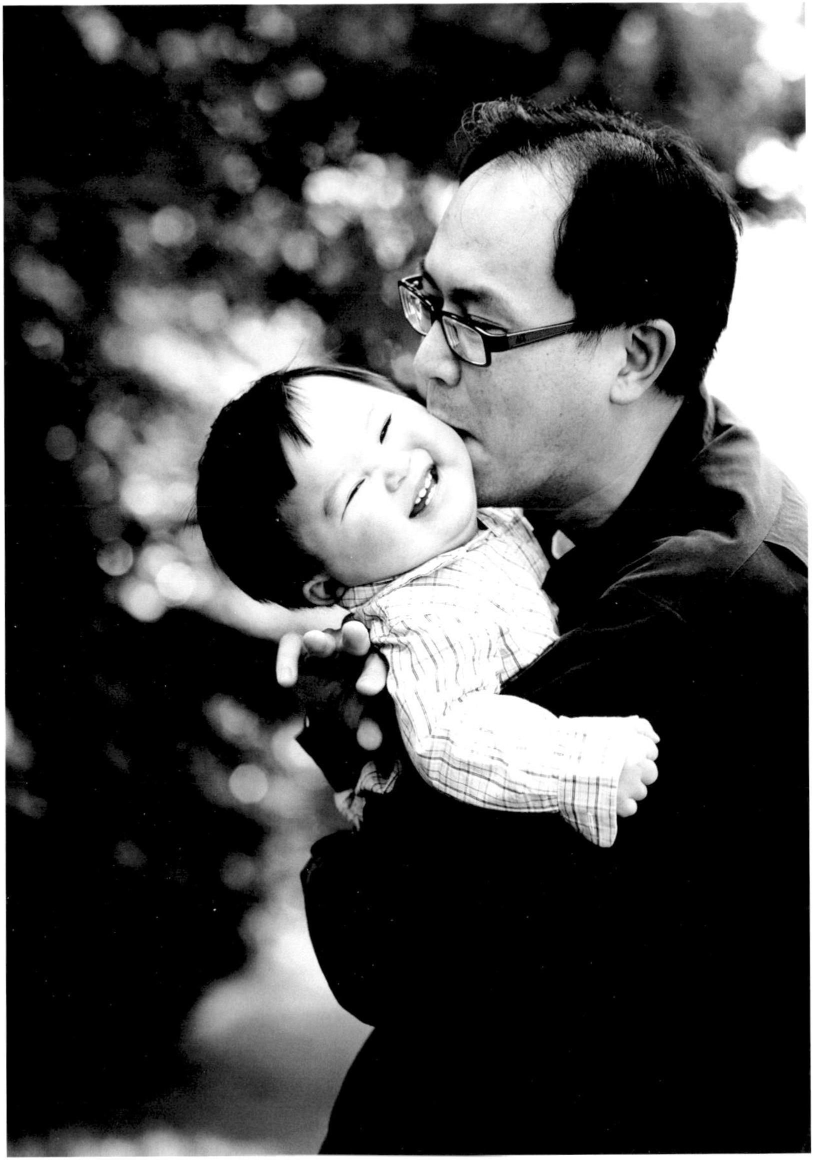

Alicia Gould Photography

Colonia, NJ

aliciagouldphotography.com

Stacey Haslem

Modesto, CA

staceyhphotography.com/blog

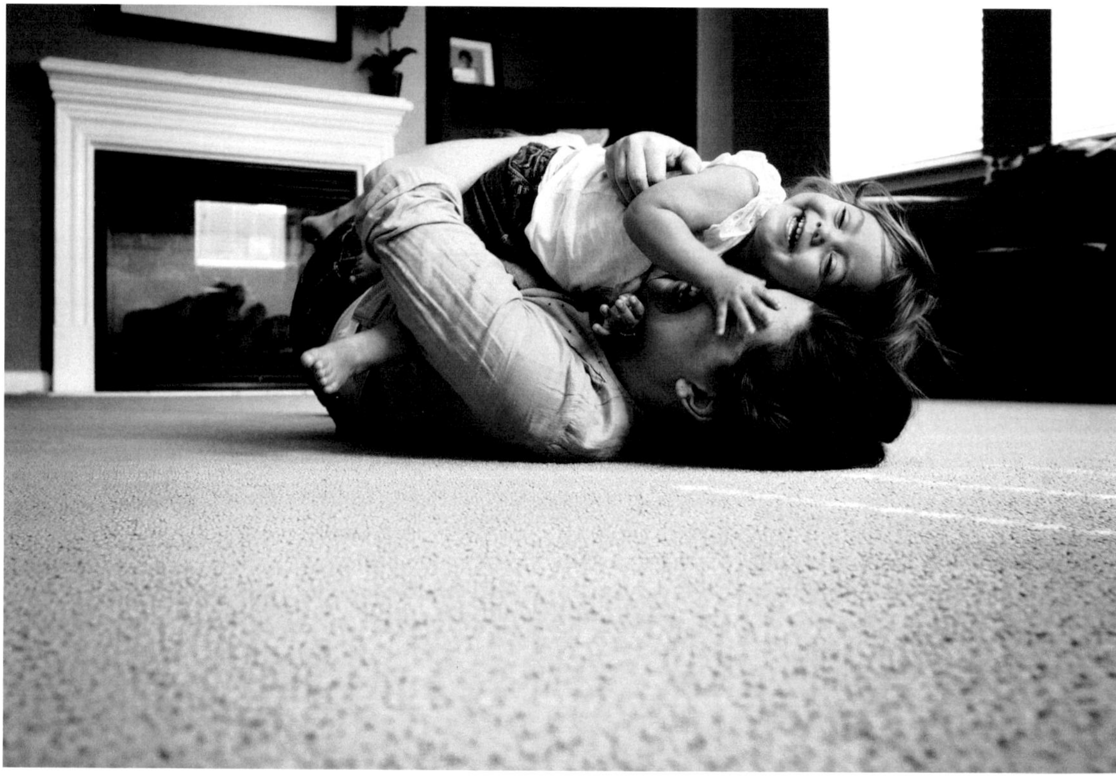

Vicki Utting

Norfolk, England

vickiutting.com

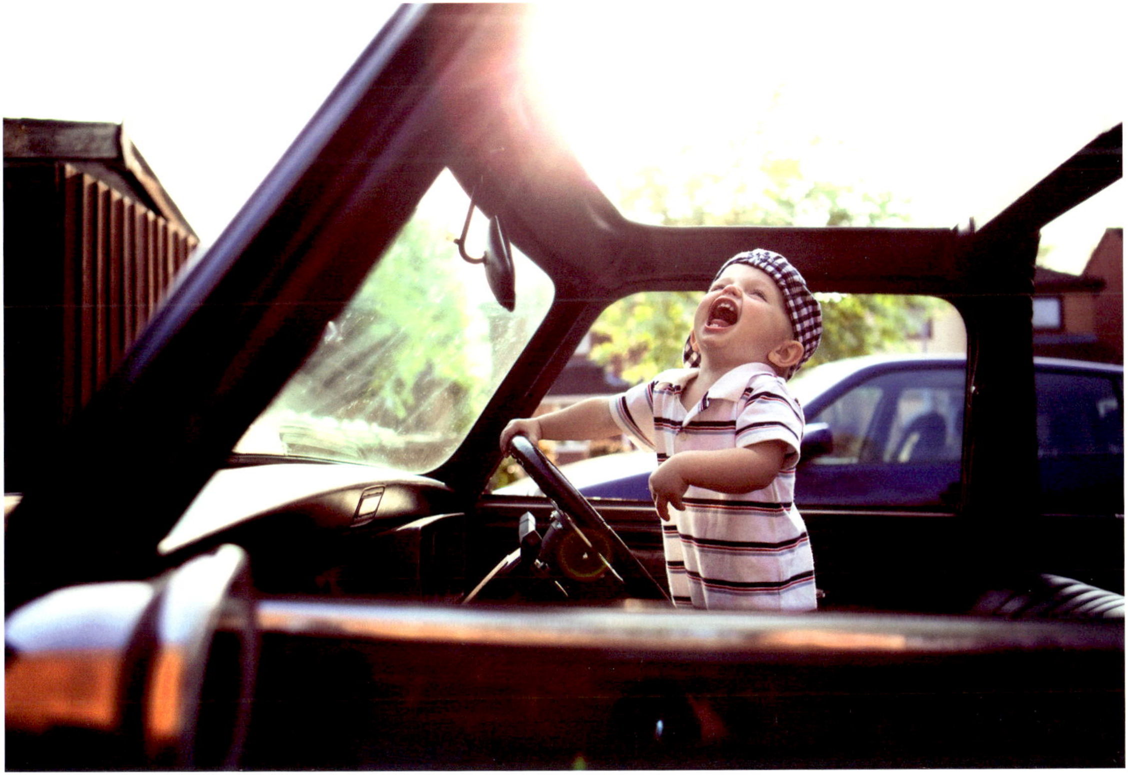

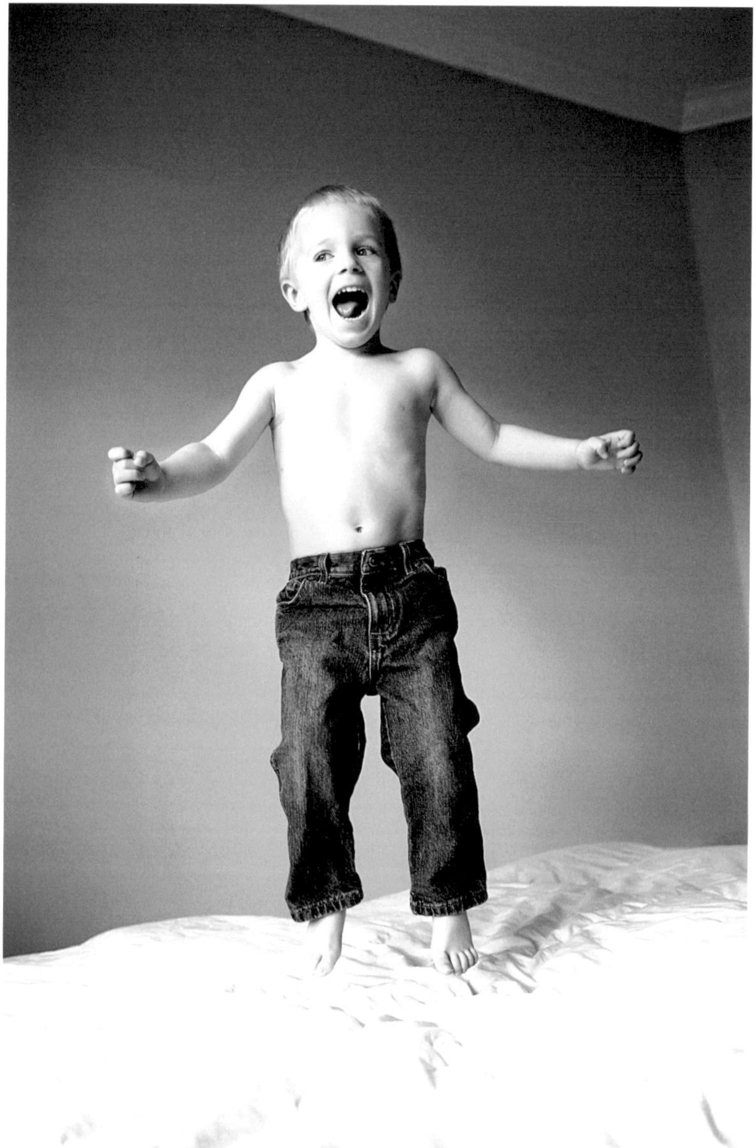

Wendy Freeman Photography

Statesville, NC

wendyfreemanphotography.com

Kelly Hopkins

Murrieta, CA

jtsphotography.net

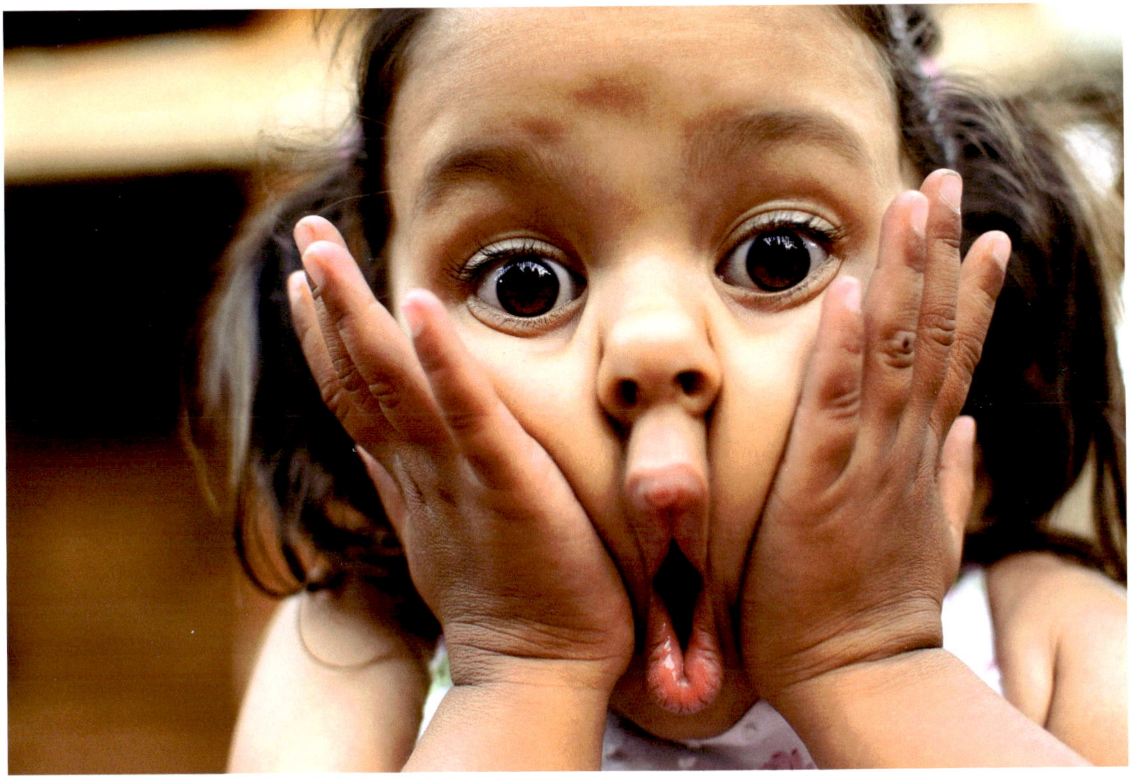

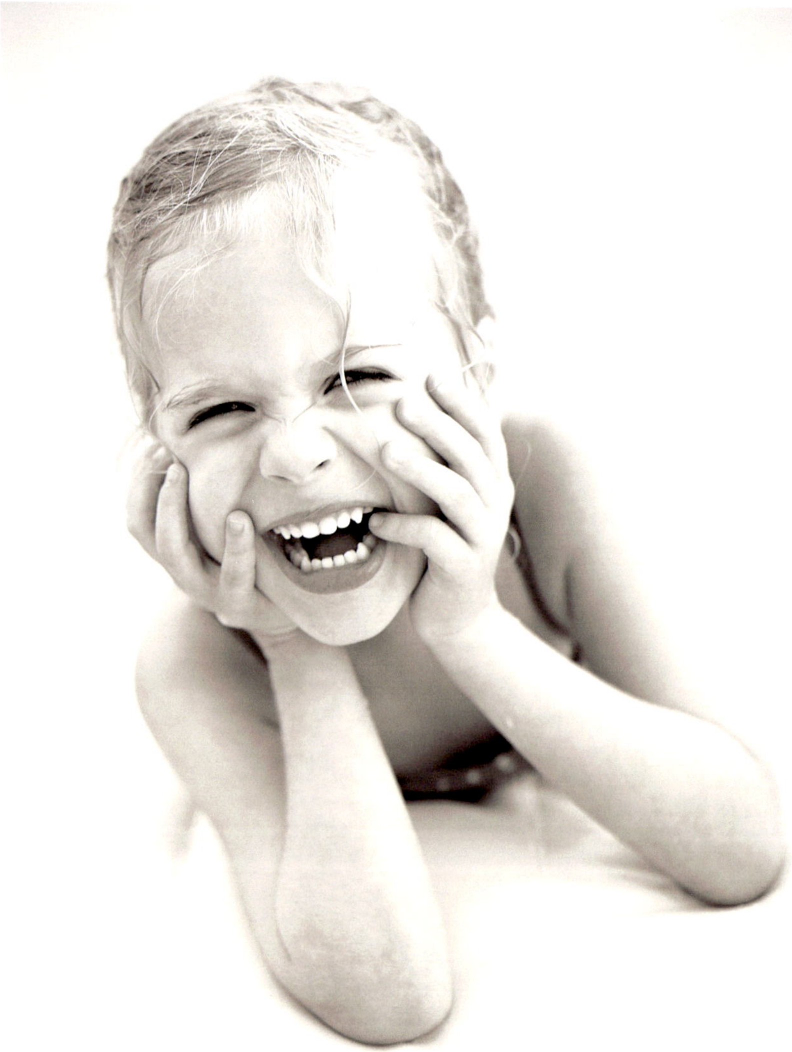

Stephanie Goulet Photography

Durham, NC

stephanie-goulet.com

Trudie Healey - Shyne Photography

Brisbane, Australia

shynephotography.com.au

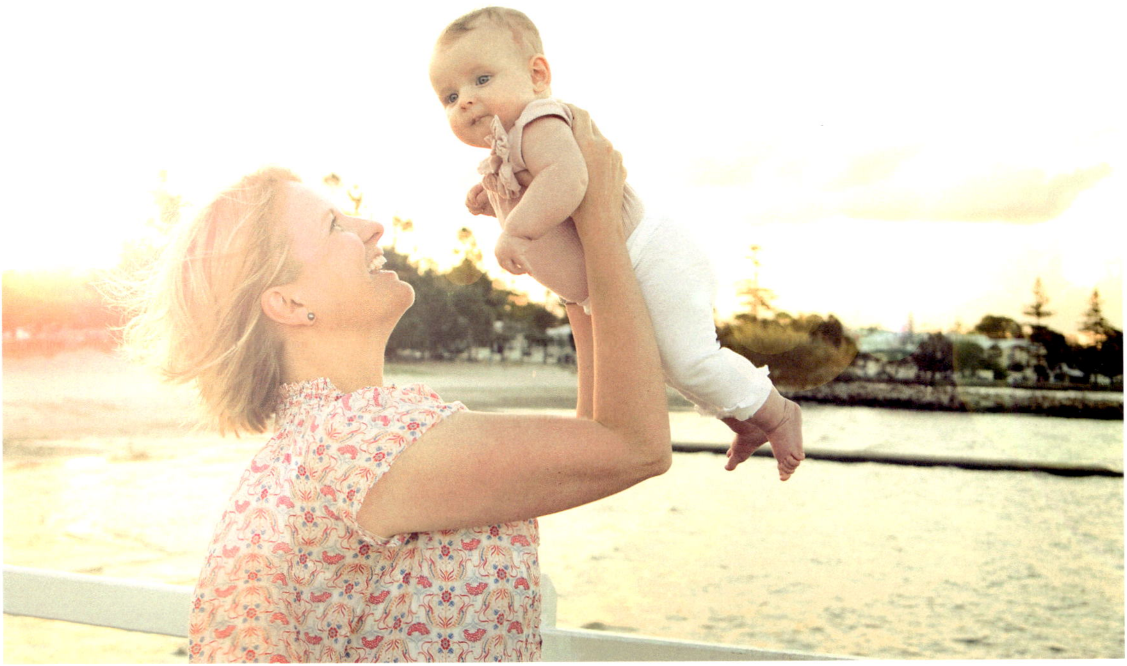

Aubri Graybeal

Canton, MI

pinkskyphoto.com

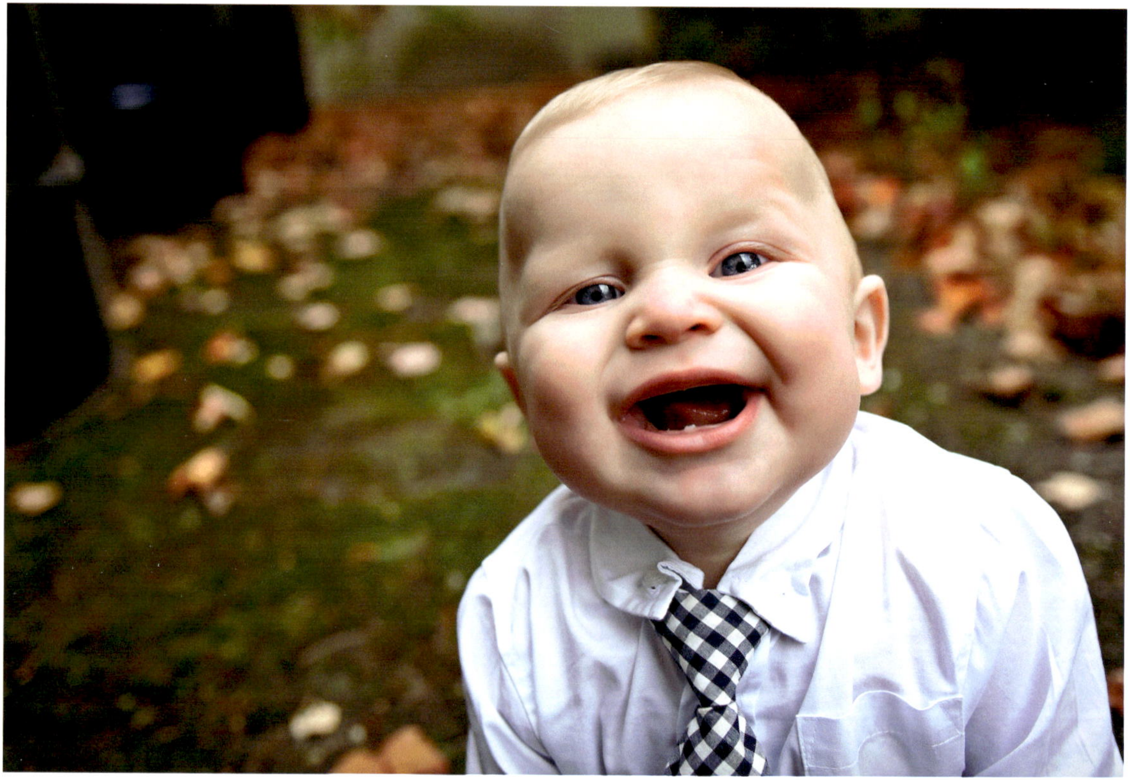

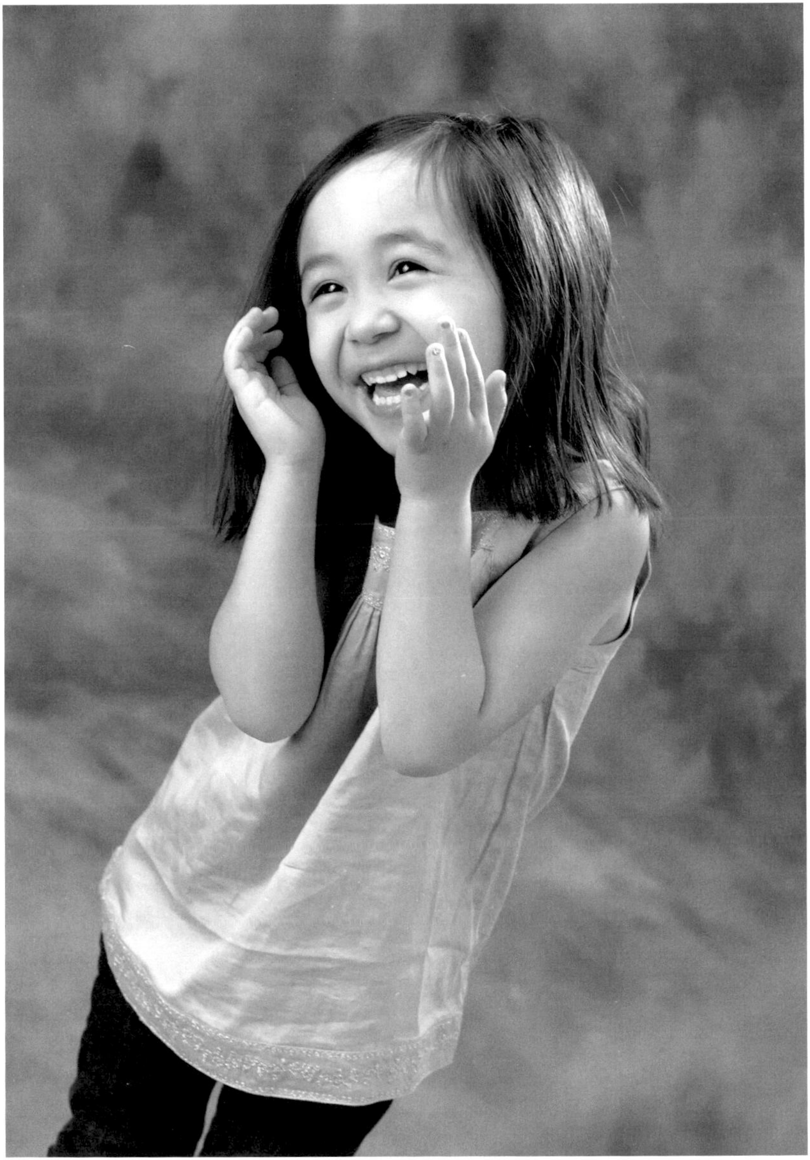

Jessica Gwozdz Photography

Chicago, IL

jessicagwozdz.com

Jessica Holden Photography

San Francisco Bay Area, CA

jessicaholdenphotography.com

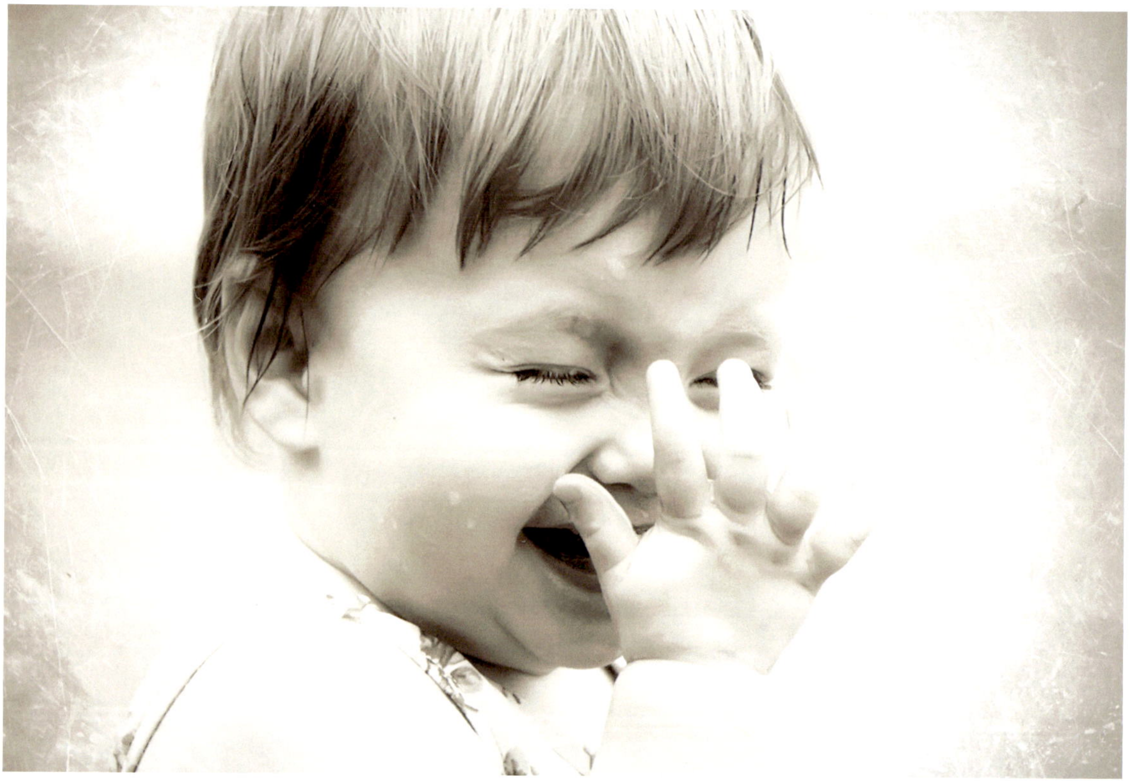

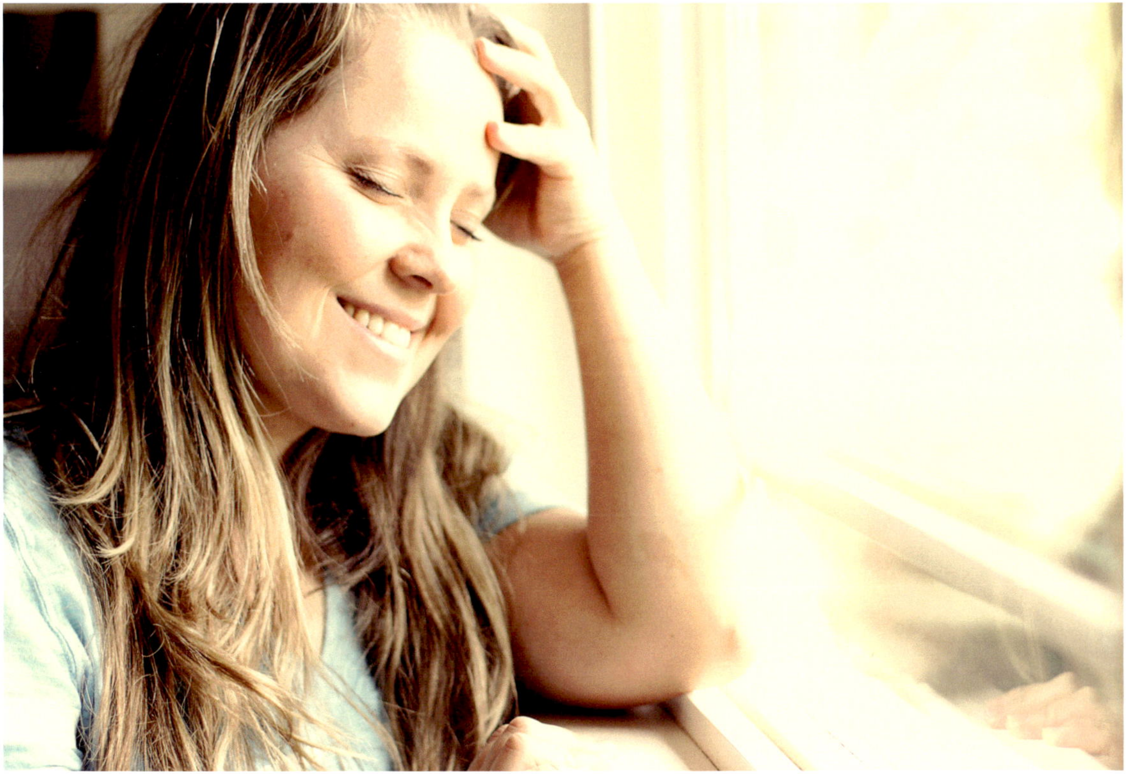

Anna Hollister Photography

Vancouver, WA

annahollister.com

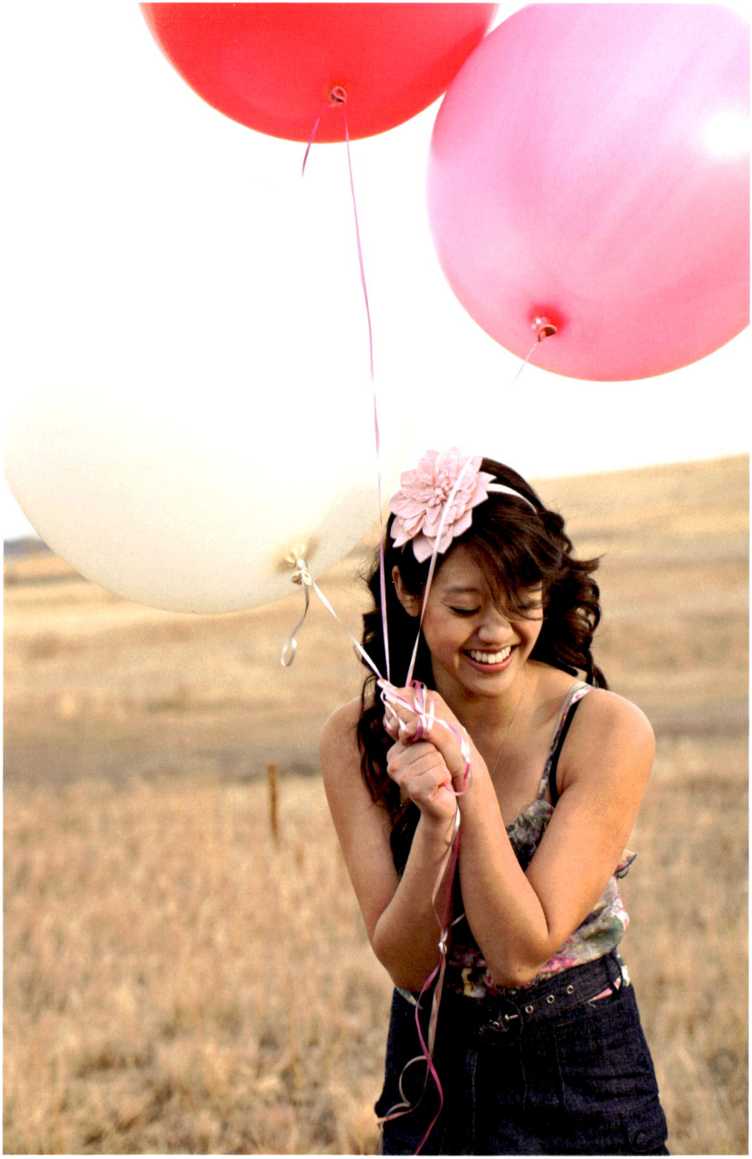

Lauren Blair Photography

Fayetteville, AR

laurenblairphotography.com

Jessica Gwozdz Photography

Chicago, IL

jessicagwozdz.com

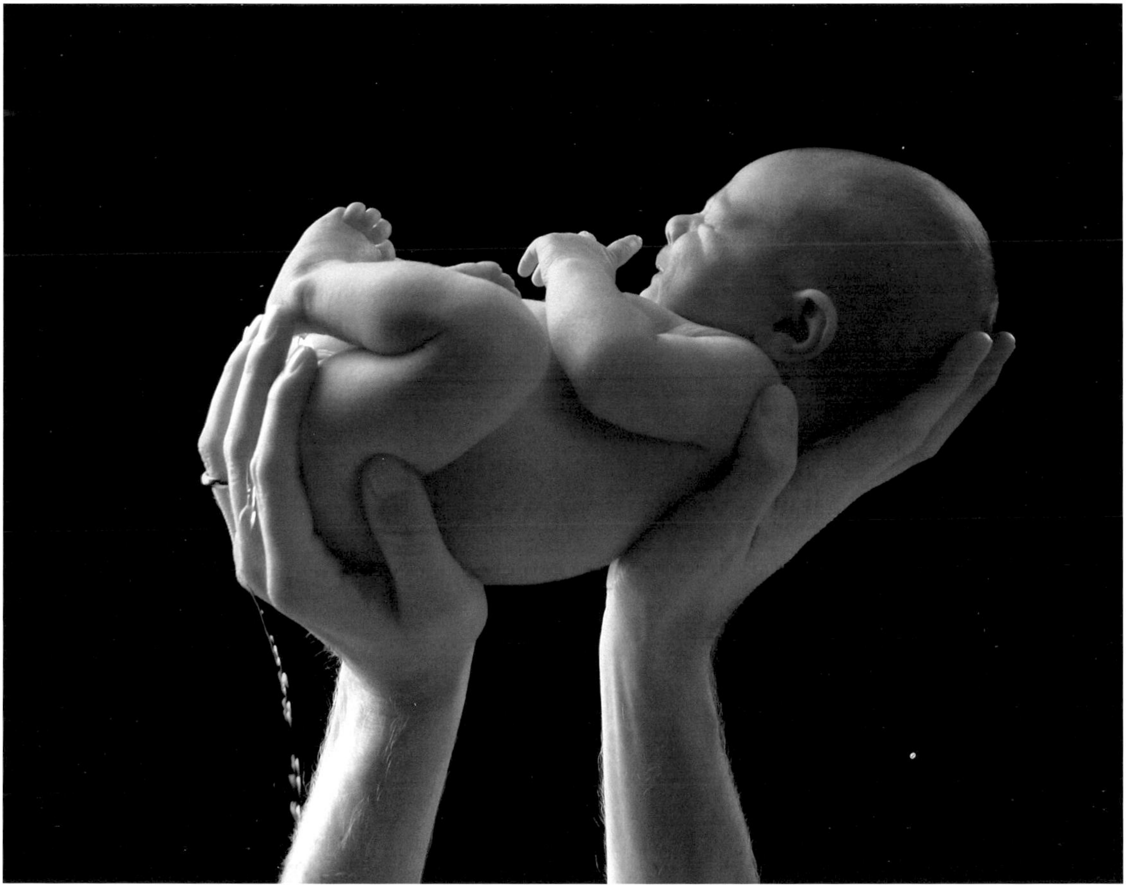

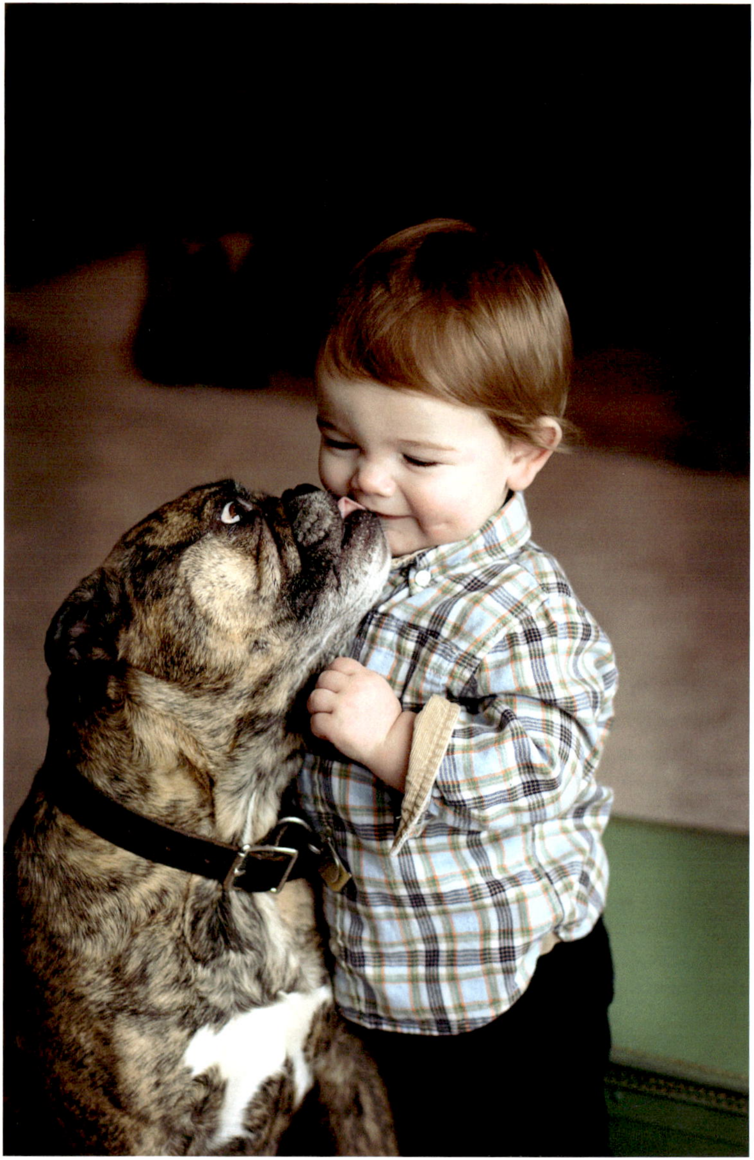

Colleen Davis Photography

Minneapolis, MN

colleendavisphotography.com

Lisa Harrison Photography

Vermont

lisaharrisonphotography.com/blog

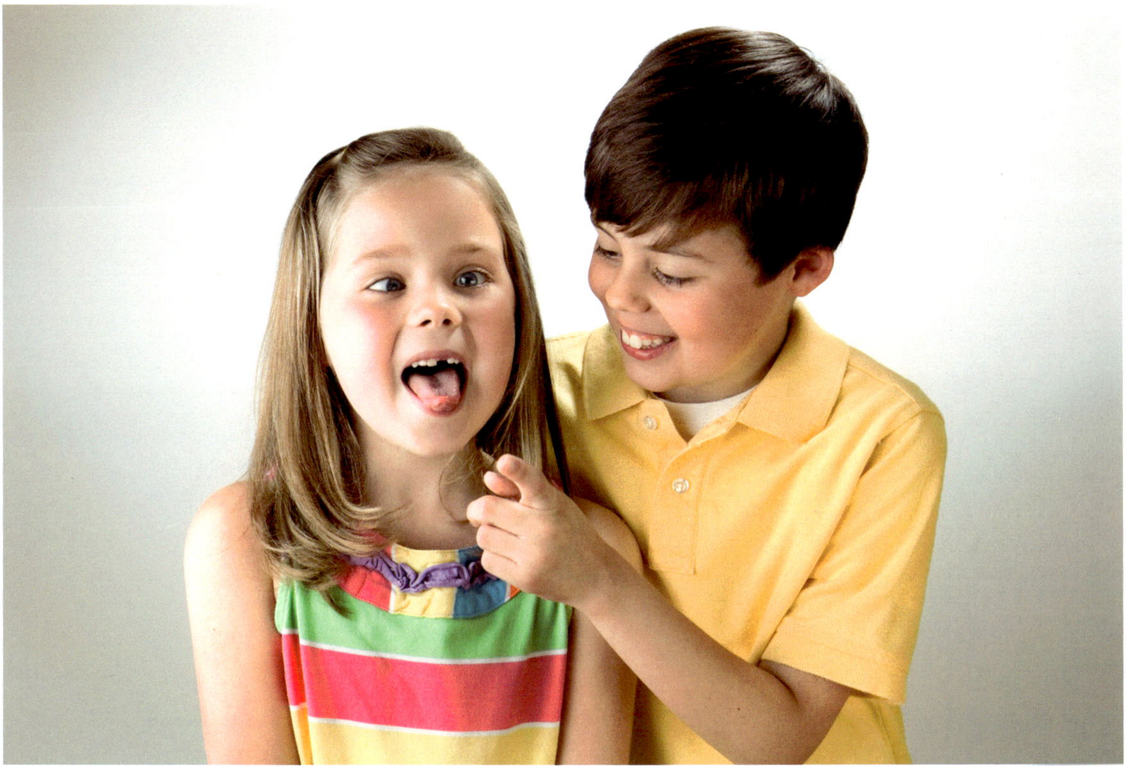

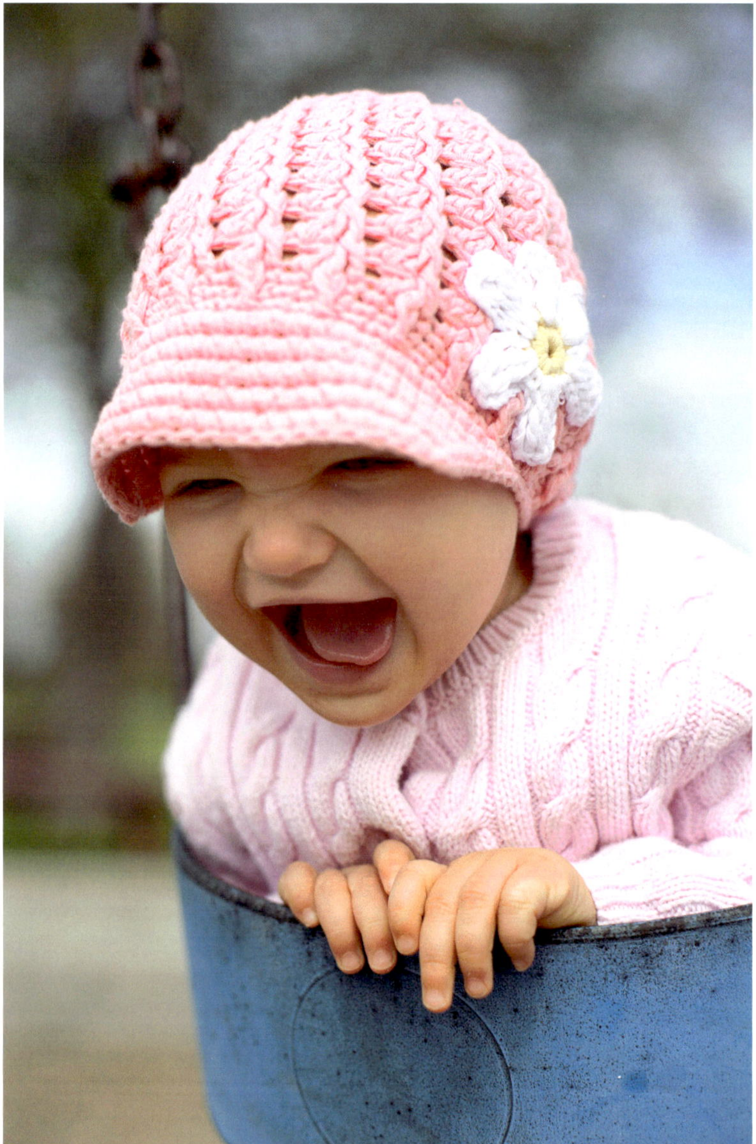

Krista Lund Photography

San Francisco Bay Area, CA

kristalundphotography.com

Stacey Haslem

Modesto, CA

staceyhphotography.com/blog

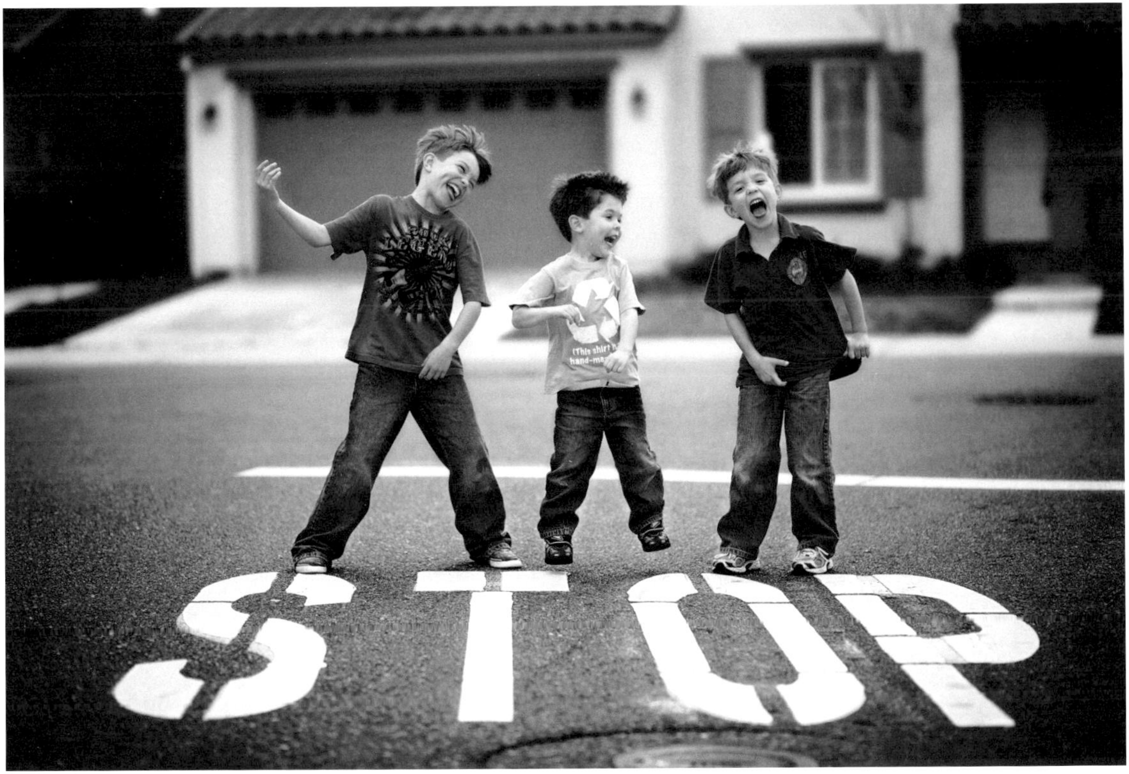

Gingersnap Photography

Anderson, IN

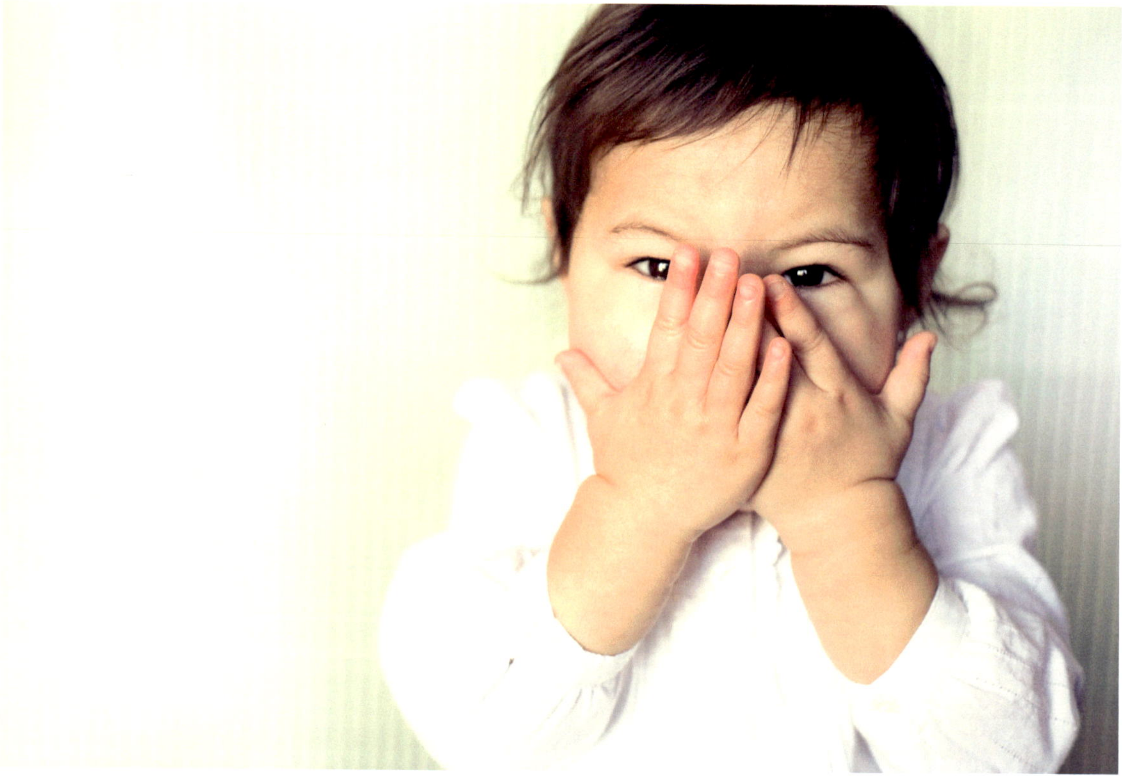

Nance Heidemann Photography

Overland Park, KS

nanceheidemannphotography.com

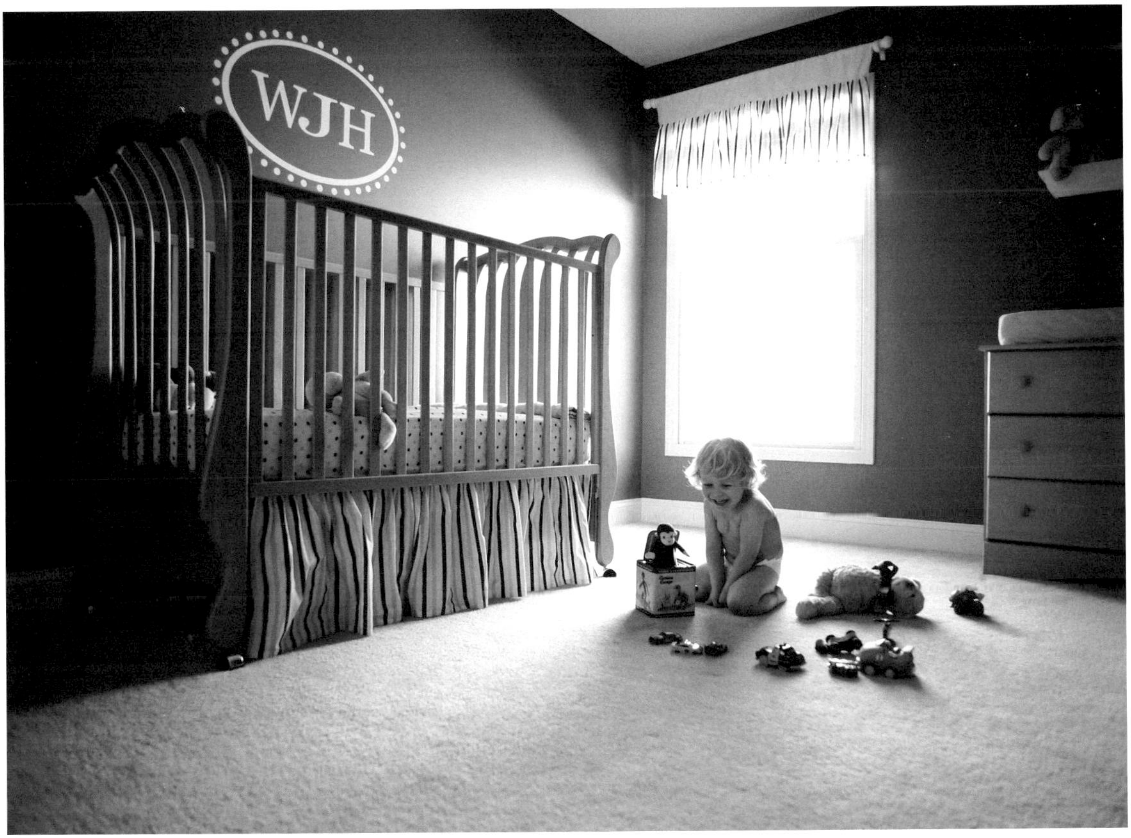

Kim Hildebrand Photography

Seattle, WA

kimhildebrand.com

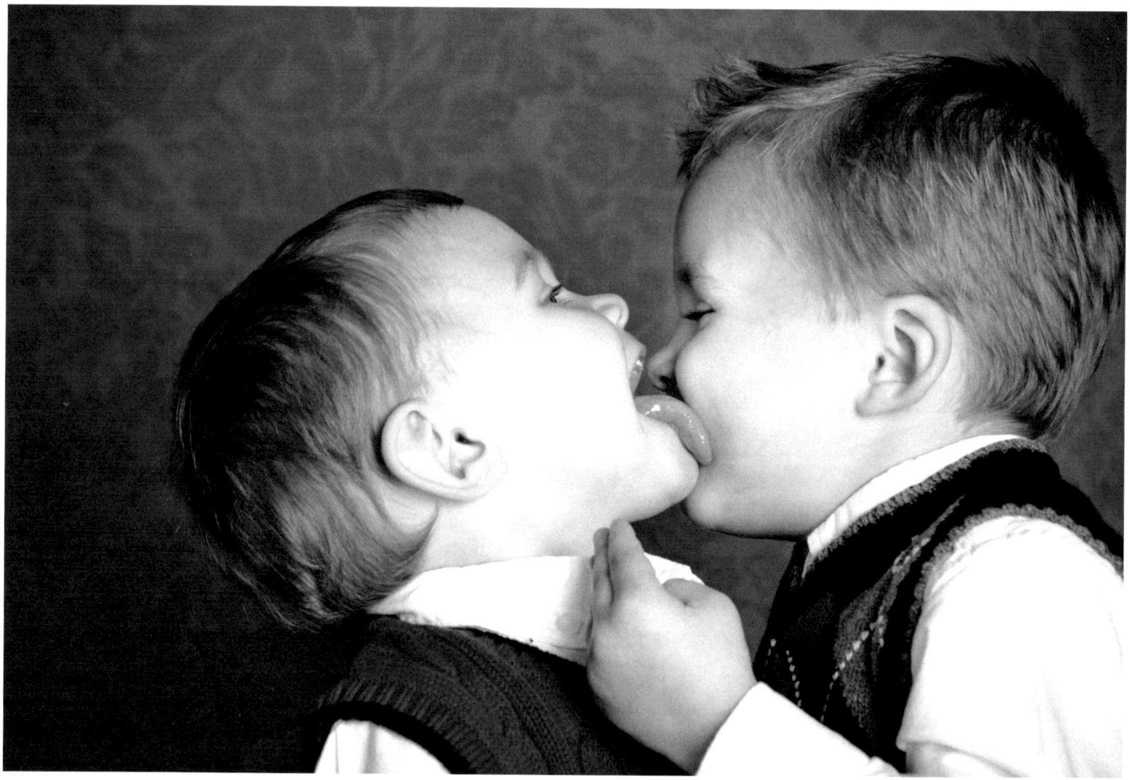

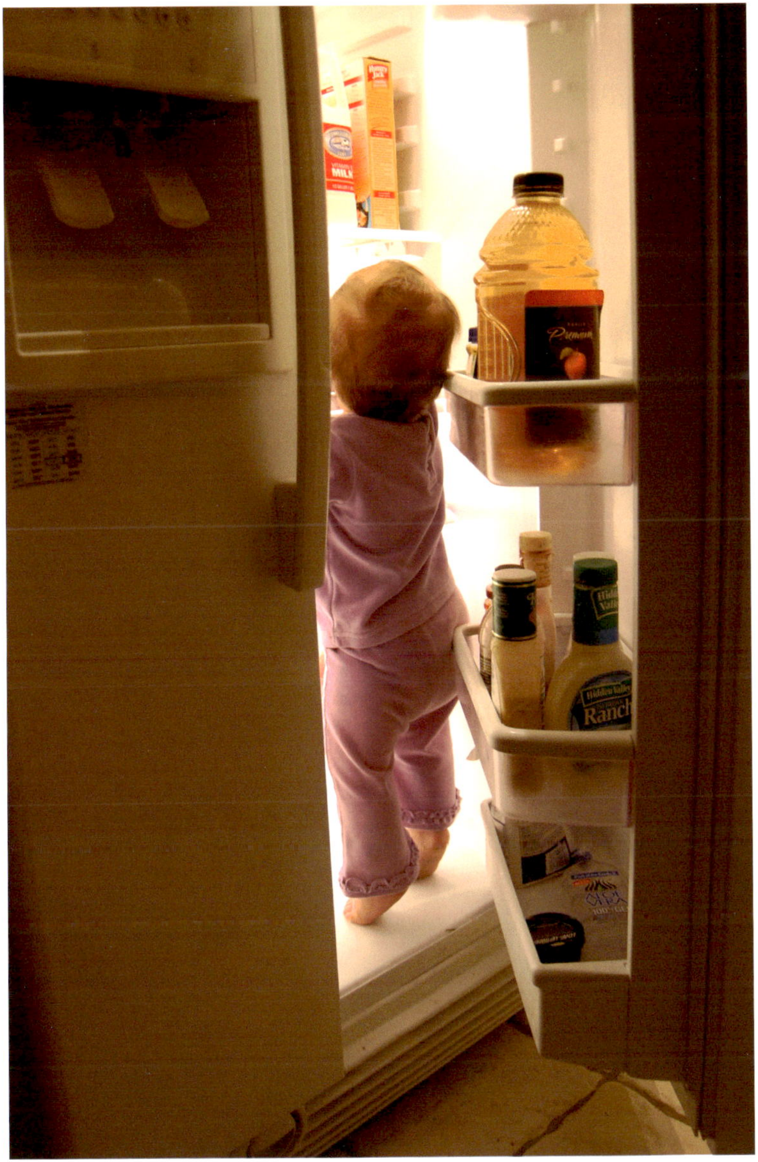

nikkinicole

Orlando, FL

nikkinicoleblog.com

KC Creations Photography

Monitor, Alberta, Canada

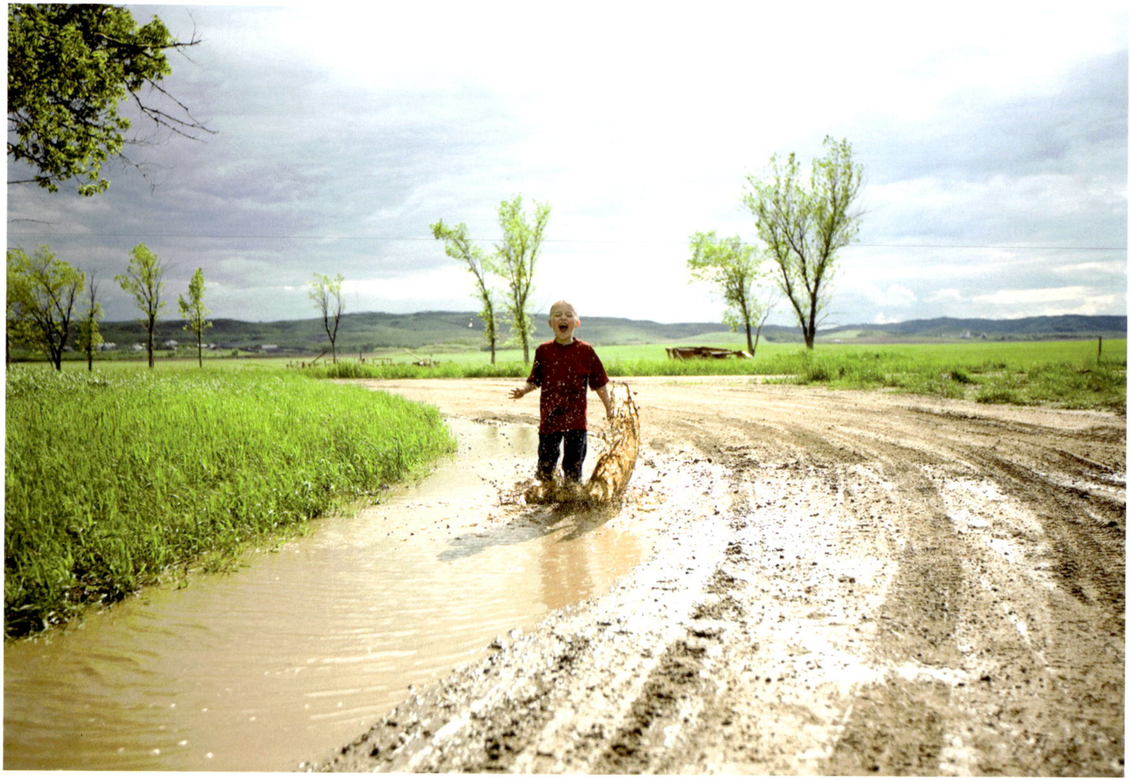

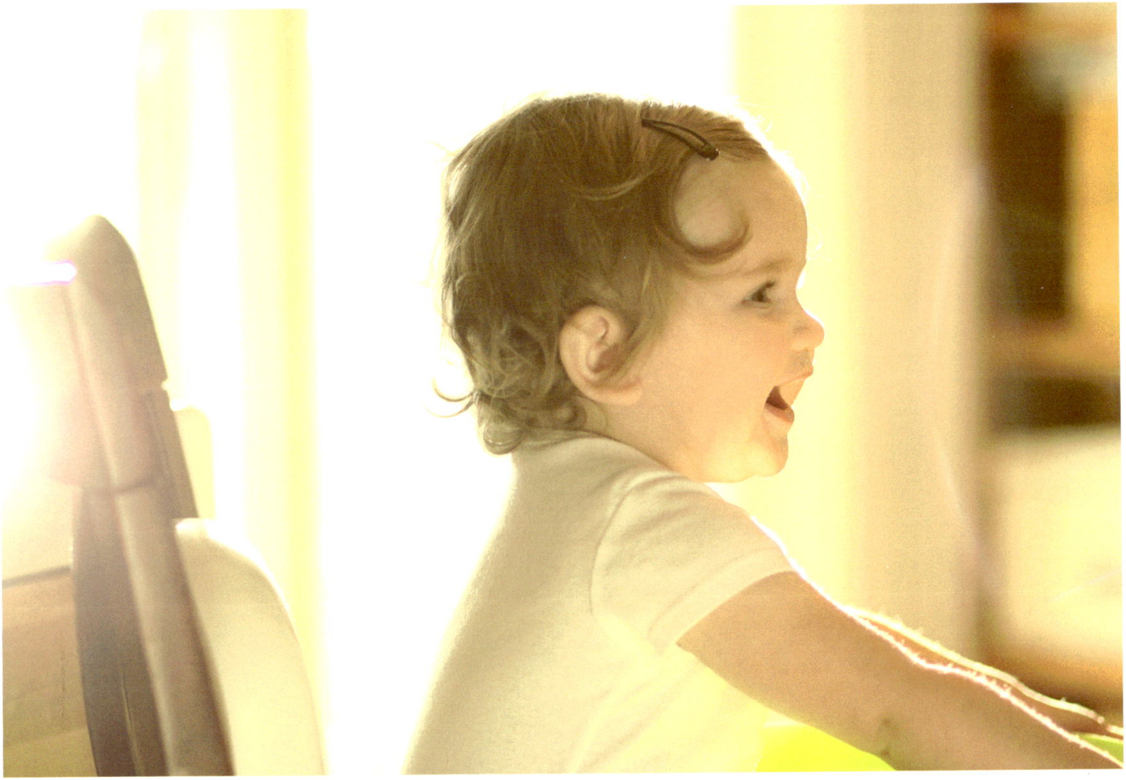

Anna Hollister Photography

Vancouver, WA

annahollister.com

Karenhalbert Photography

Nashville, TN

karenhalbertphotography.com

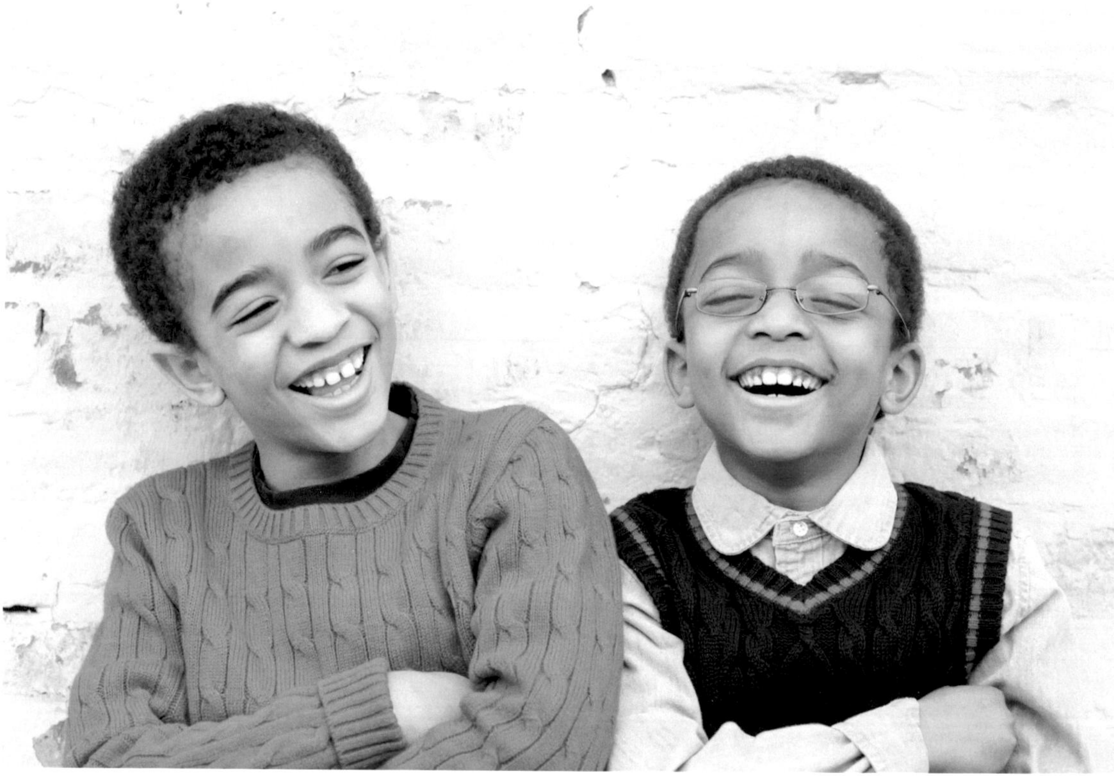

Ariana Falerni Photography

Rockland County, NY

arianafalerni.com

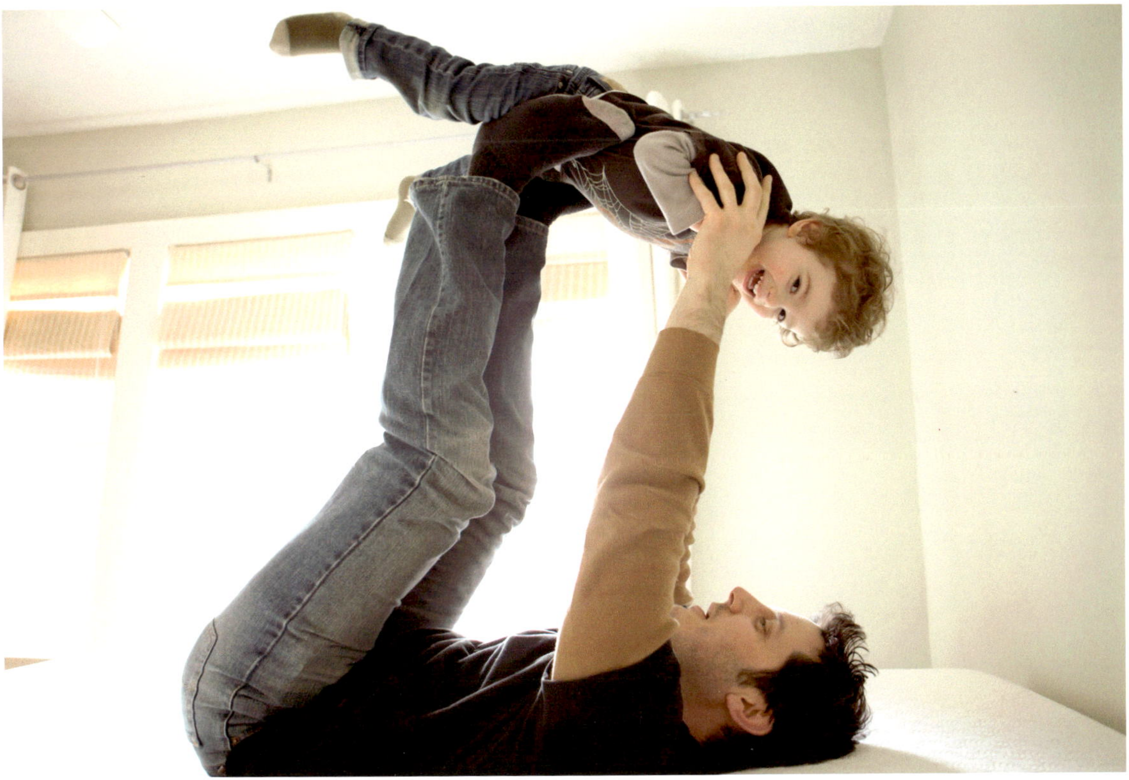

Leesa Perry Photogrpahy

Brisbane, Australia

leesaperryphotography.com

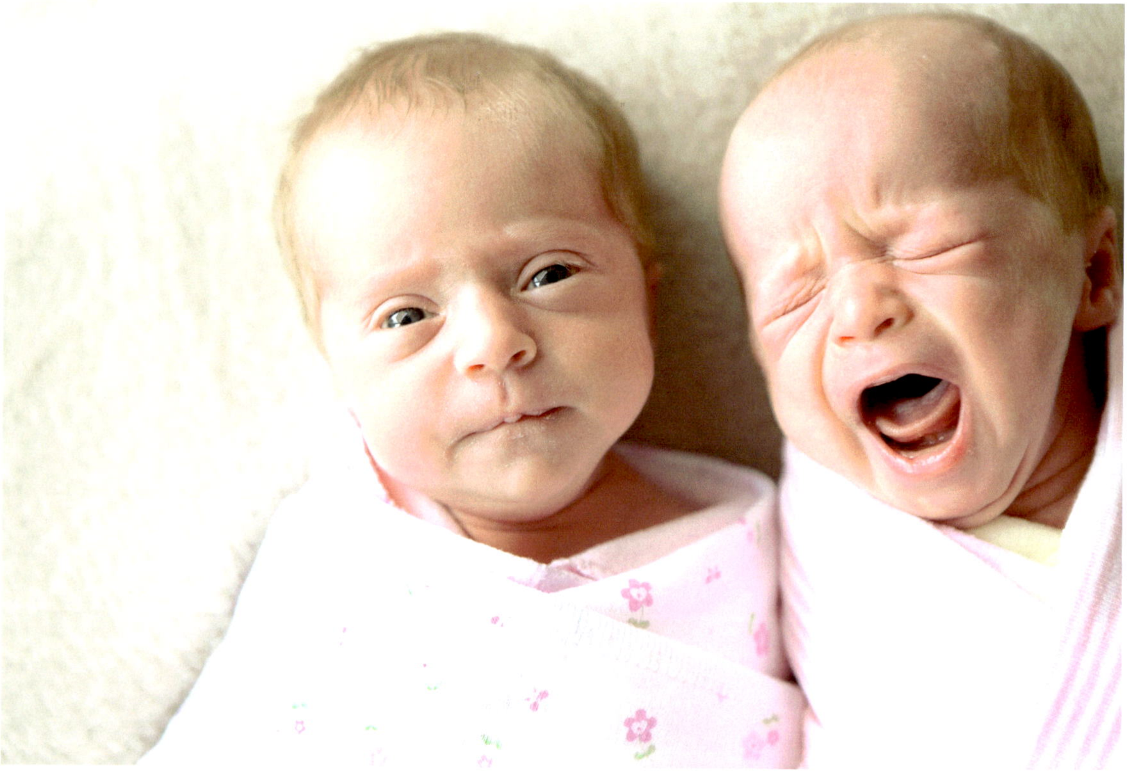

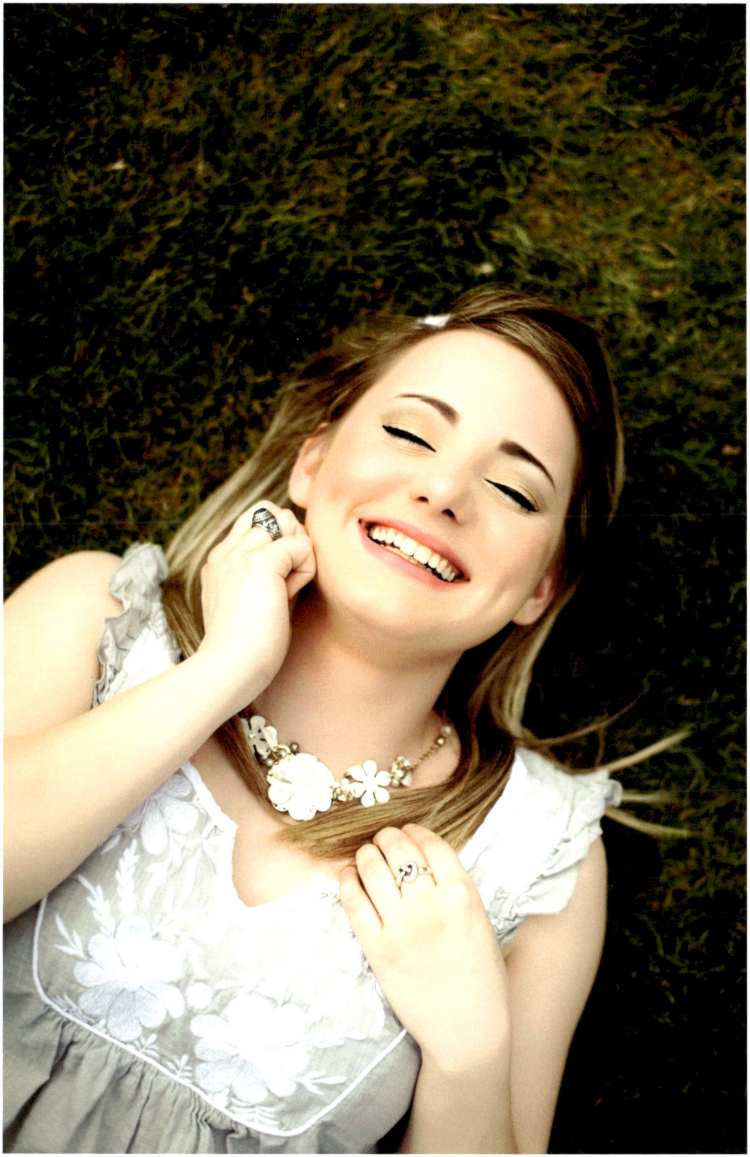

Amanda Holloway Photography

Huntsville, TX

amandahollowayphotography.com

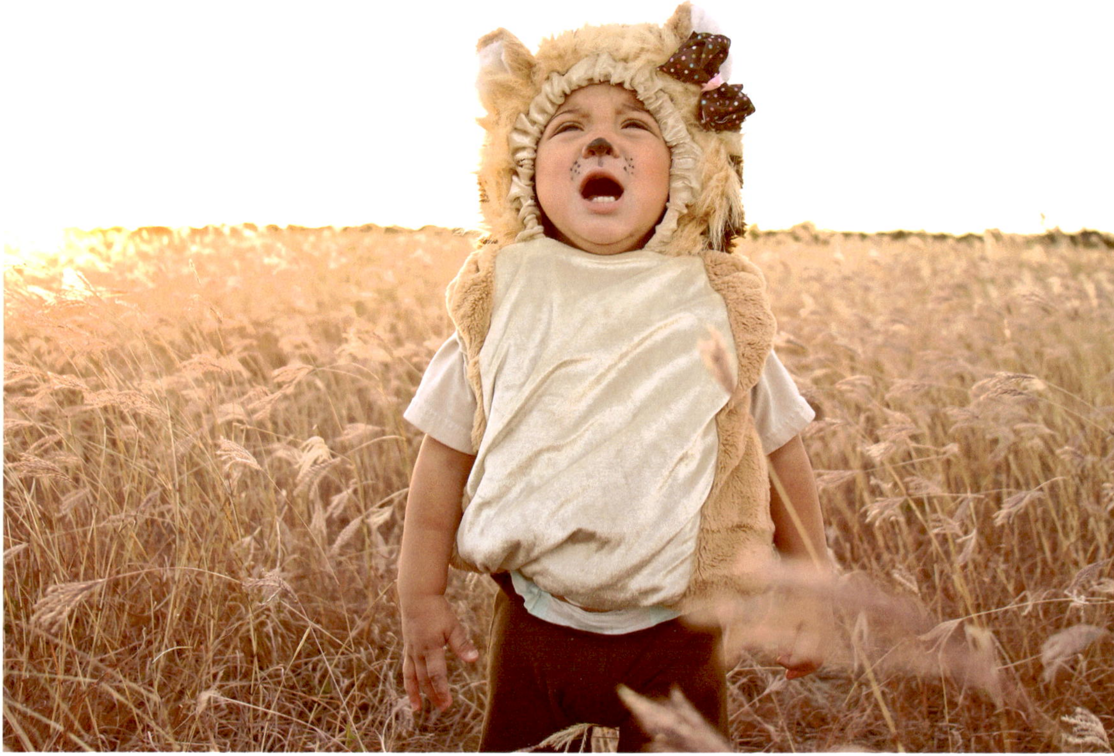

Rochelle Scutt Photography

Amarillo, TX

April Nienhuis Photography

Cleveland, OK

aprilnienhuis.com

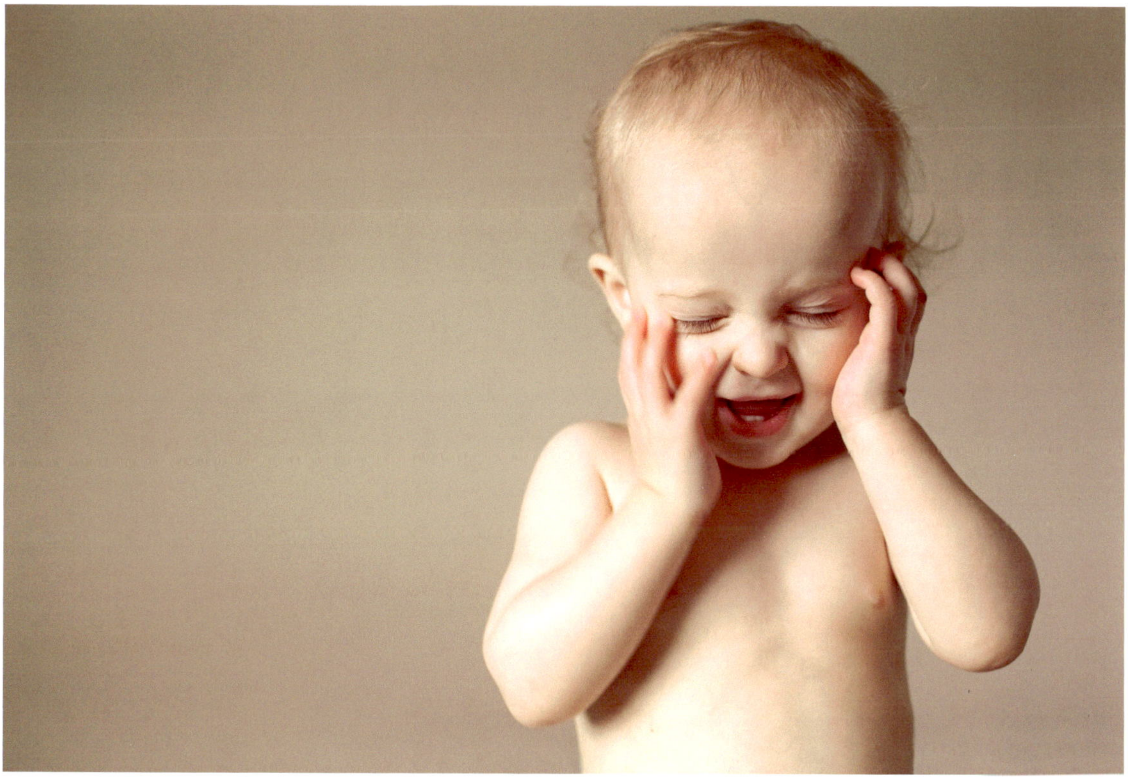

Kathy Howard Photography

Raleigh, NC

kathyhowardphotography.com

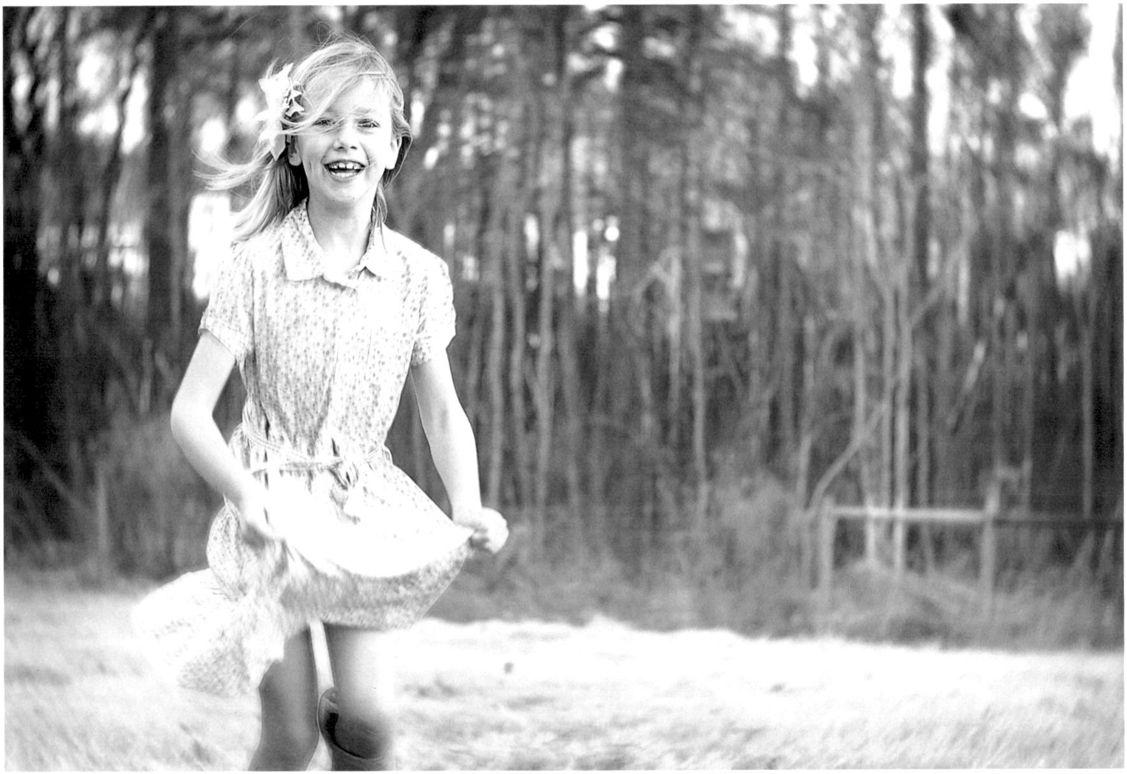

Katherine D Photography

Fayetteville, NC

katherinedphotography.com

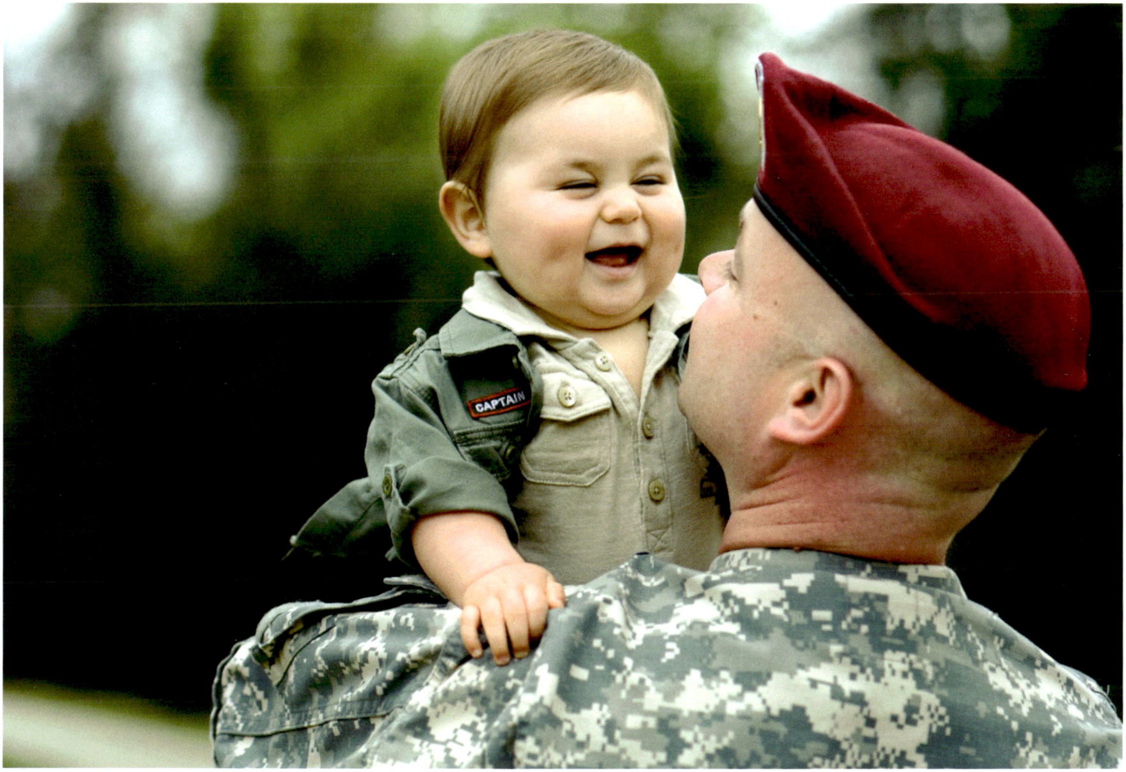

Jennifer Witt Photography

Minneapolis, MN

jenniferwittphotography.com

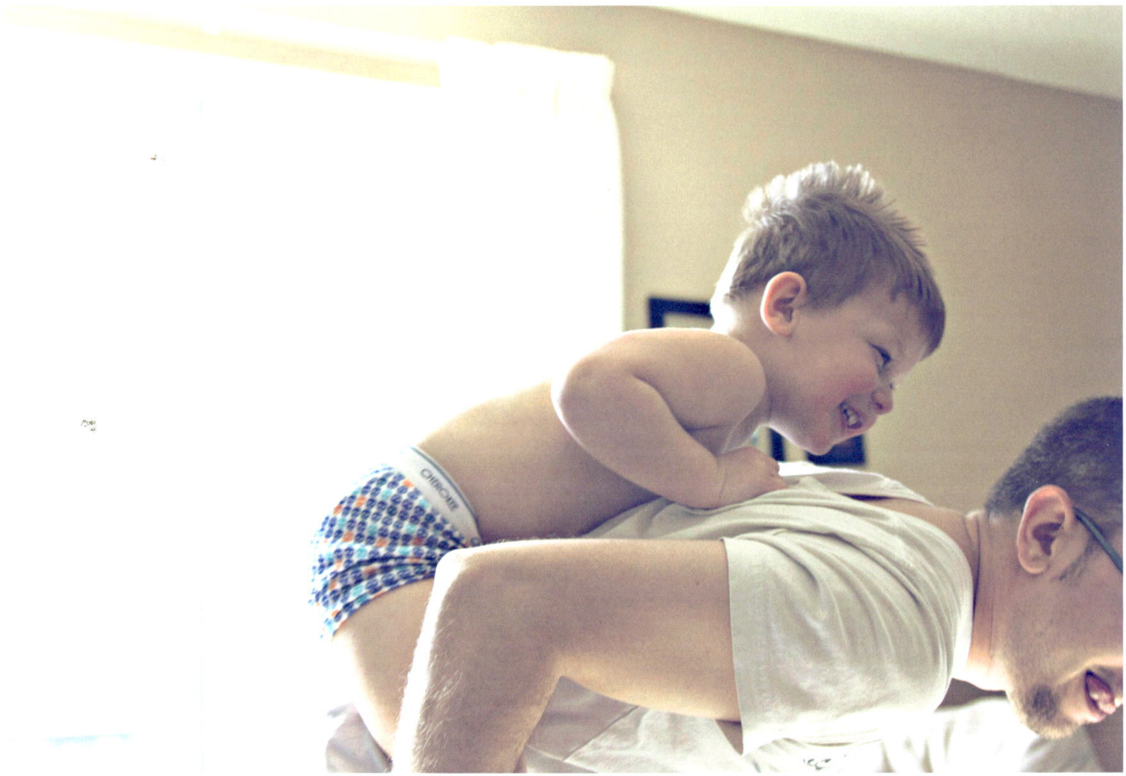

Kristin Ingalls

Kirkland, WA

kristiningalls.com

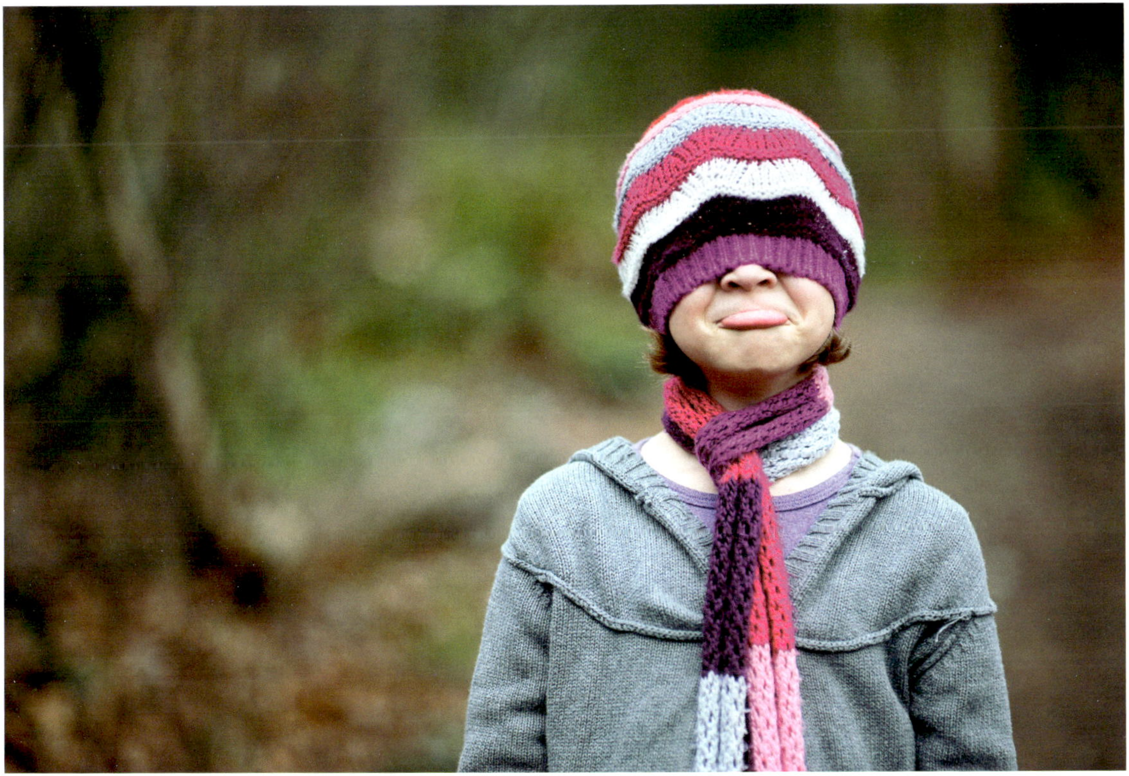

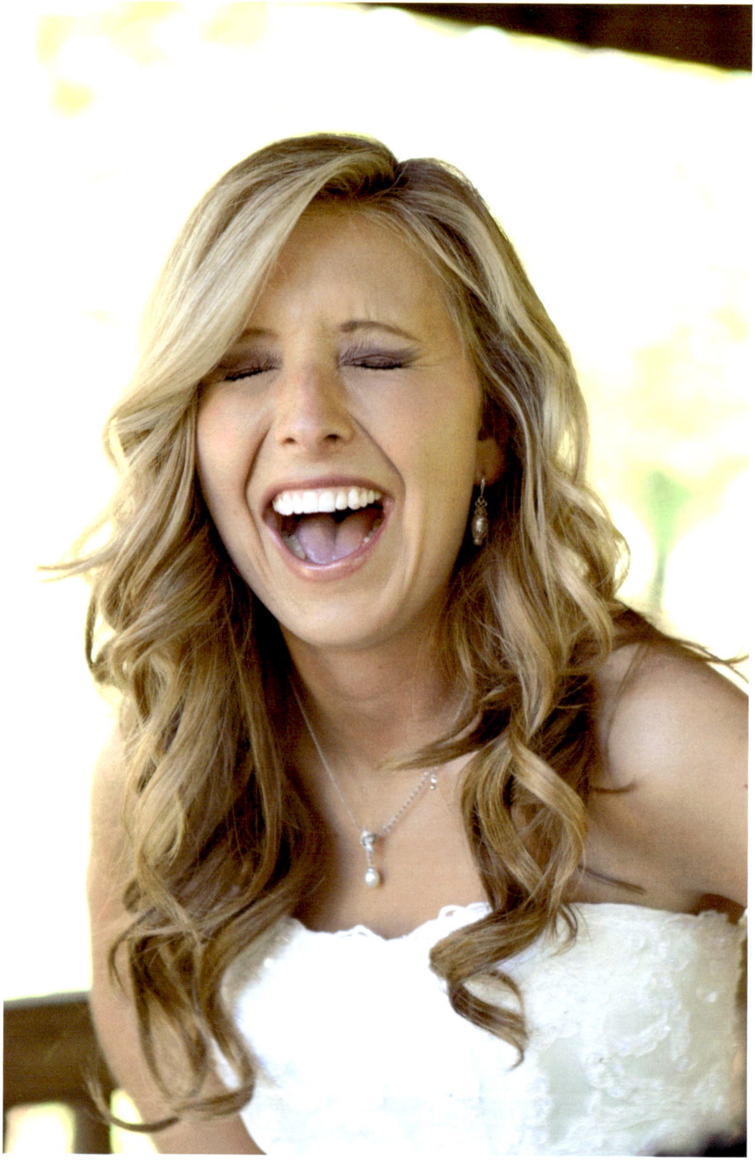

Susan Kelly Photography

Charlotte, NC

susankellyphotography.com

Jessica Hamlin Photography

Seattle, WA

jessicahamlinphotography.com

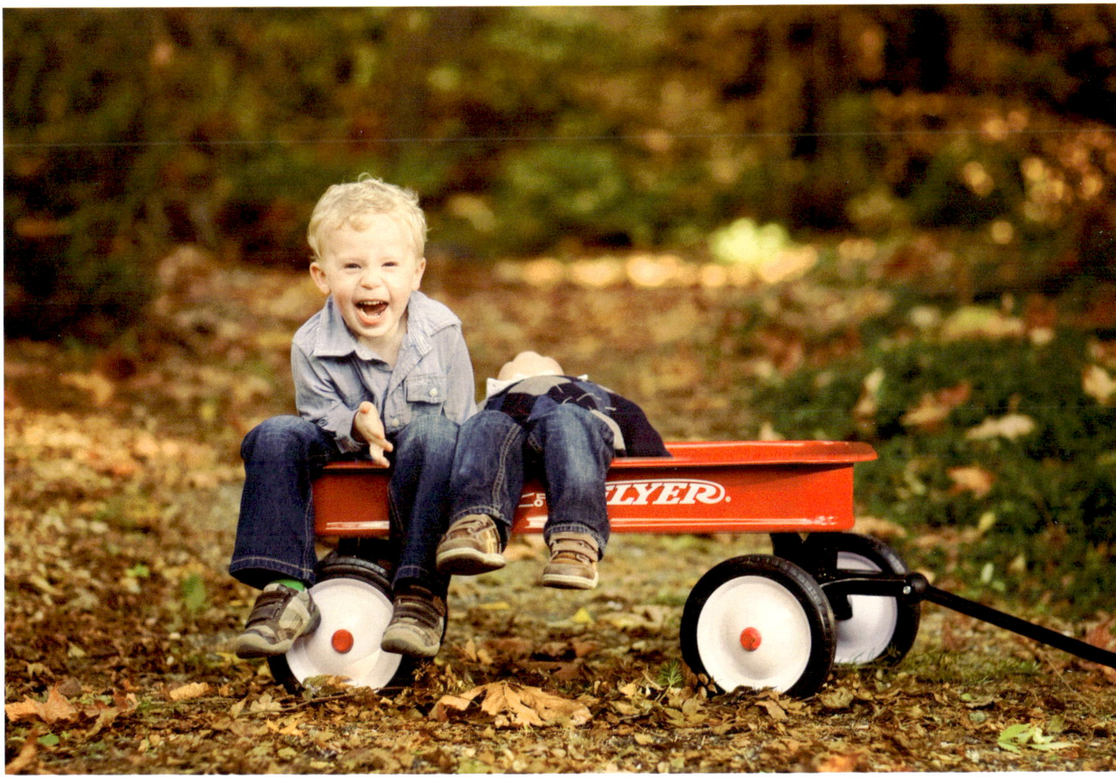

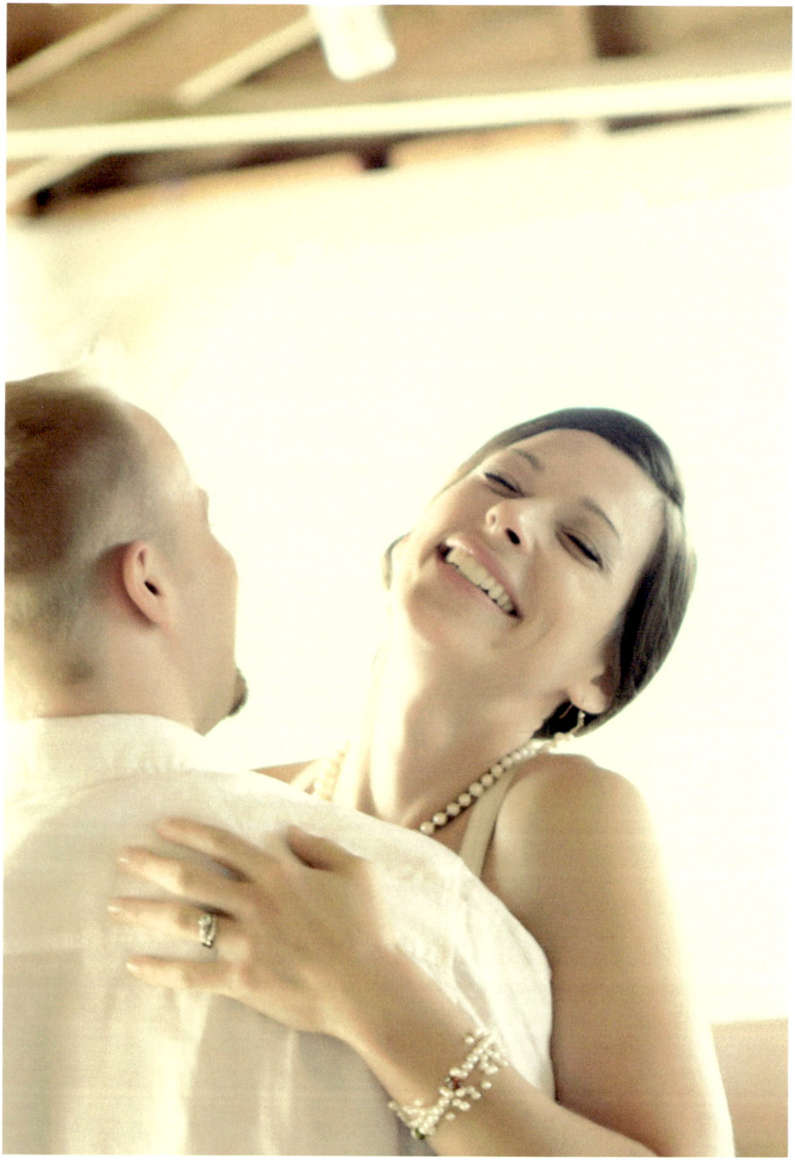

Liz Hayford - Windy Hill Photography

Mid Coast Maine

windyhillphotography.com

Kristine Kraft Photography

Columbia, PA

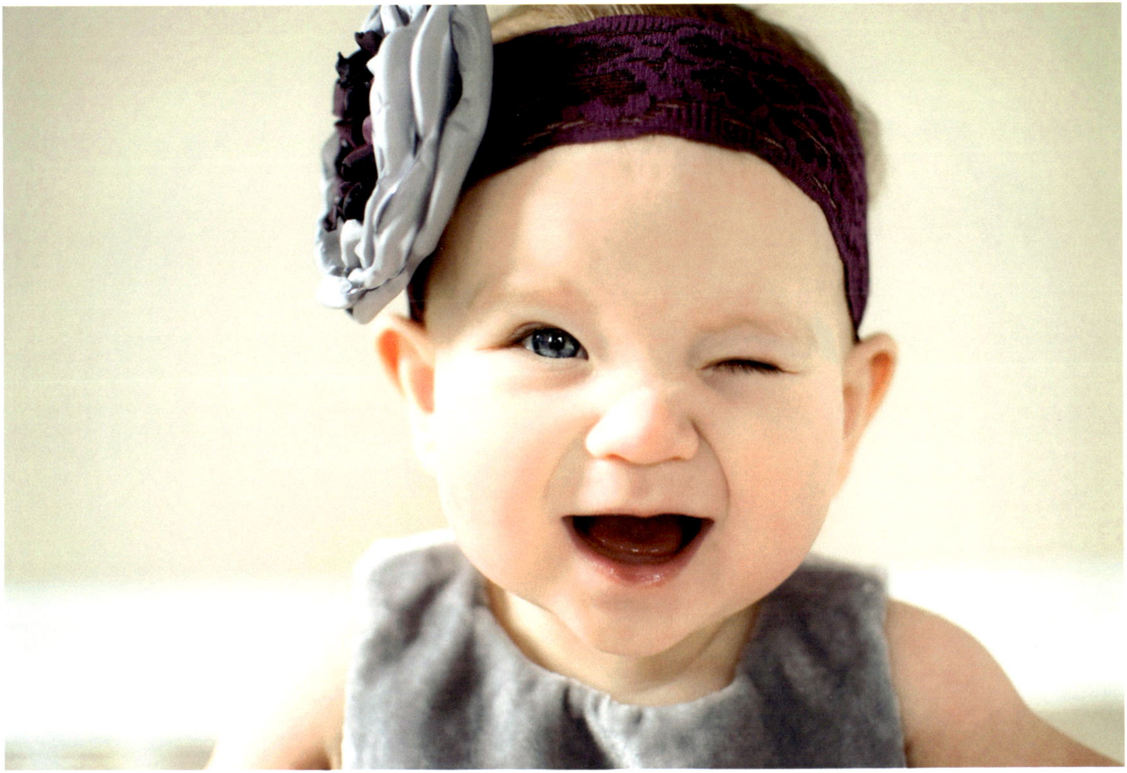

Tiffany Krieger Photography

Olney, MD

tiffanykrieger.com

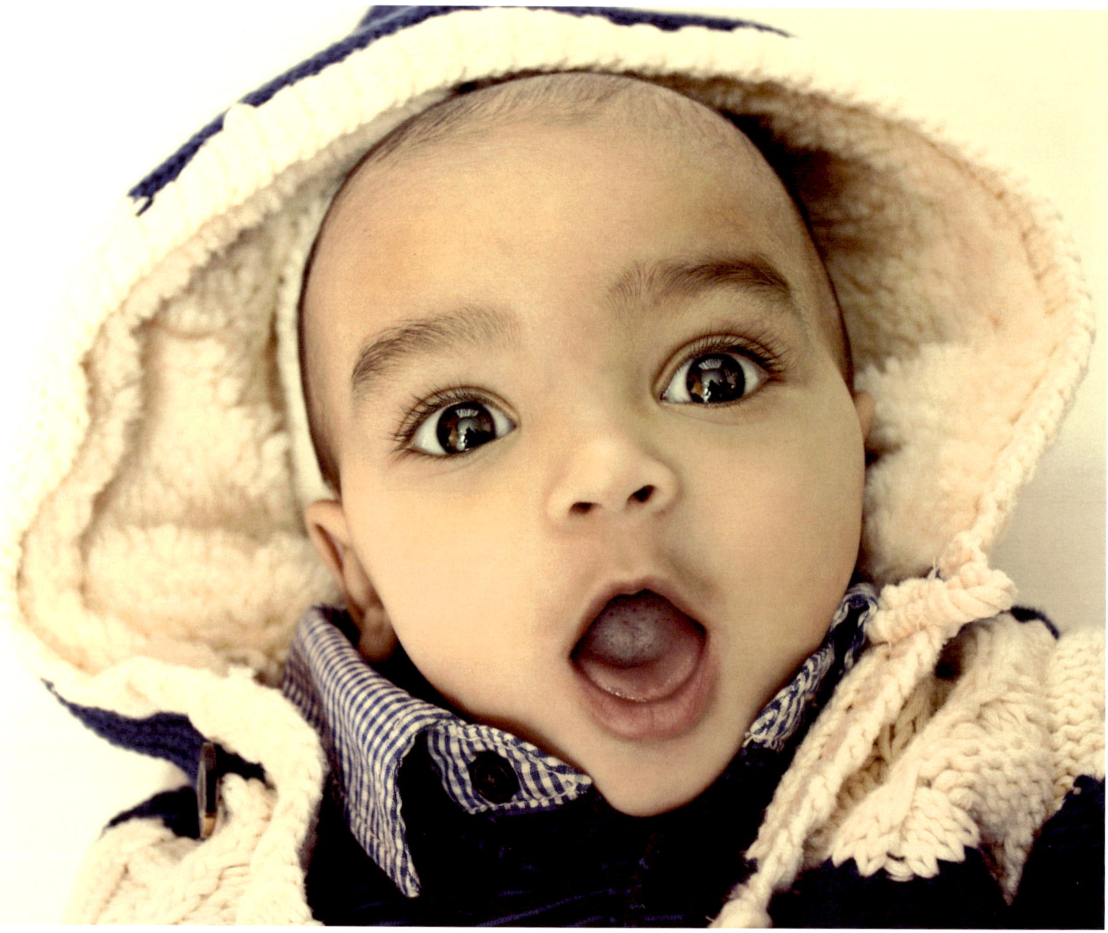

Shannon King Photography

Holly Springs, NC

shannonkphoto.com

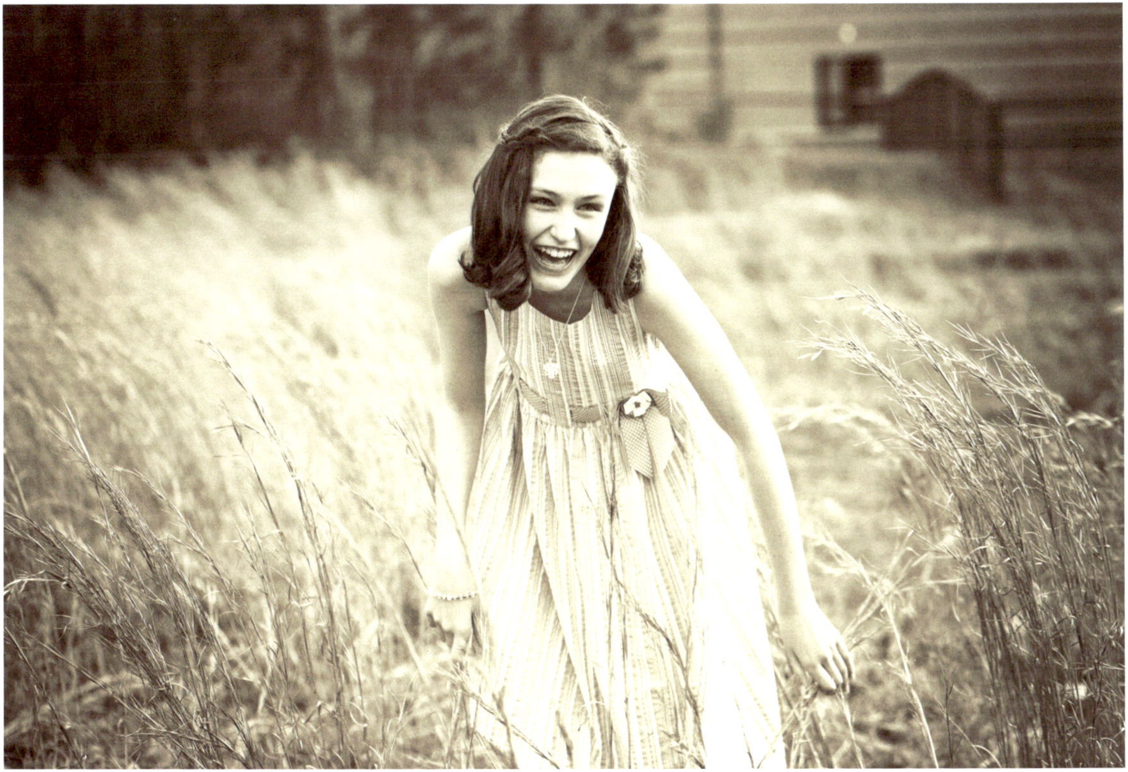

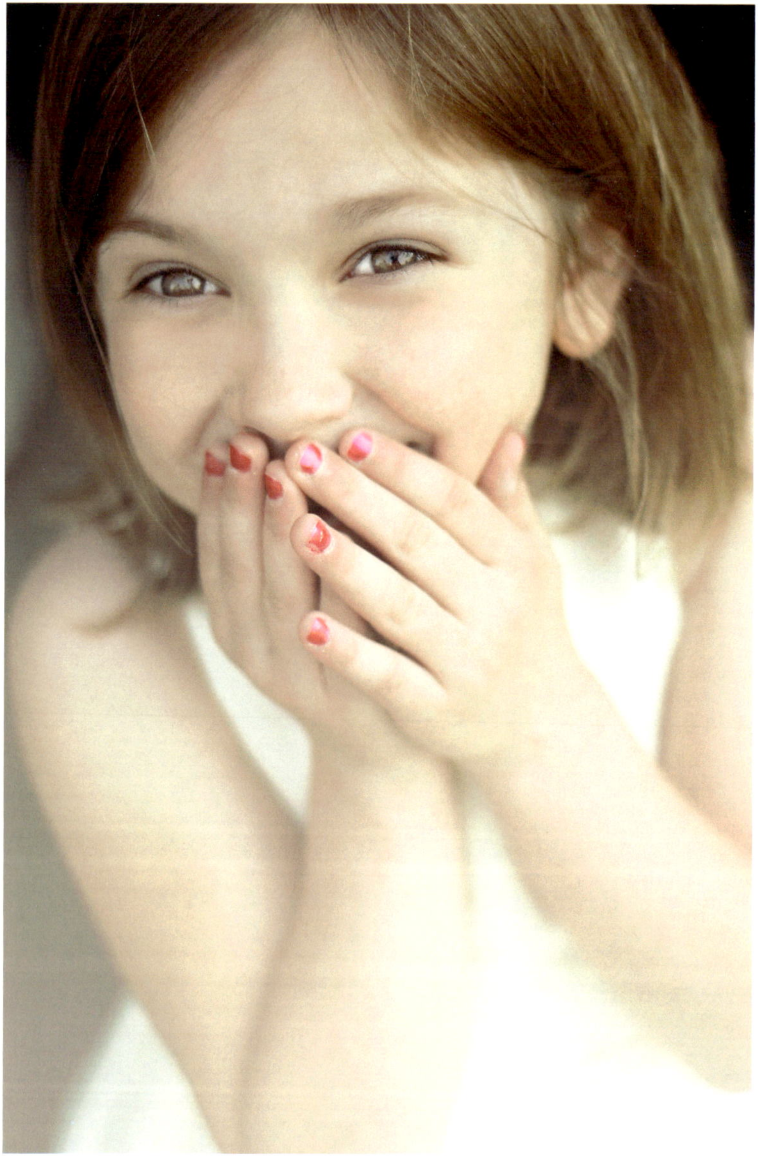

vicphotography

Minonk, IL

vicphotography.net

Landis Photography

Raleigh, NC

amylandisphotography.com

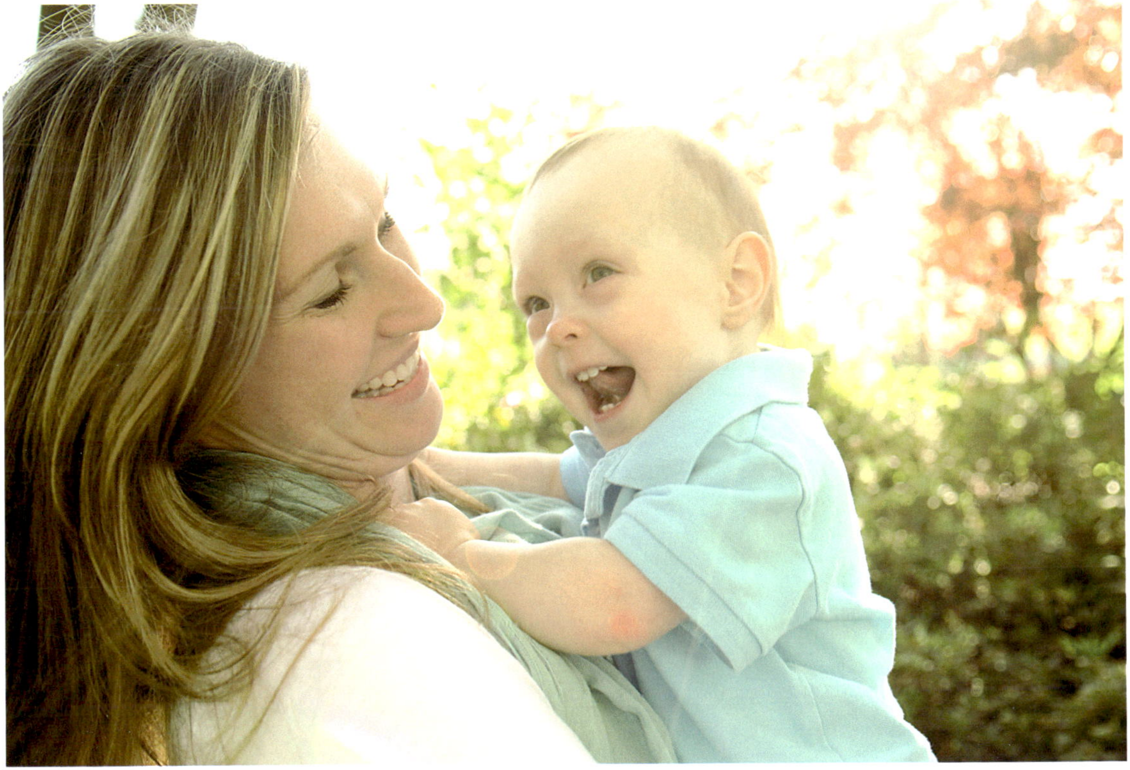

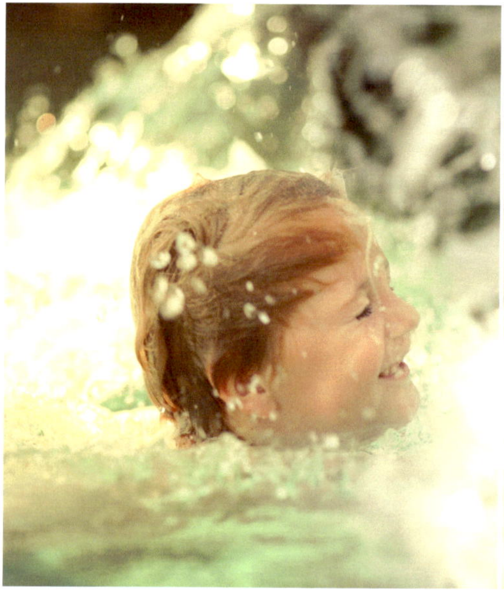

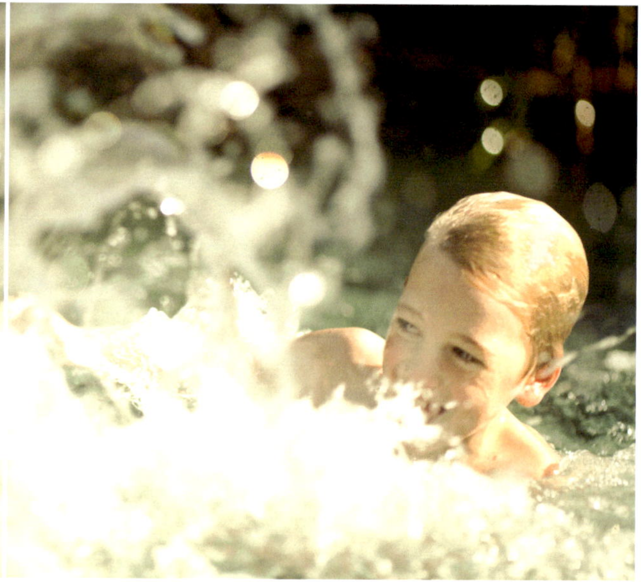

Lynne Rigby

Orlando, FL

lynnerigby.com

Holly Thompson

Austin, TX

hollyanissa.com

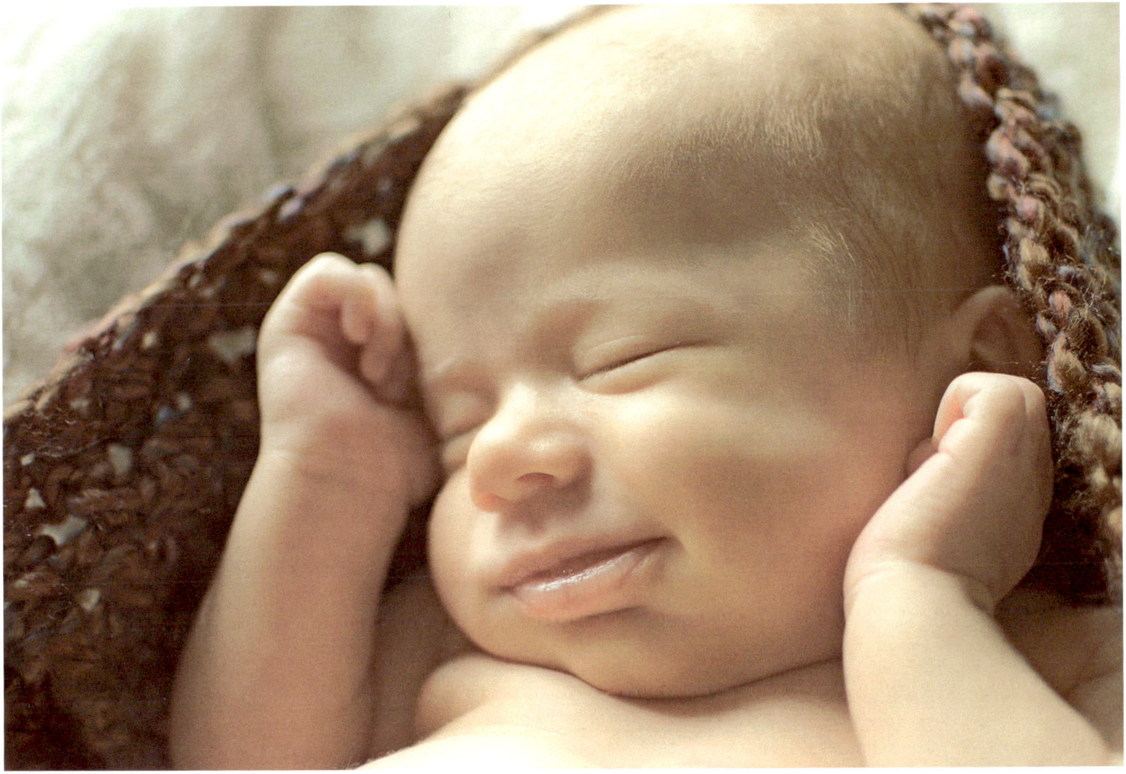

Megapixie

Chapel Hill, NC

megapixie.com

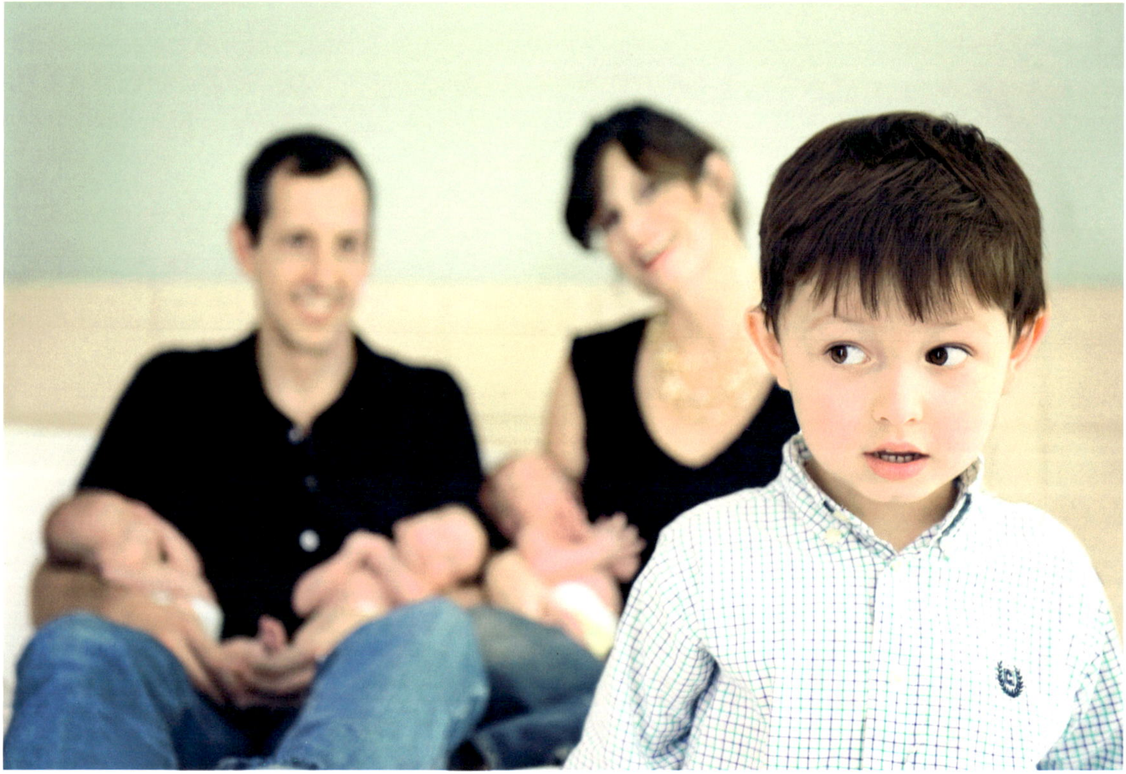

Jennifer Likes

thelikesfamily.com

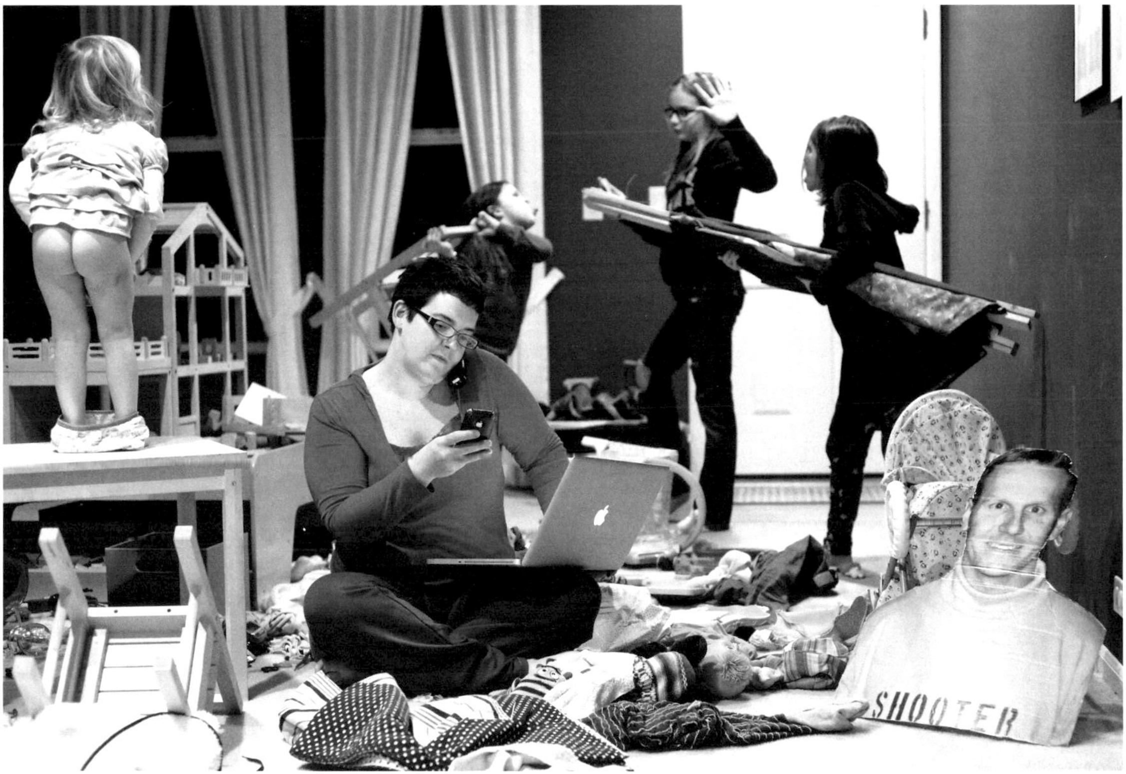

Lia Lotito Fotografia

Rio de Janeiro, Brazil

lialotito.com.br

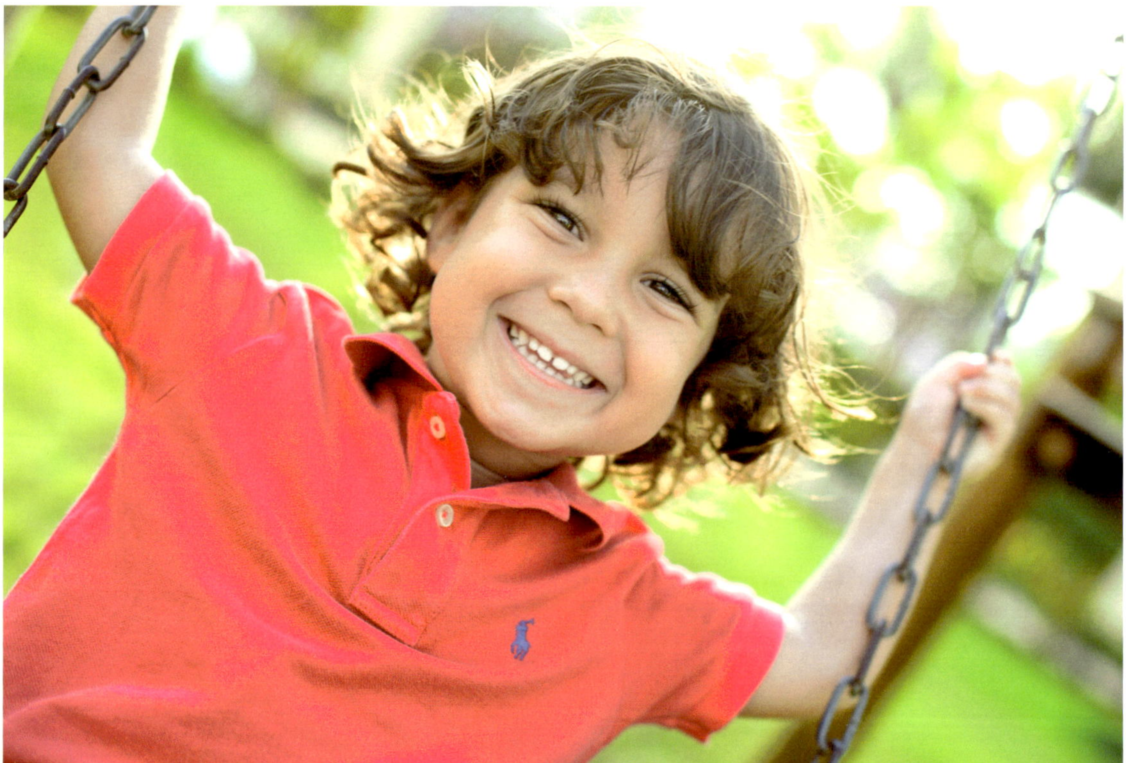

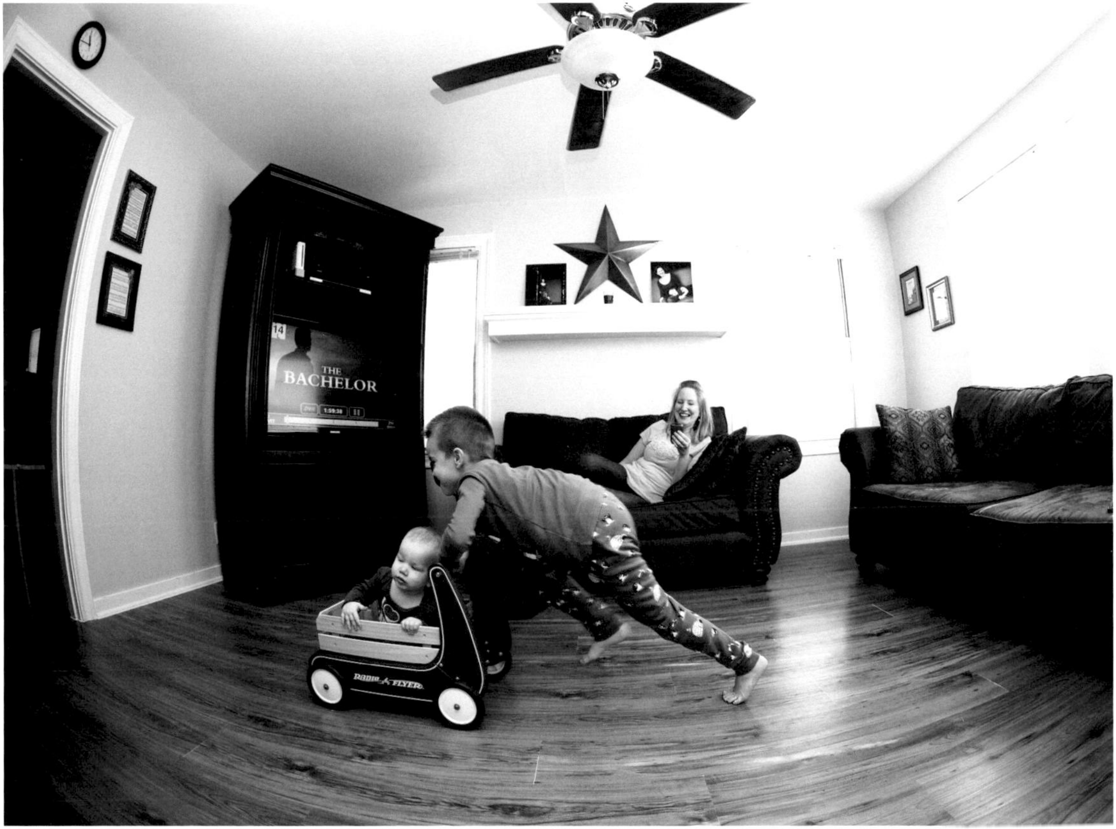

Elisabeth Ross

Brownsboro, TX

elisabethrossphotography.com

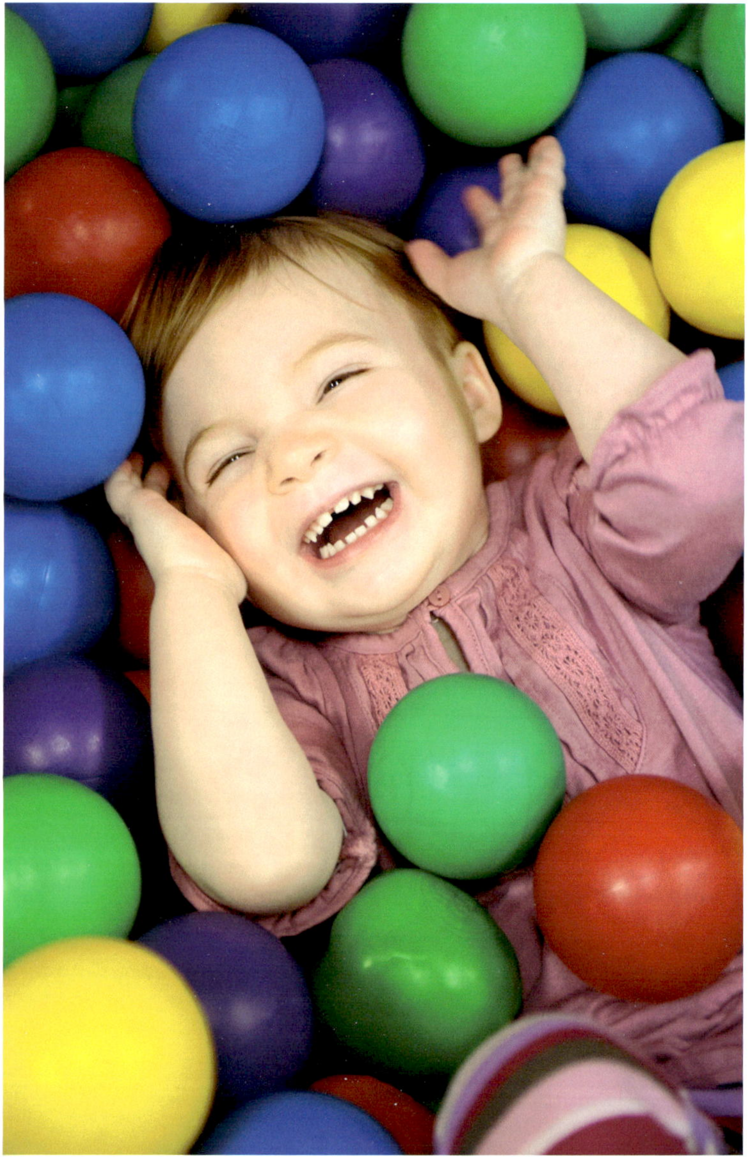

Megan Moore - Megan Jane Photography

Boston, MA

meganjanephotography.com

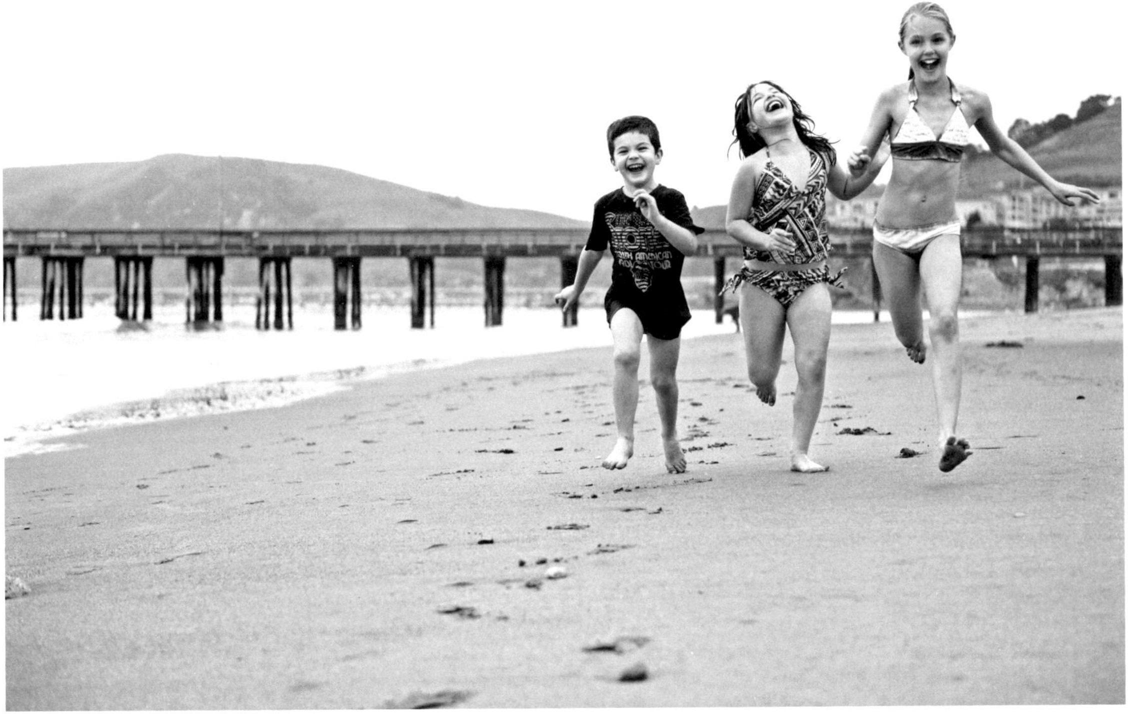

Tami Wilson Photography

Denver, CO

tamiwilsonphotography.com

Christina McGuire Photography

Novi, MI

christinamcguire.com

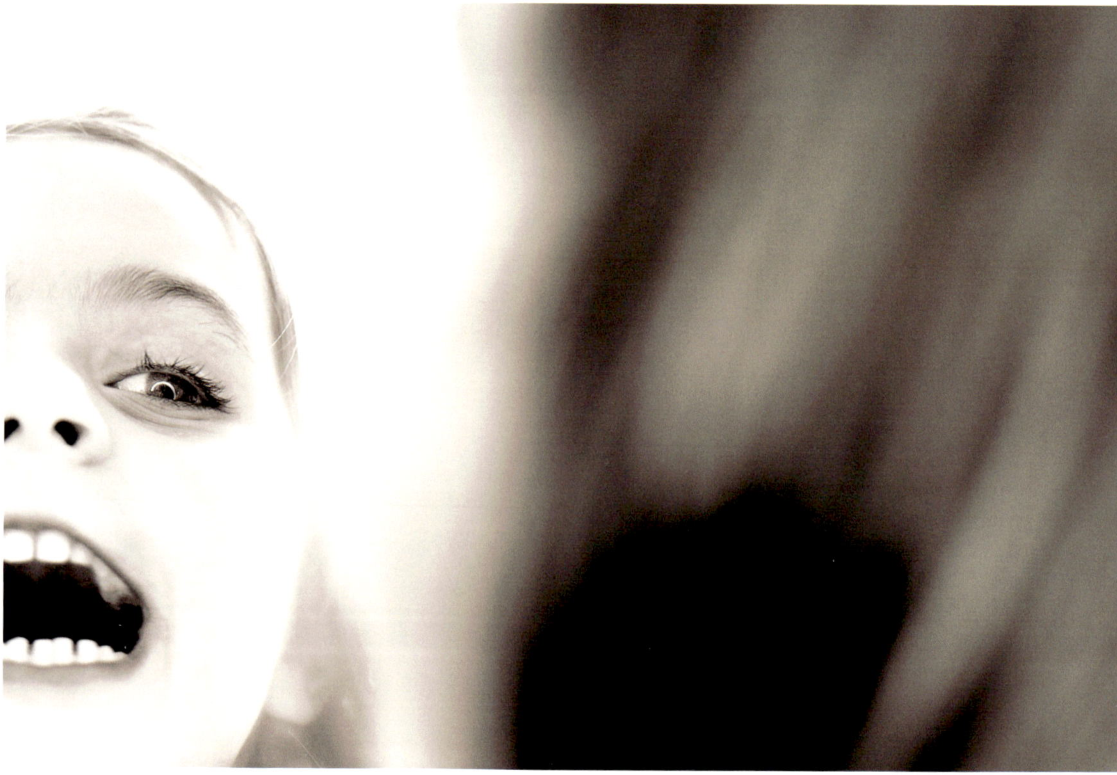

Marsha Mifsud - The Savvy Photographer

McLean, VA

thesavvyphotographerblog.com

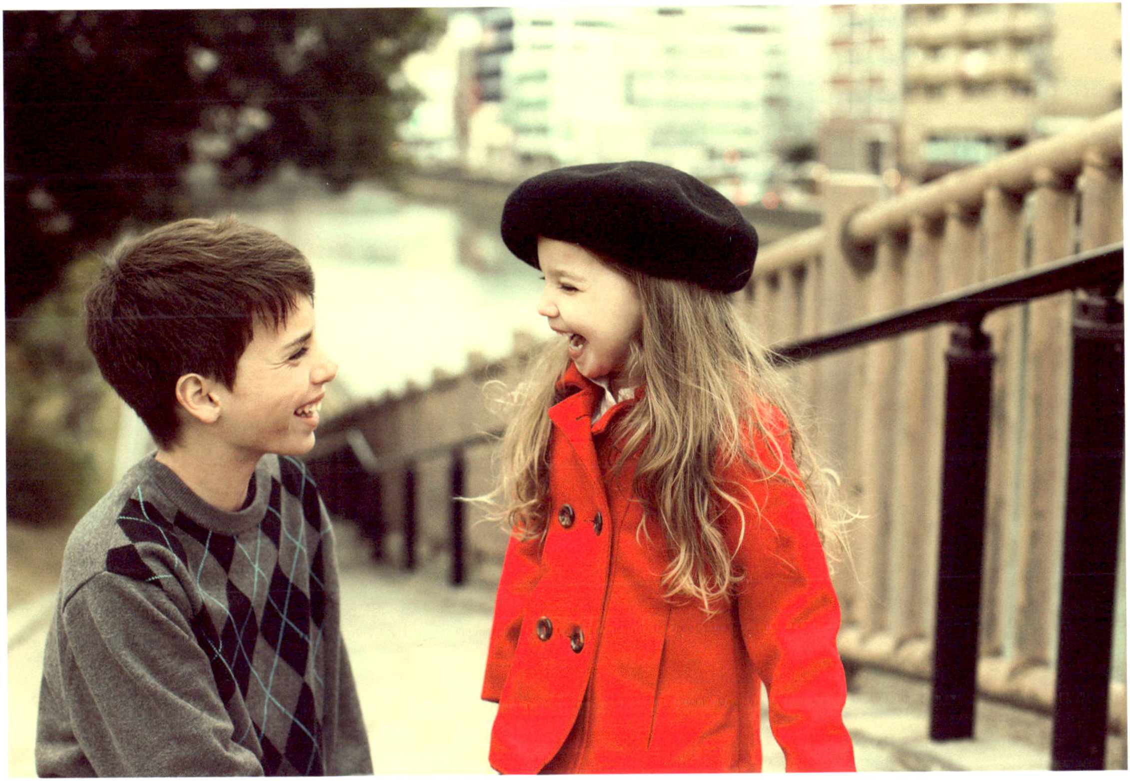

Emily Sara Photography

Lafayette, CA

emilysaraphoto.com

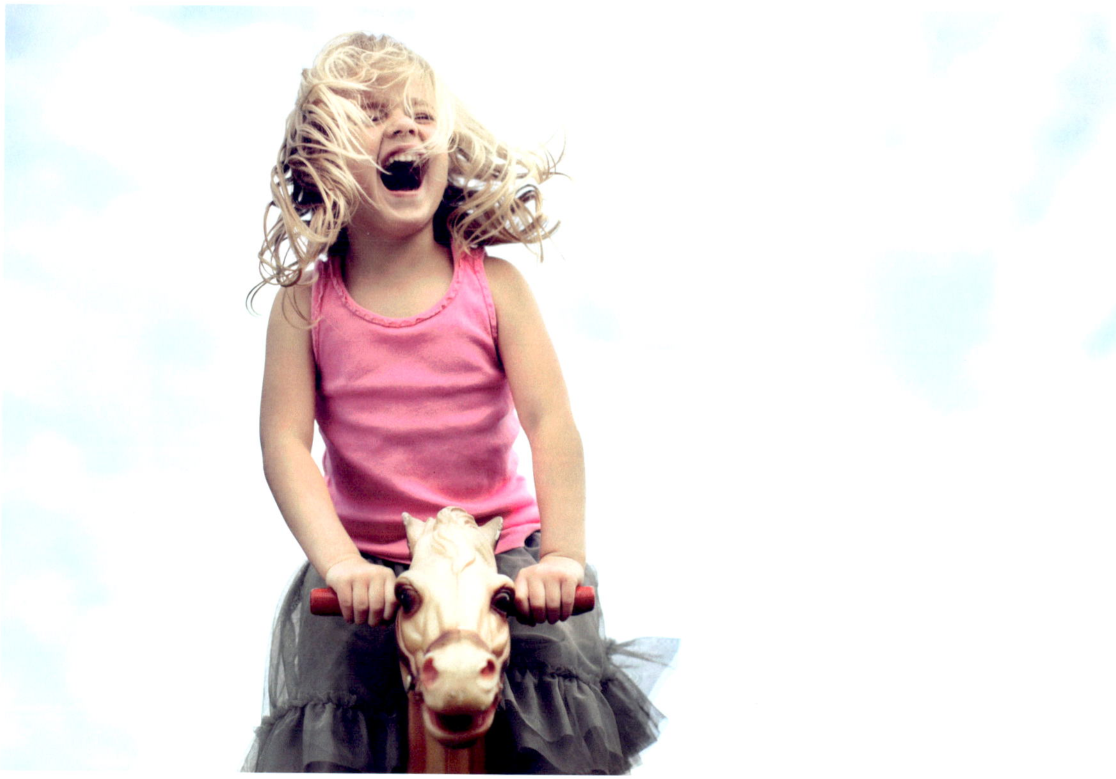

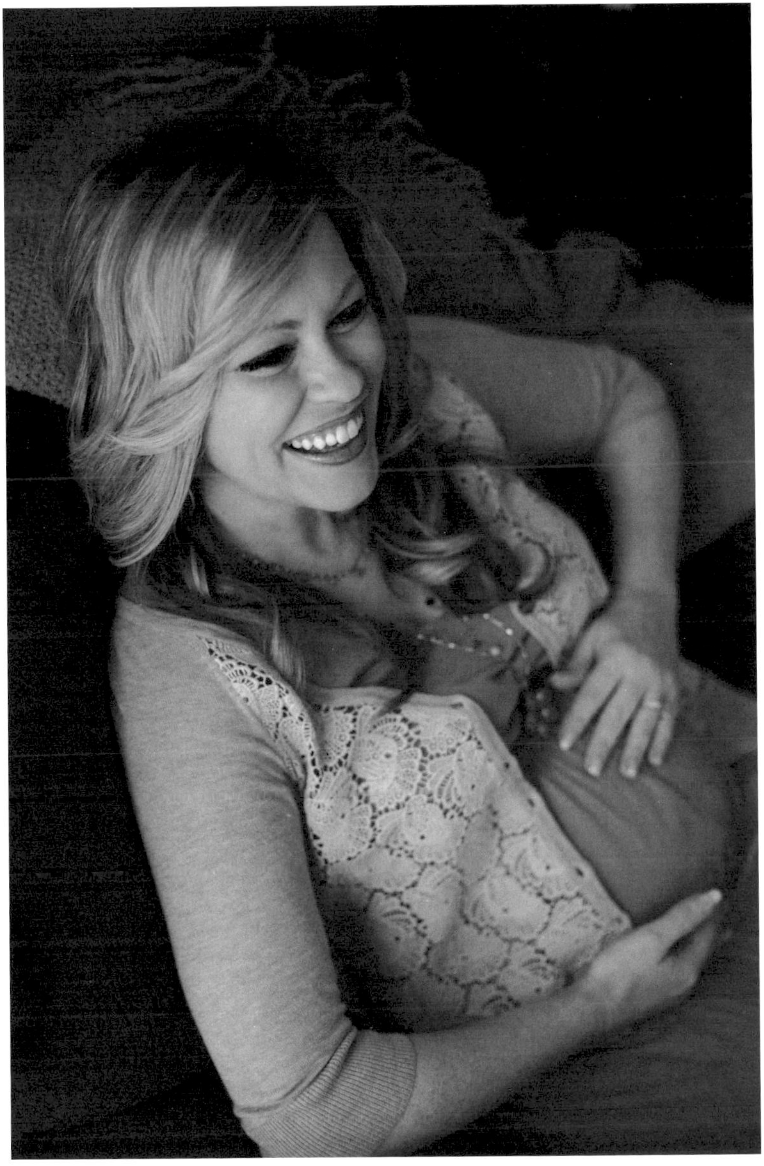

Darien Aislee Photography

Royse City, TX

darienaislee.com

Monica Wilkinson Photography

Seattle, WA

monicawilkinson.com

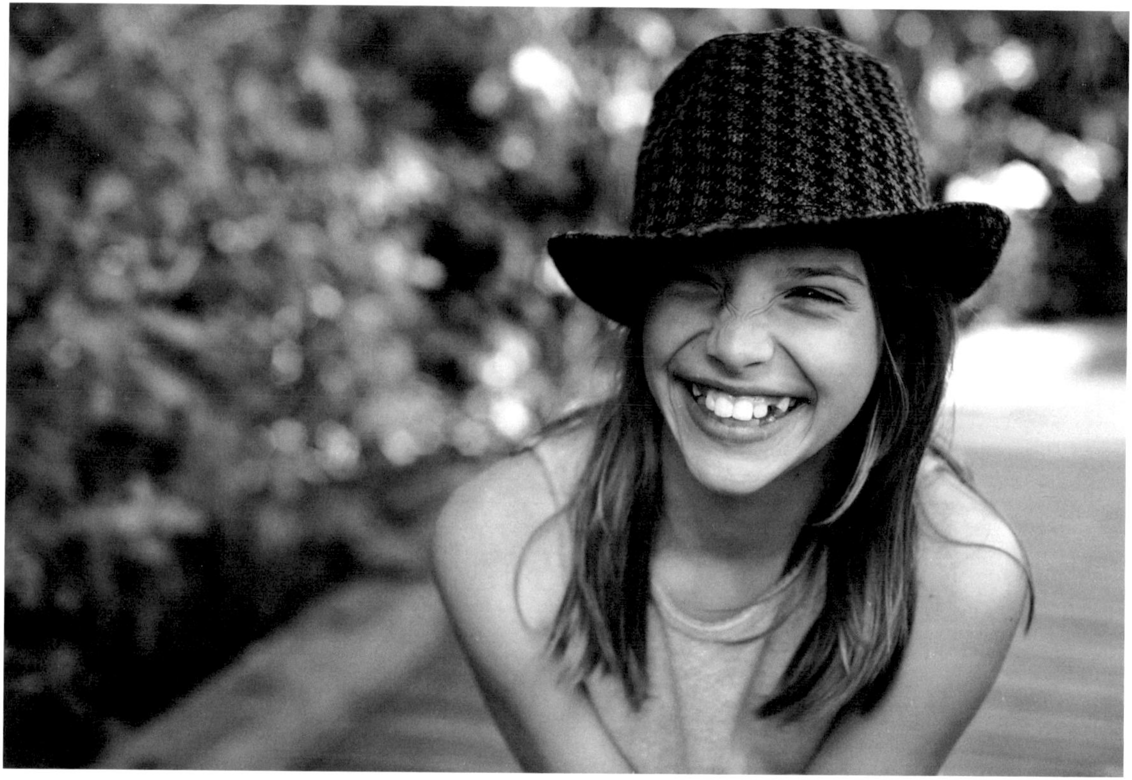

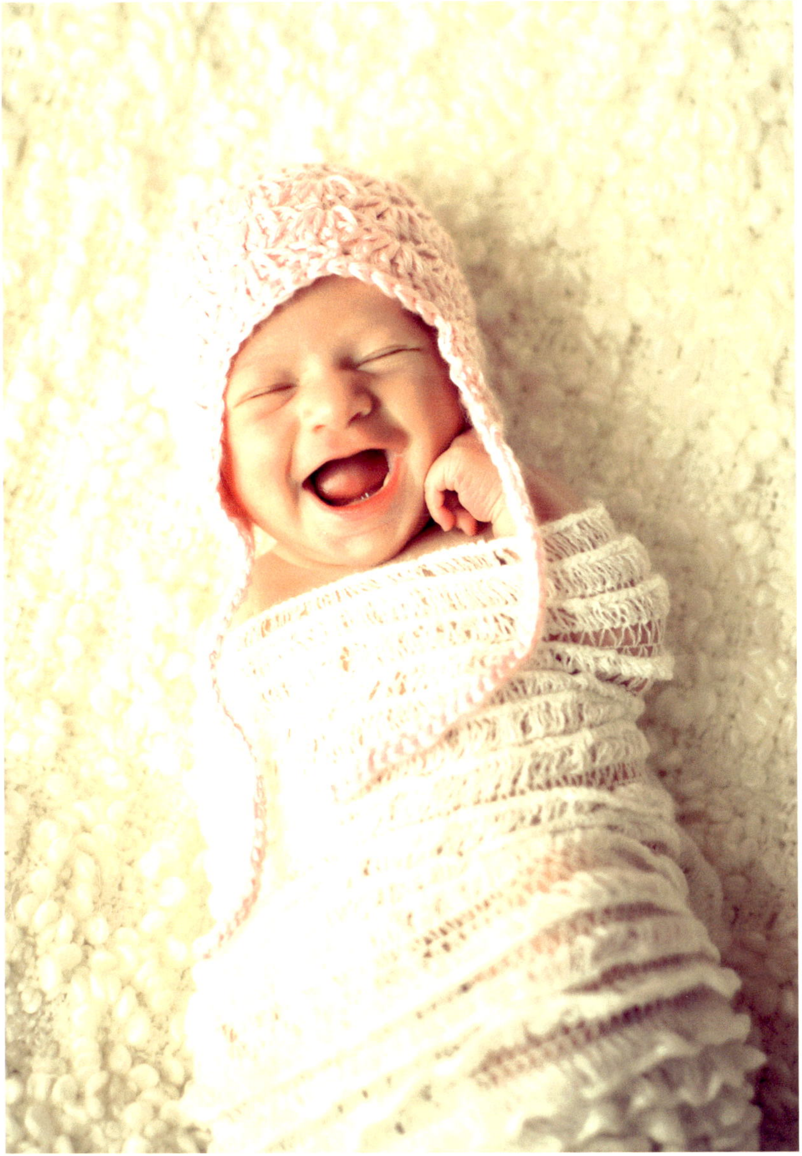

Jolie Anne Photography

Phoenix, AZ

jolieannephotography.com

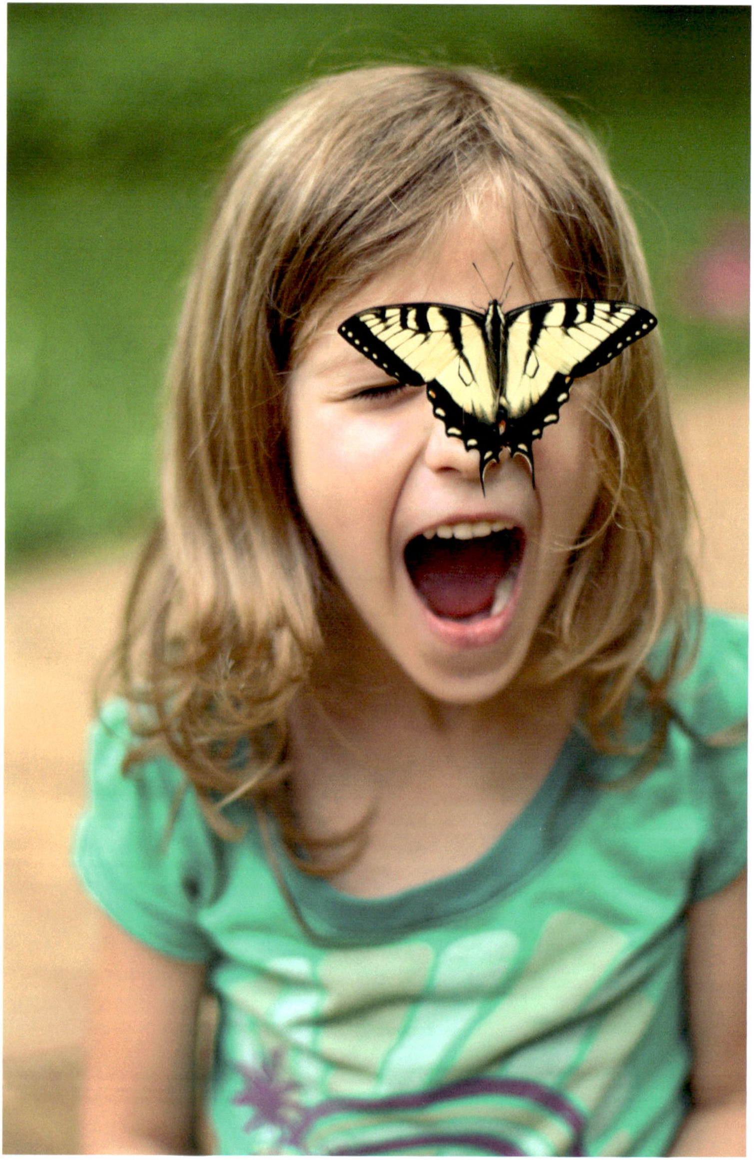

Jody McKitrick Photography

Washington, DC

jodymphotography.com

Hannah Mayo

West Palm Beach, FL

hannahmayophotography.com

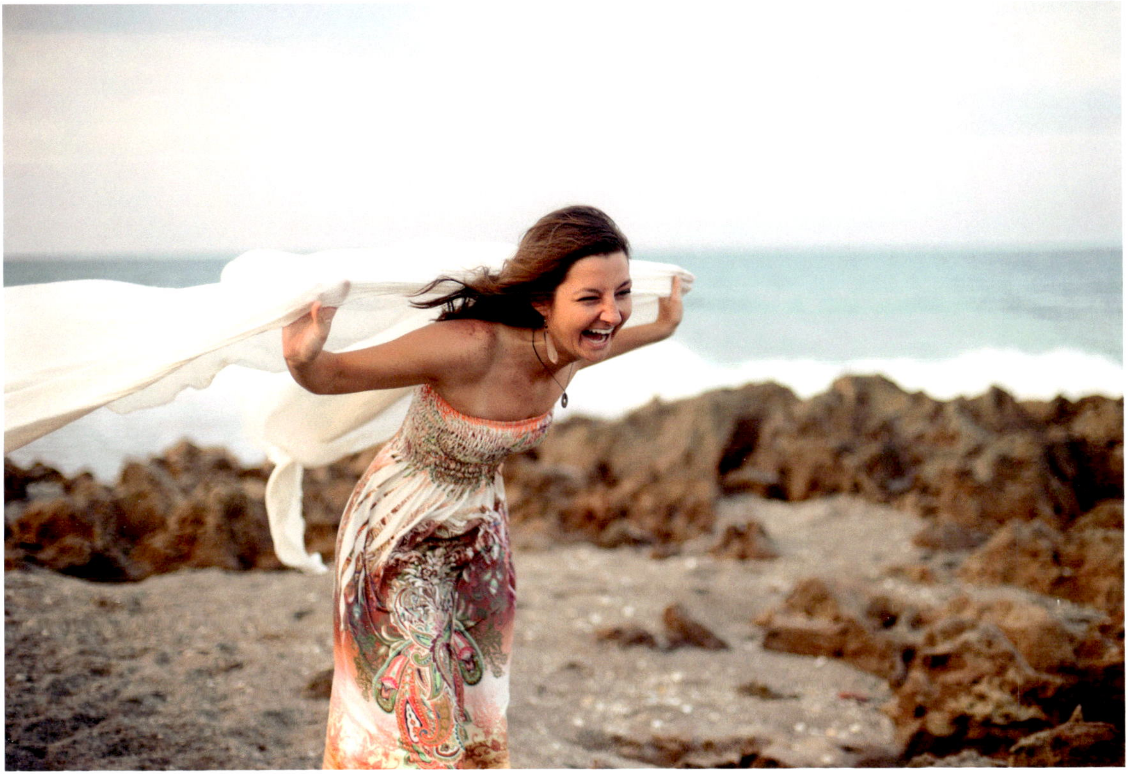

Lacey Meyers Photography

Molalla, OR

laceymeyersphotography.com

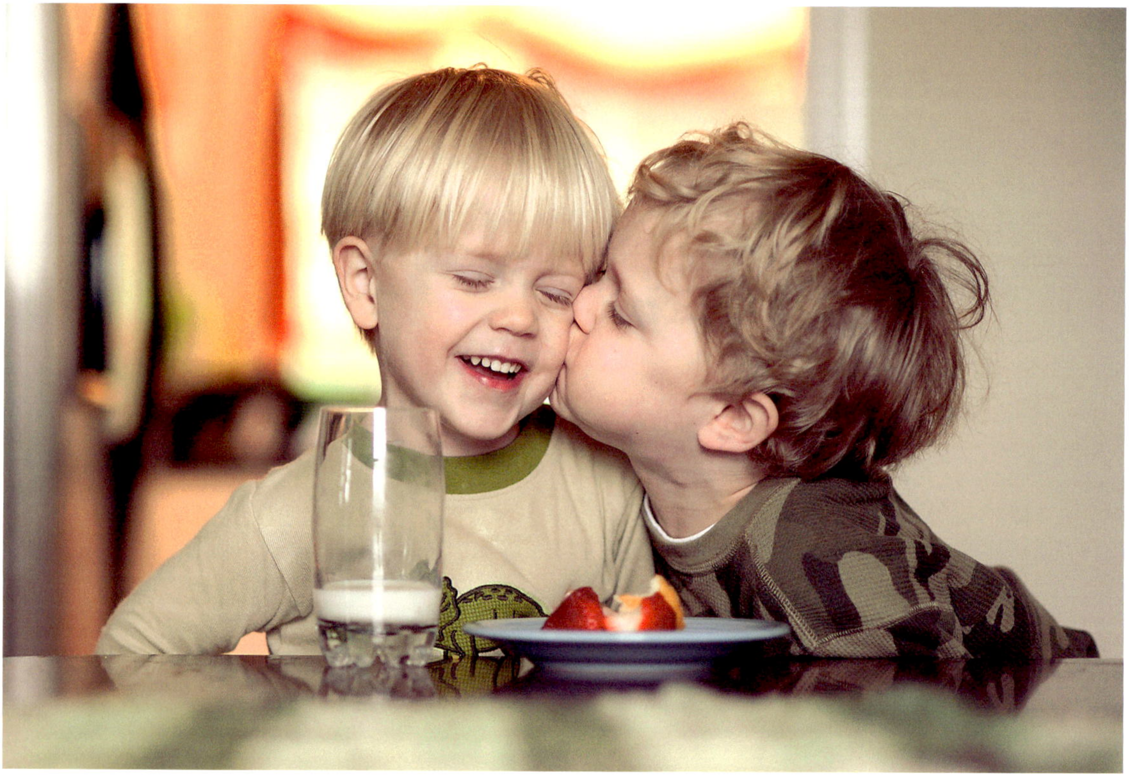

Gina Maxine Photography

Arroyo Grande, CA

ginamaxinephotography.com

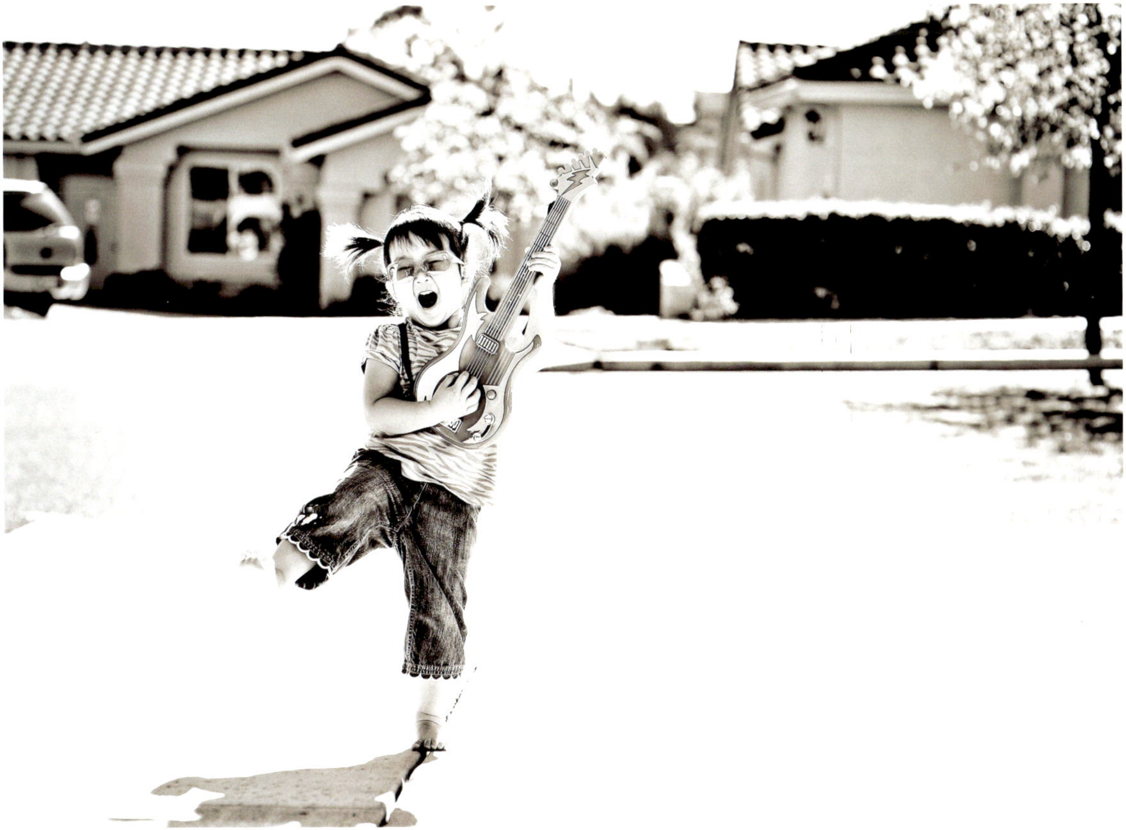

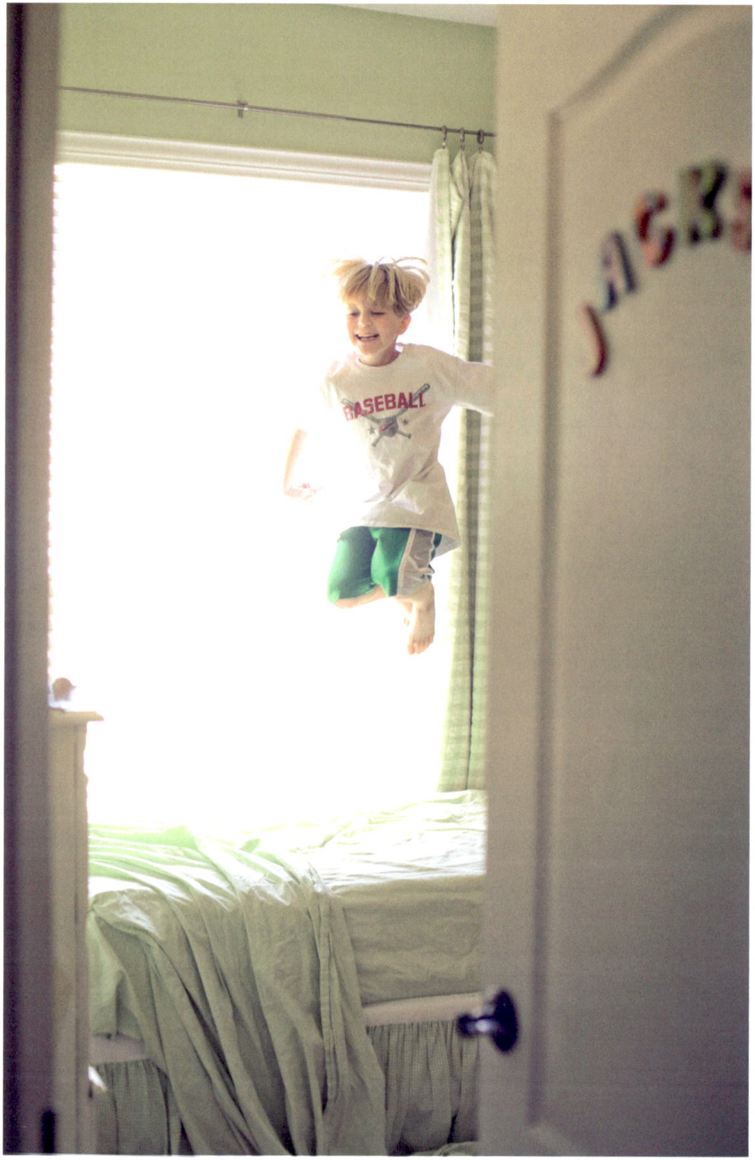

Lynne Rigby

Orlando, FL

lynnerigby.com

Chikadeez Photography

Atlanta, GA

photography.chikadeez.com

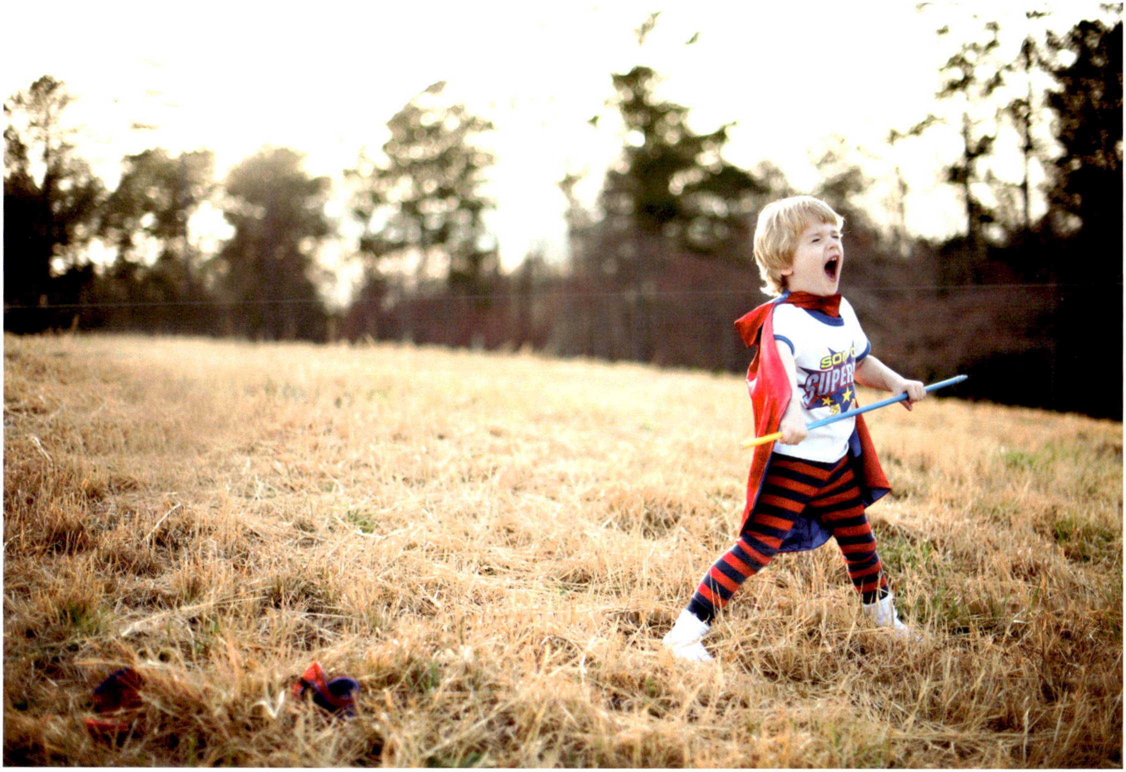

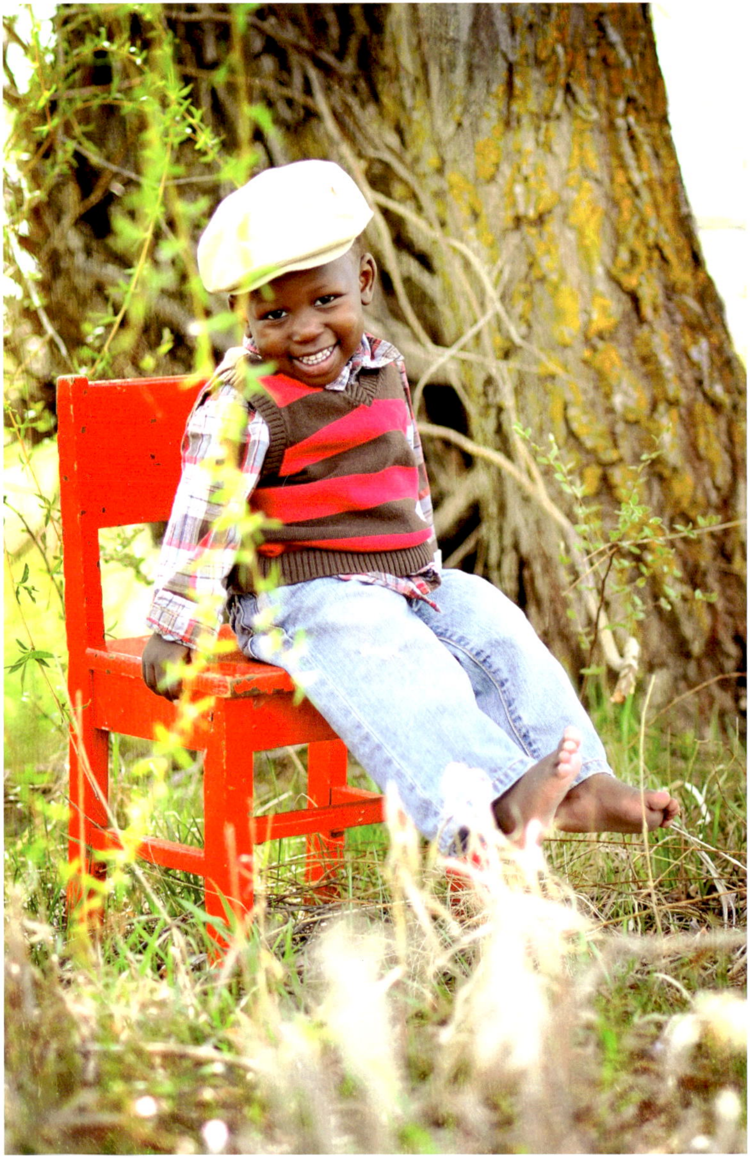

Laura Holmquist - Laura Lu Photography

Fergus Falls, MN

lauraluphotography.com

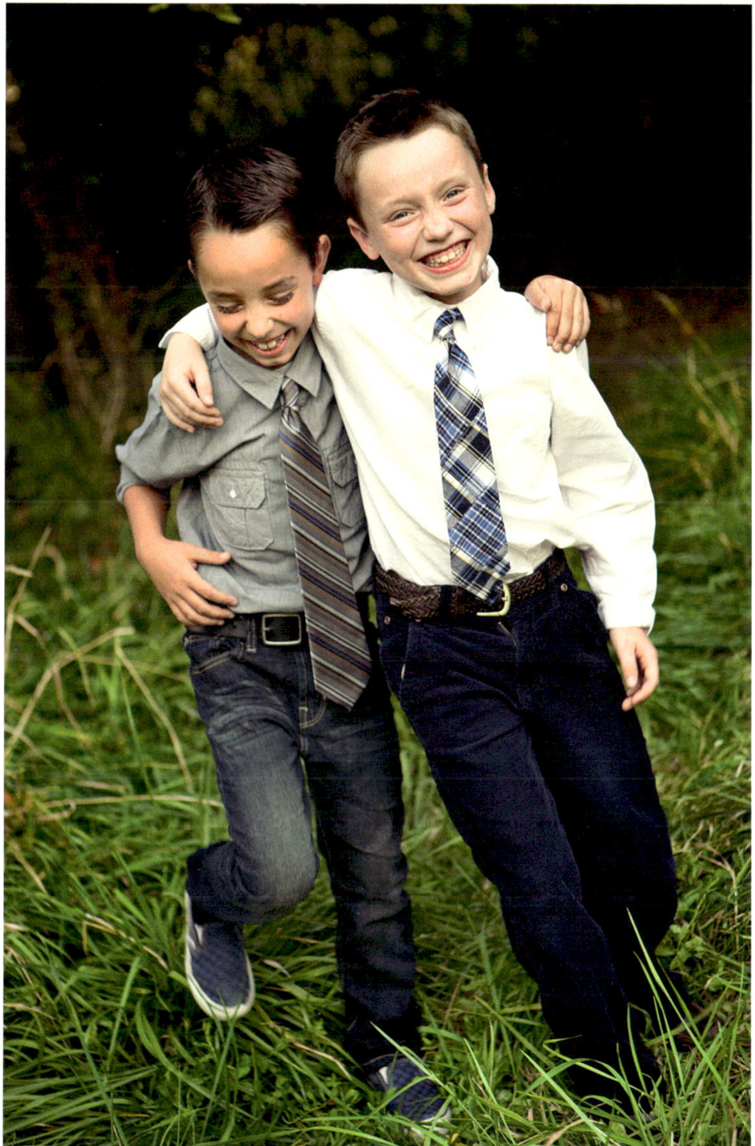

Summer Murdock Photography

Salt Lake City, Utah

summershoots.blogspot.com

Sarah Wilkerson

Colorado Springs, CO

sarahwilkerson.com

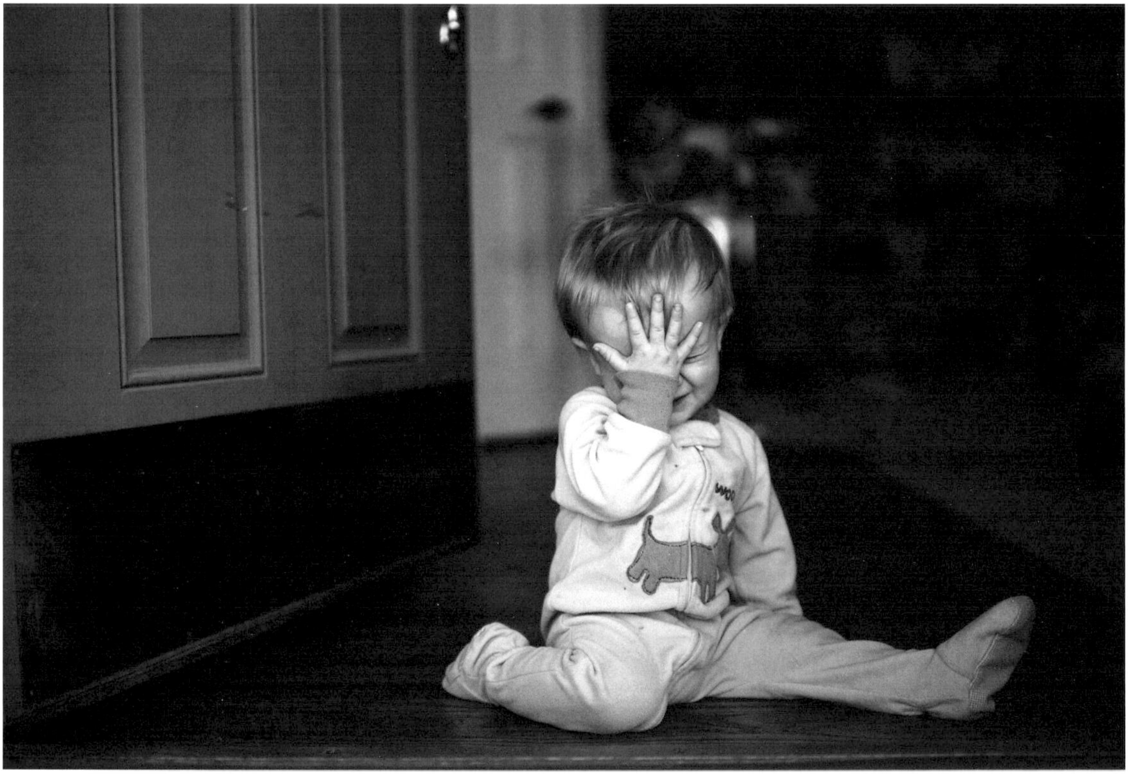

Amy Hoogstad - Asher Images

Hamilton, ON

asherimages.com

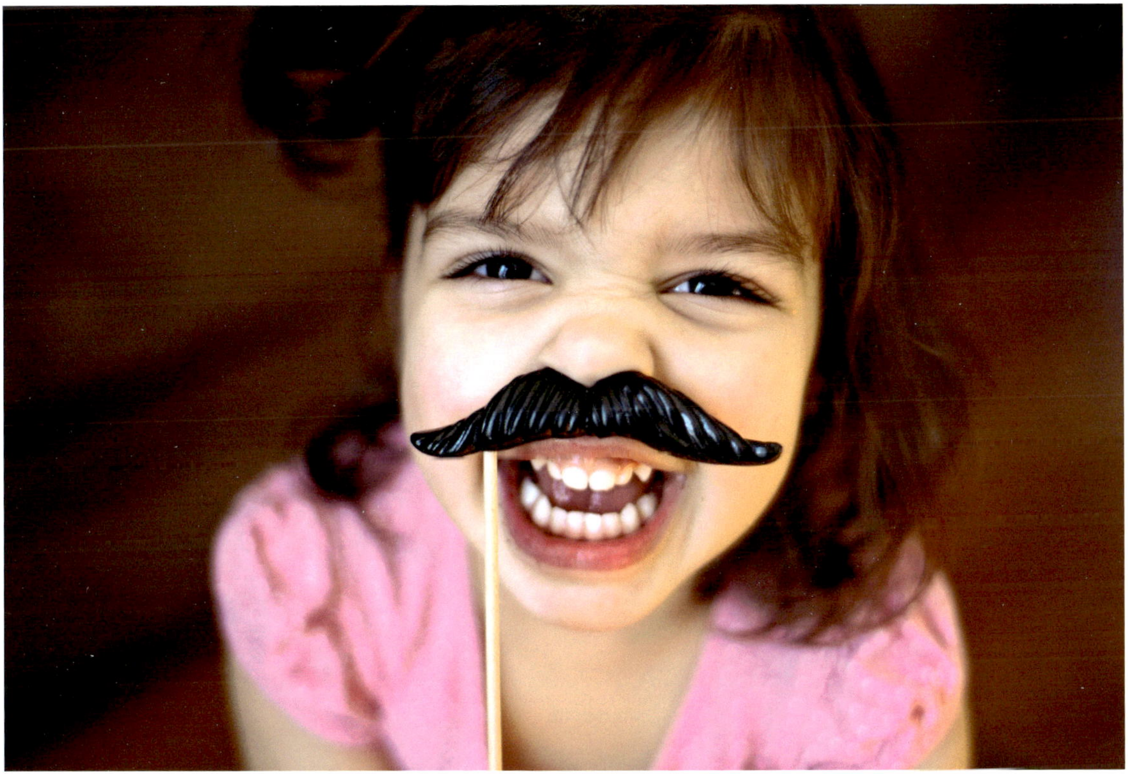

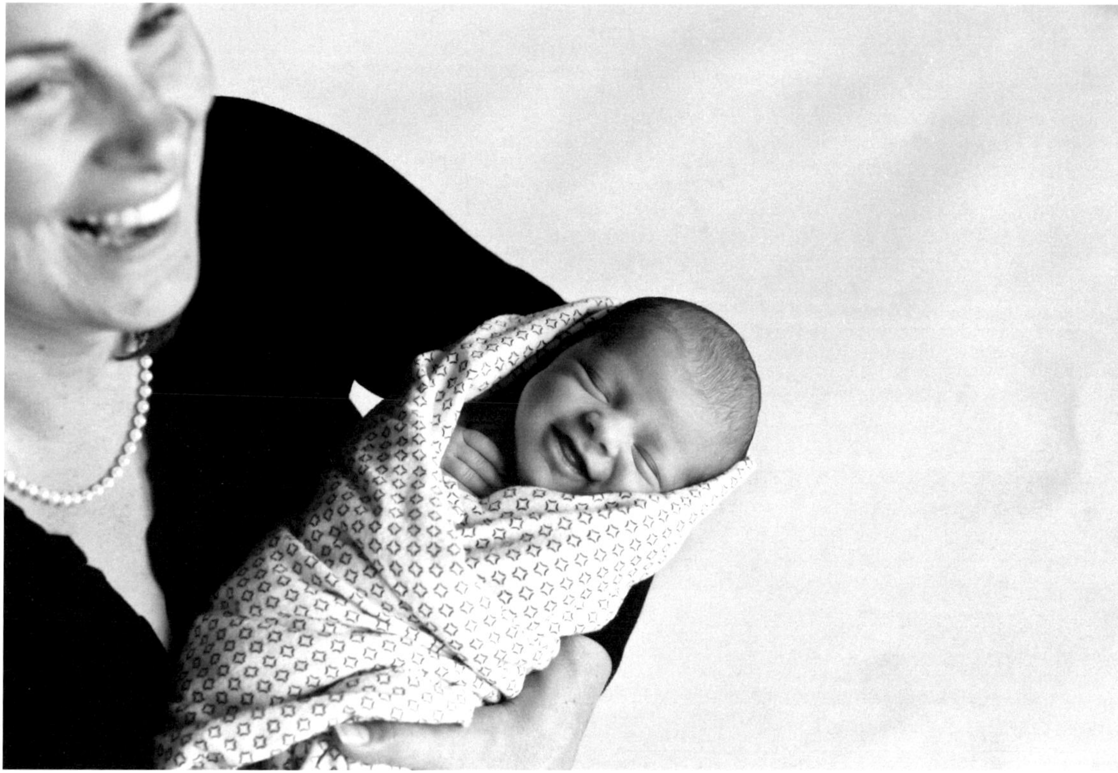

Breanna Peterson Photography

Kodiak, Alaska

breannapetersonphotography.com

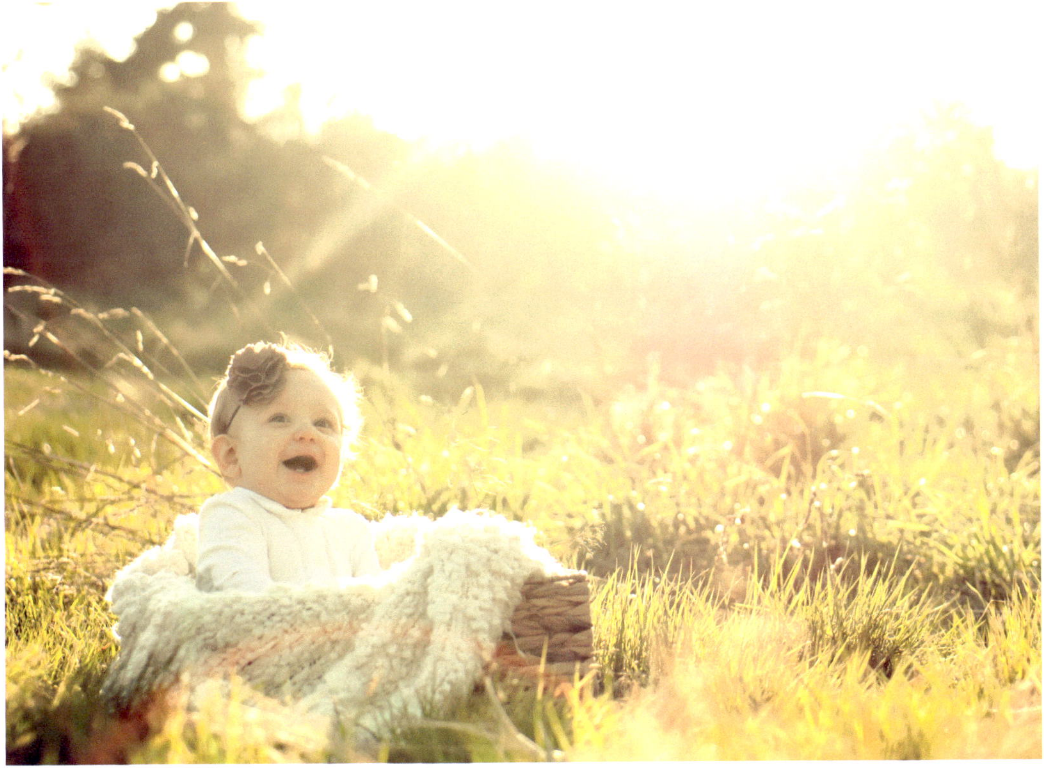

Krysten O'Coffey of Sweet Fields Photography

Victoria, BC, Canada

sweetfieldsphotography.com

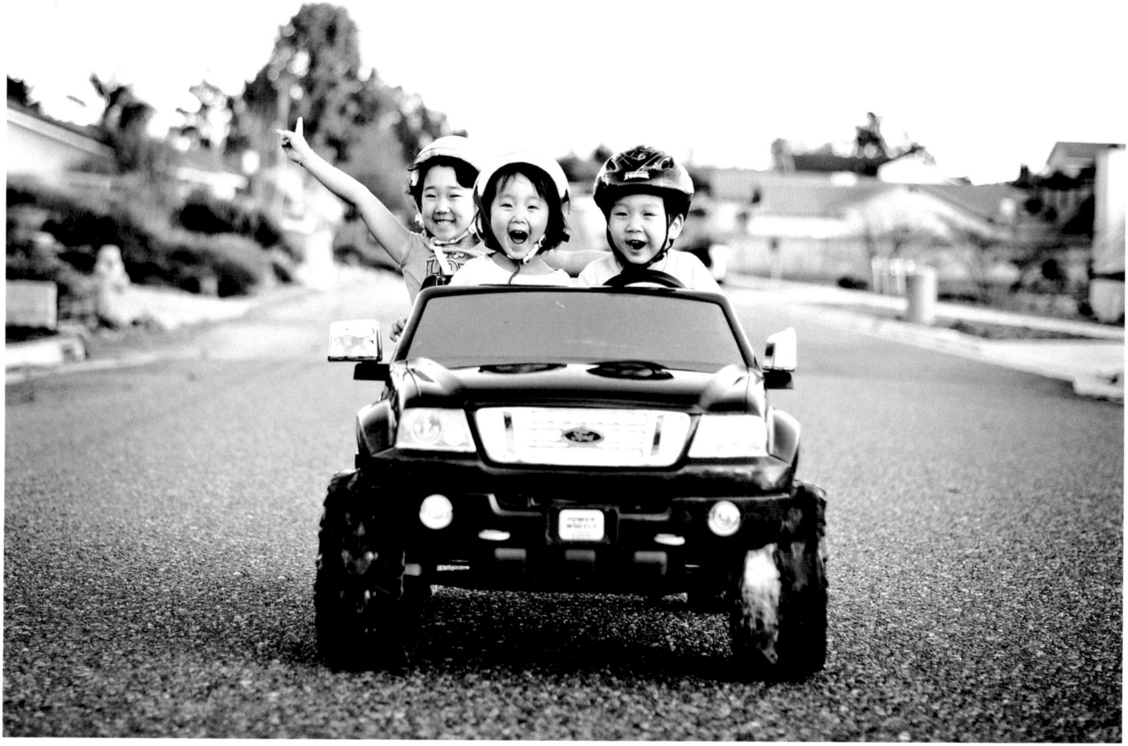

Gina Maxine Photography

Arroyo Grande, CA

ginamaxinephotography.com

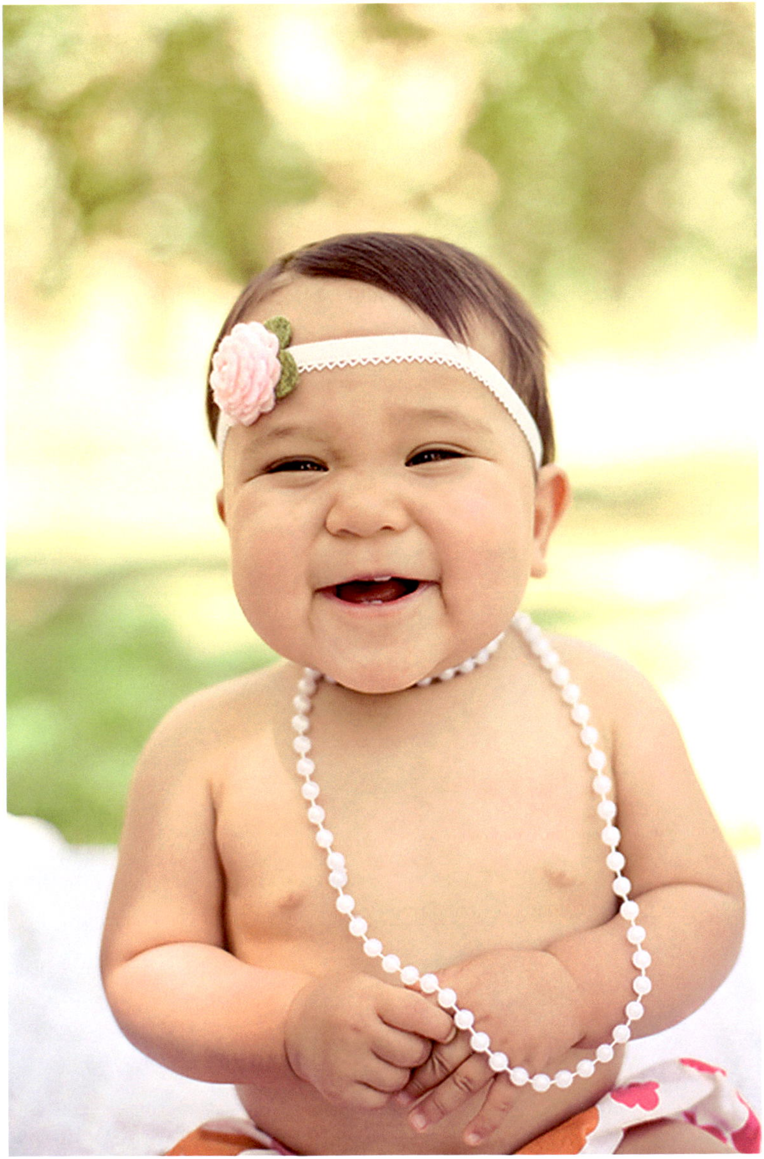

Krista Lund Photography

San Francisco Bay Area, CA

kristalundphotography.com

Tina Palmer Photography

Newcastle, WA

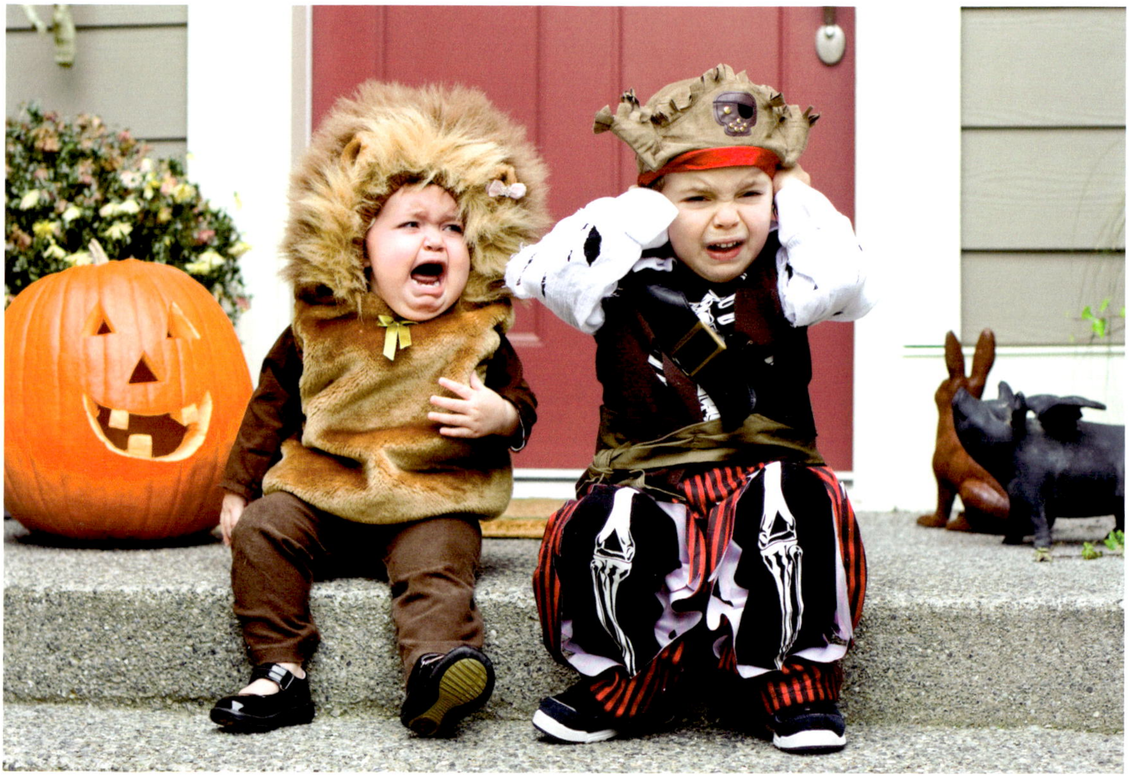

Kristen Parker - KE Portraits

McMinnville, OR

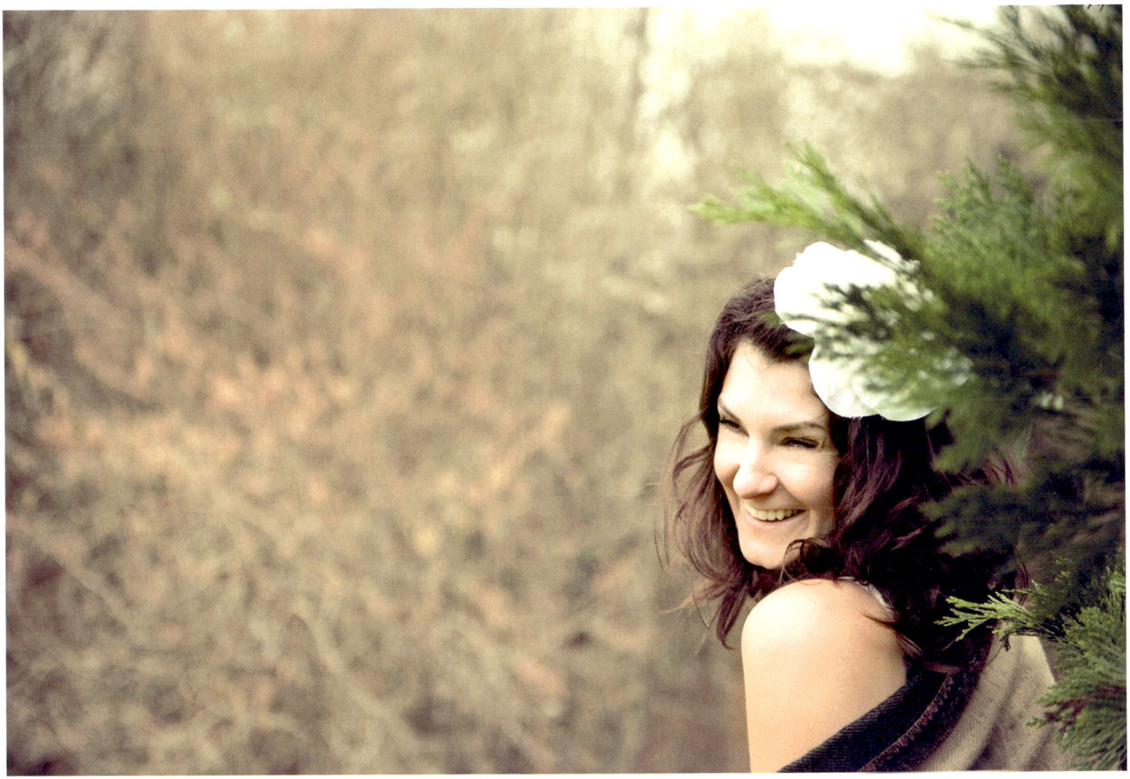

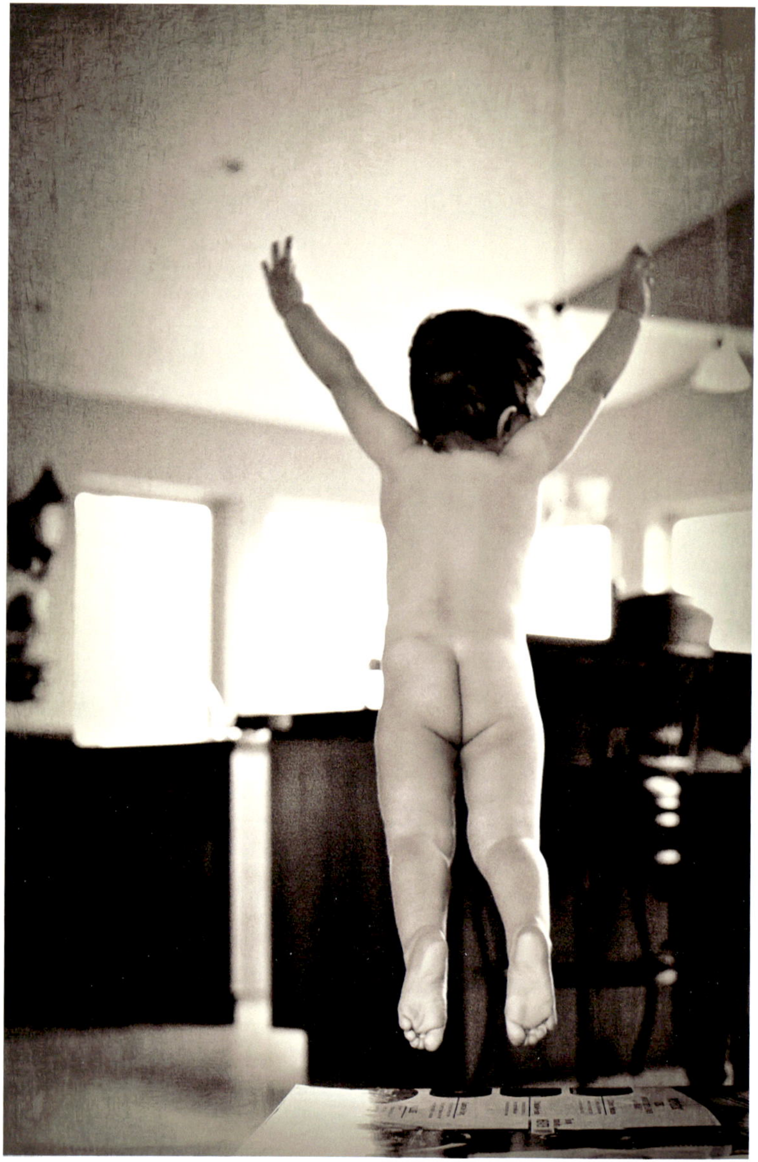

Linsey Wilt Photography

Bailey, CO

linseywiltphotography.com

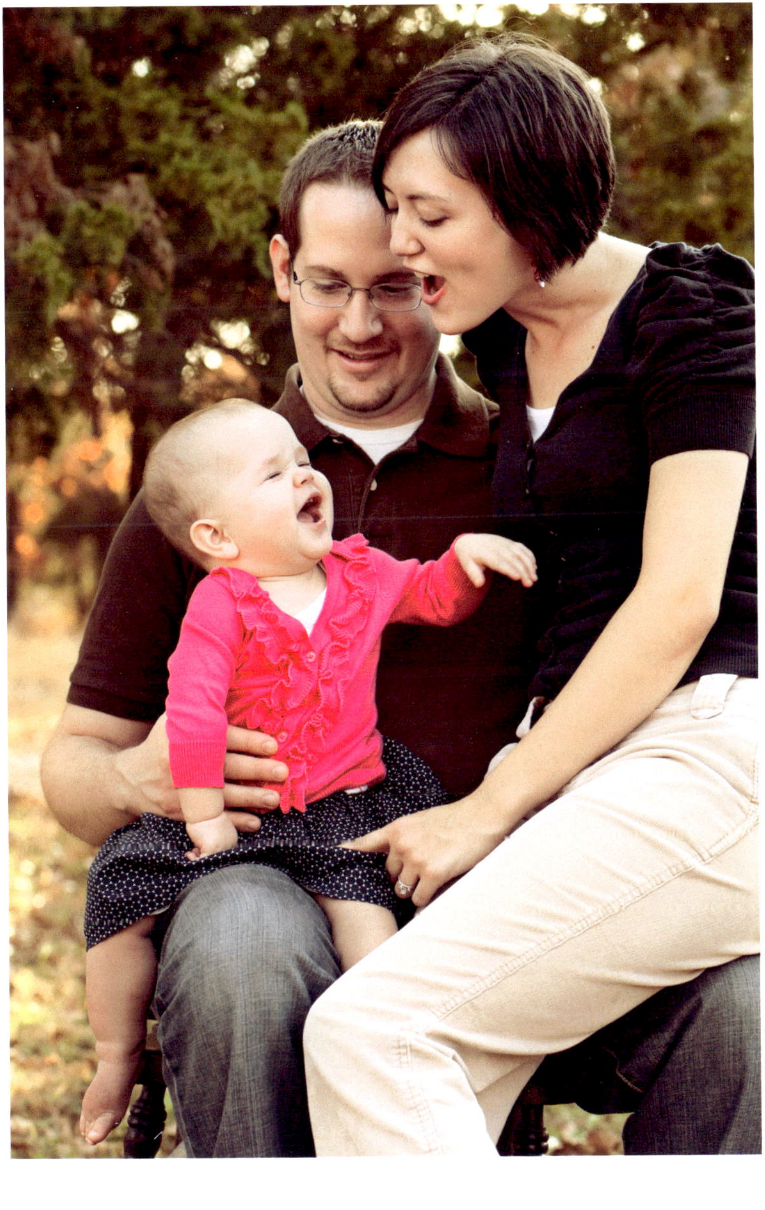

April Nienhuis Photography

Cleveland, OK

aprilnienhuis.com

Marisa Reda

Montreal, Quebec - Canada

marisareda.blogspot.com

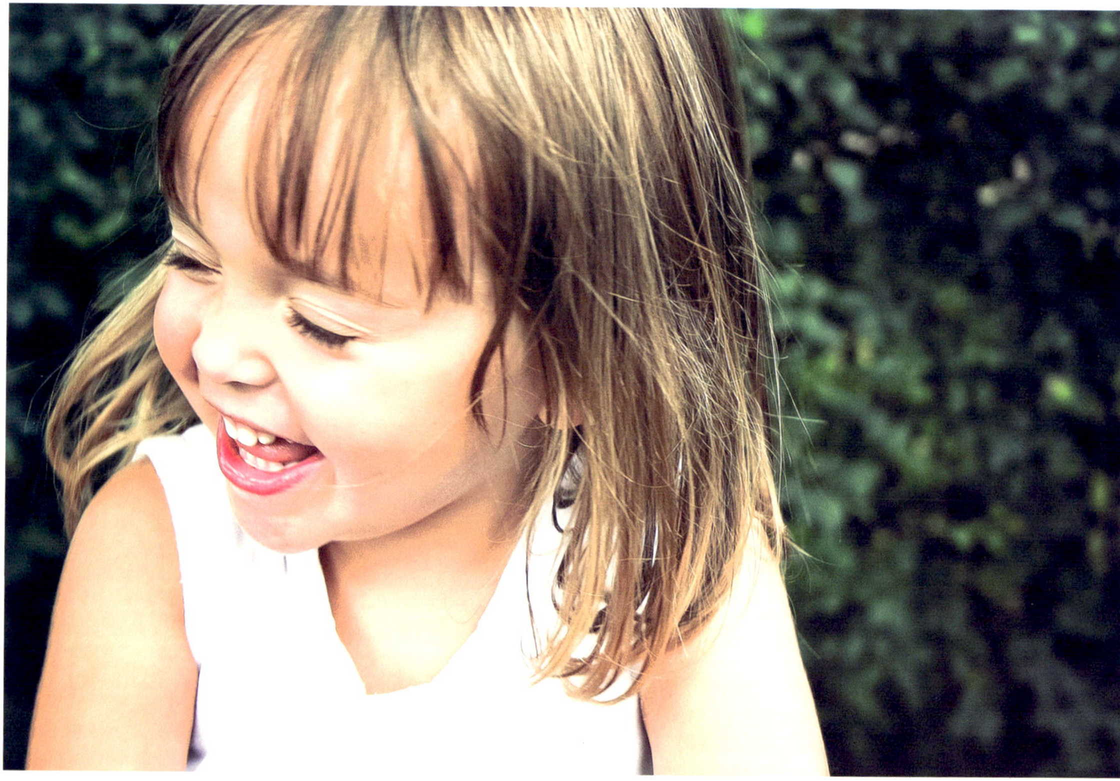

Andy & Jenna Photodesign

Bluffton, IN

andyandjenna.com

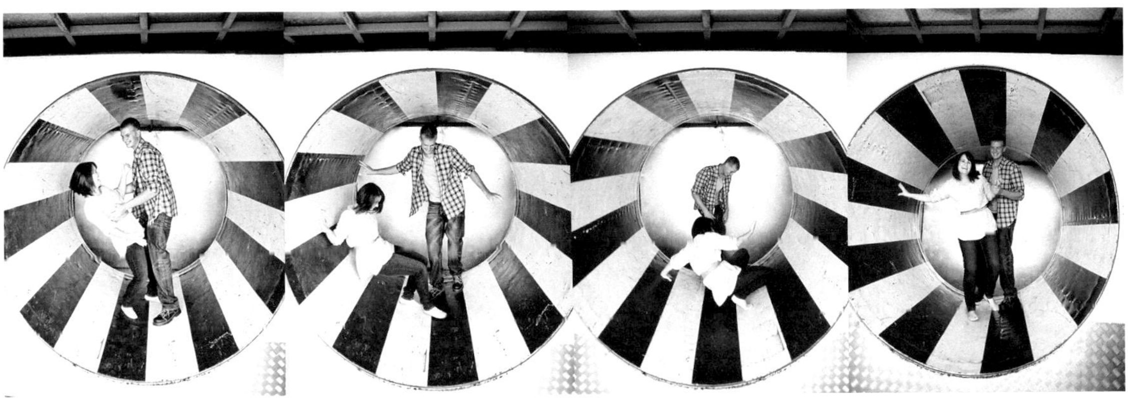

Laura Reive Photography

Elmvale, Ontario - Canada

laurareivephotography.com

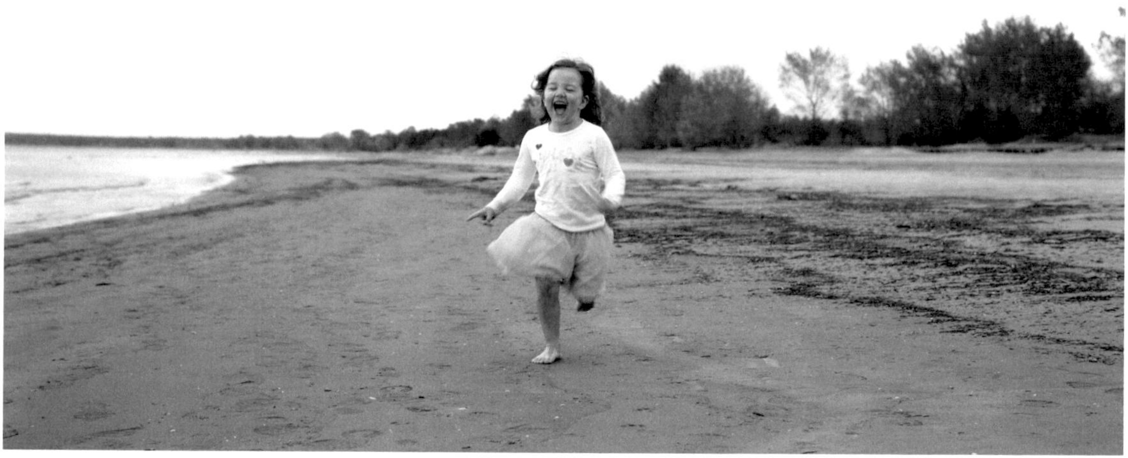

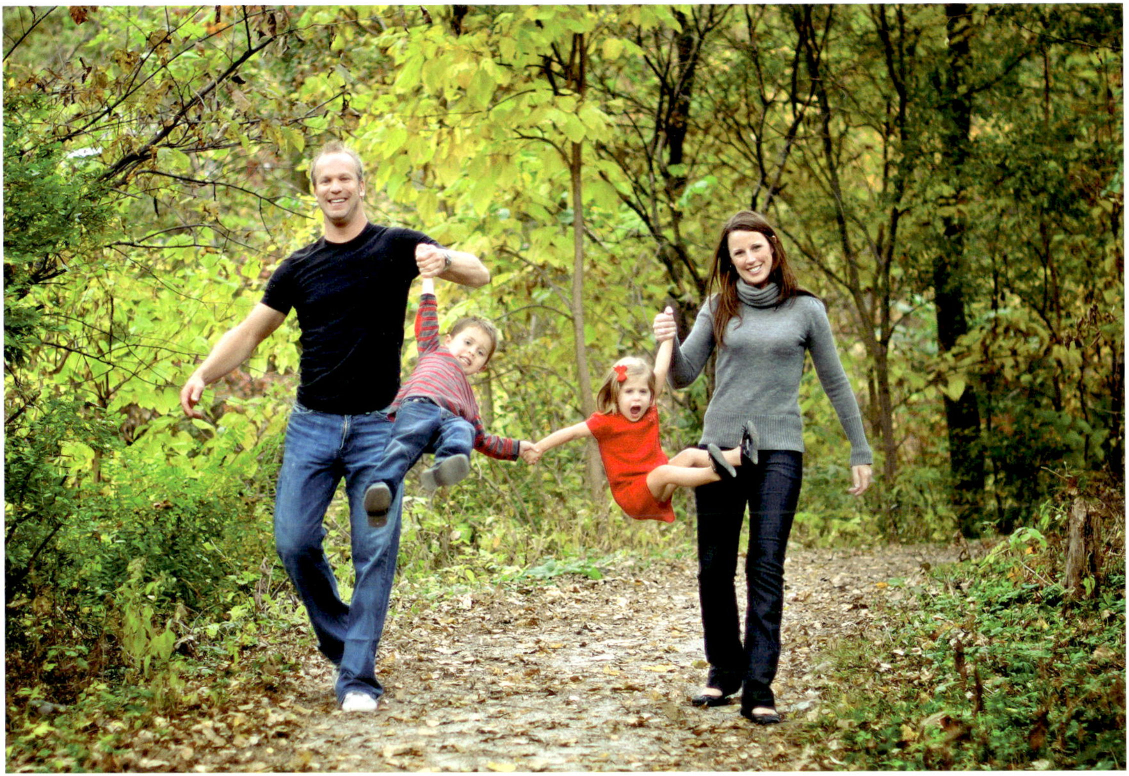

Beth Ritchie

Omaha, NE

bethritchie.com

Kitty Rogers Photography

Minneapolis, MN

kittyrogers.com

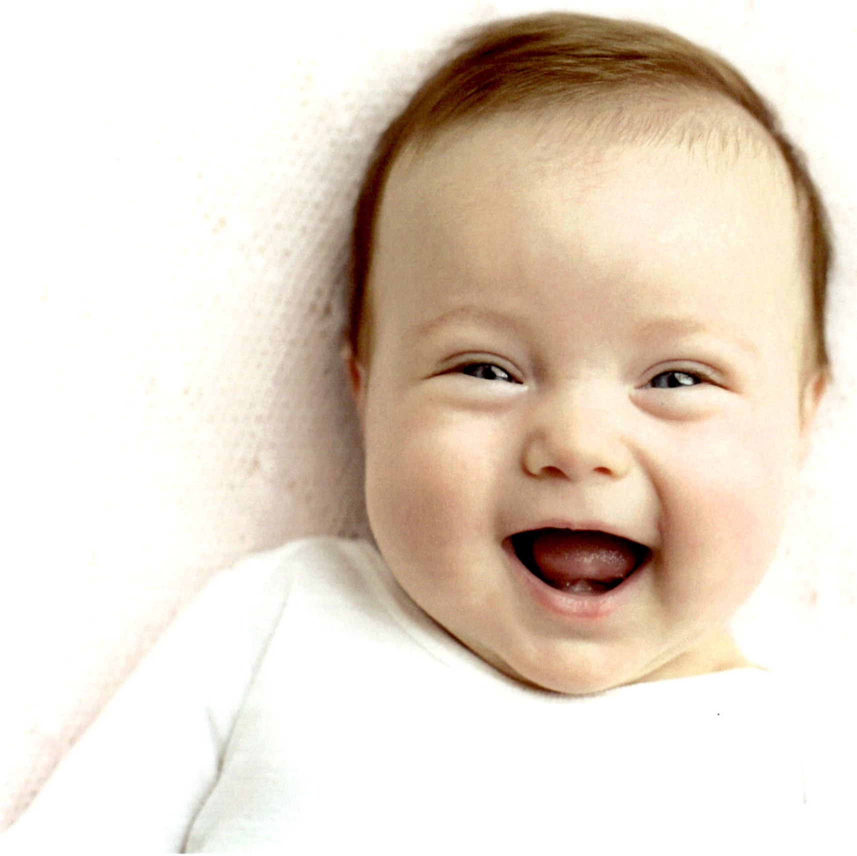

Vitty Robinson

London, UK

vittyrobinson.com

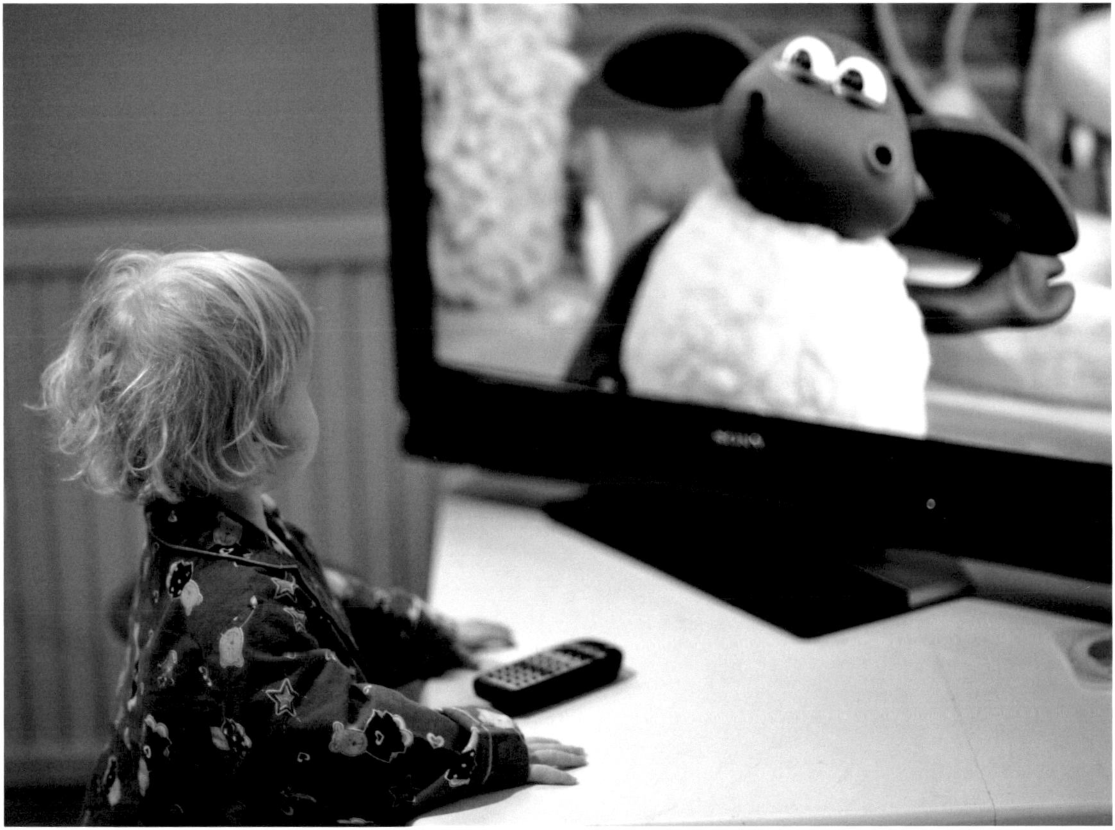

Anne Scherrer Photography

Washington DC

annescherrer.fr

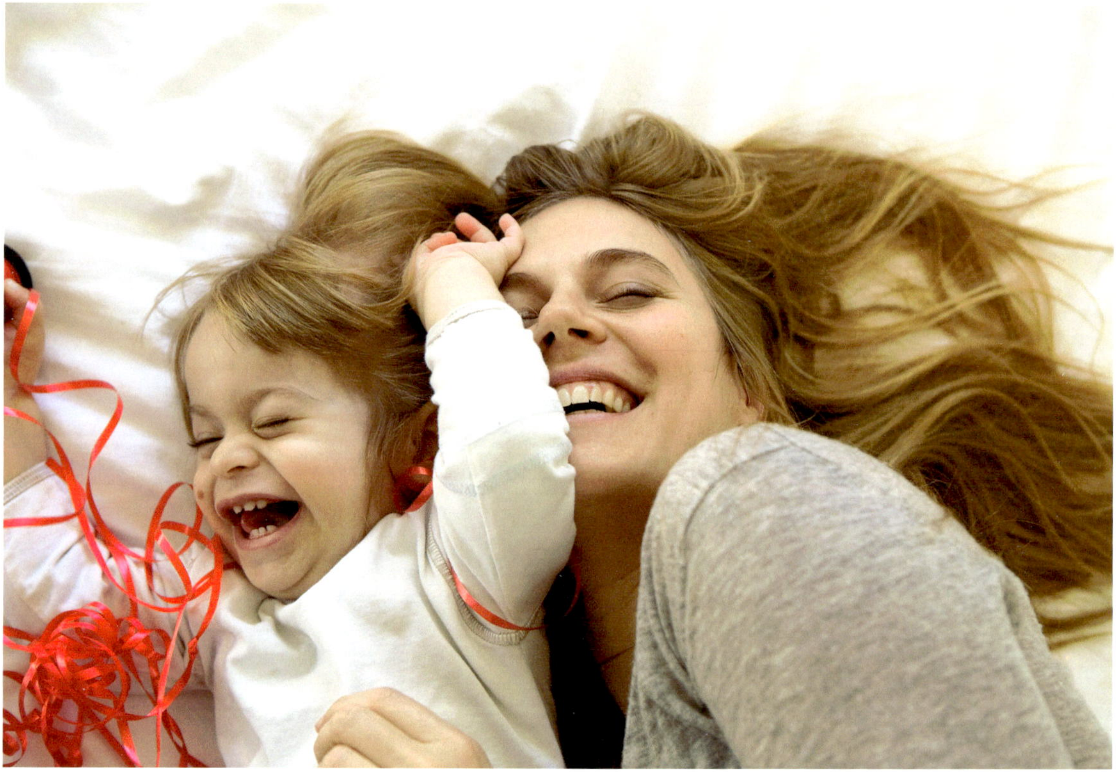

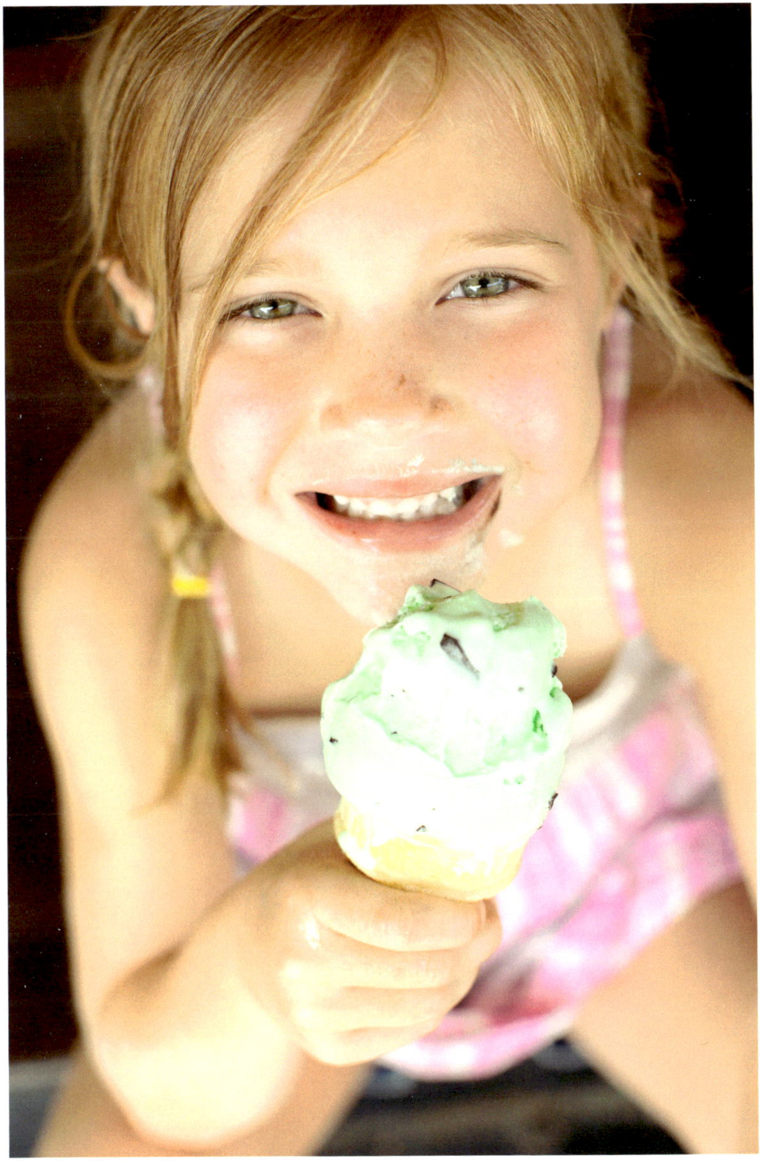

Kendra Okolita

Geneva, IL

lulubirdphotography.com

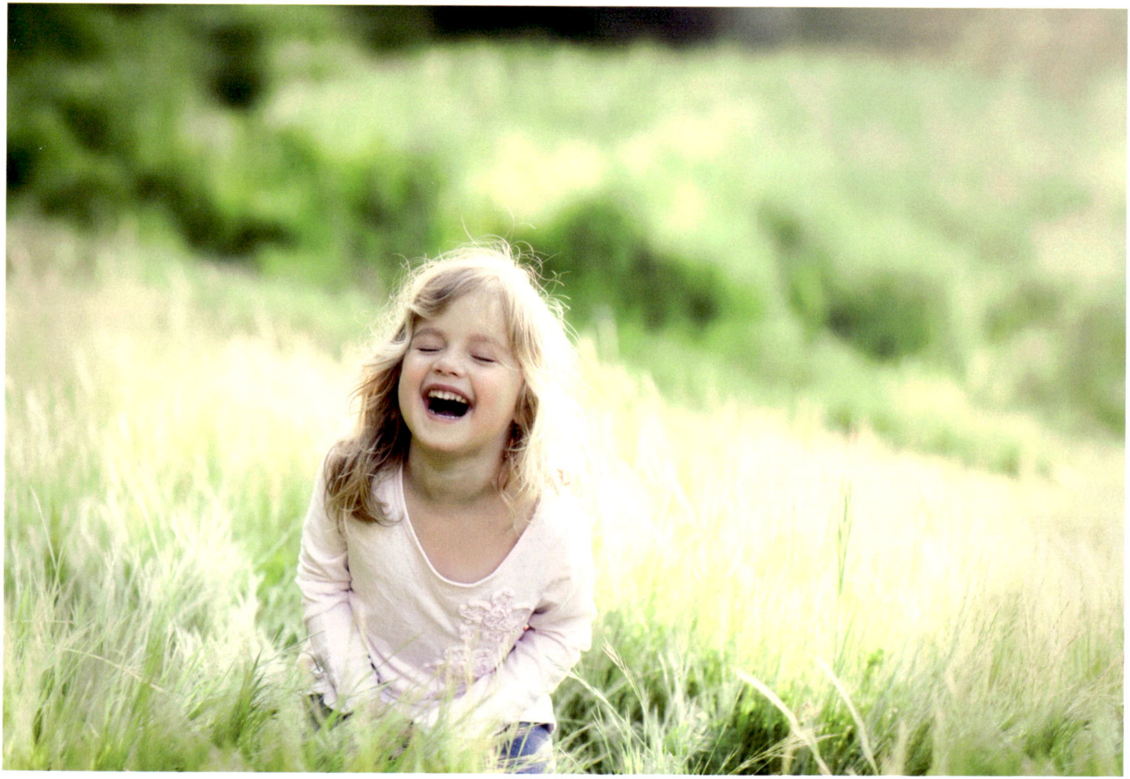

Emily Sara Photography

Lafayette, CA

emilysaraphoto.com

Sheryl Salisbury Photography

Weatherford, OK

kbimagery.com

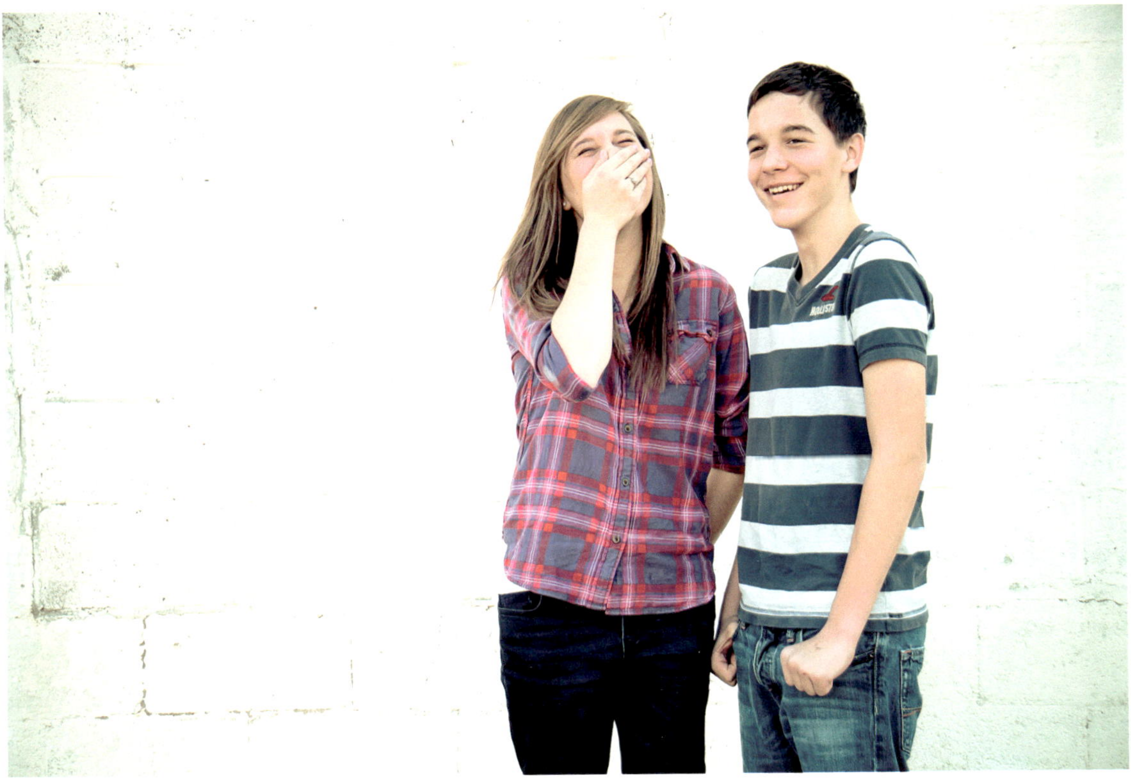

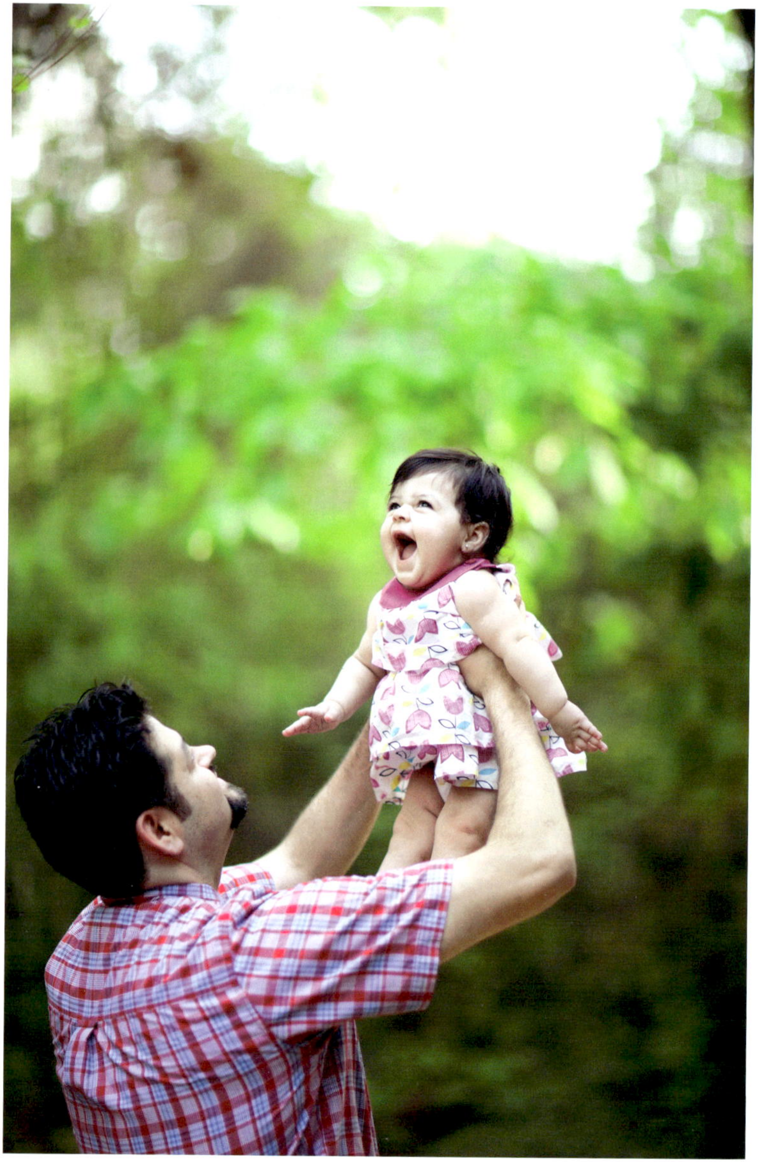

Sara Seeton Photography

Dallas/Fort Worth, TX

saraseetonphotography.com

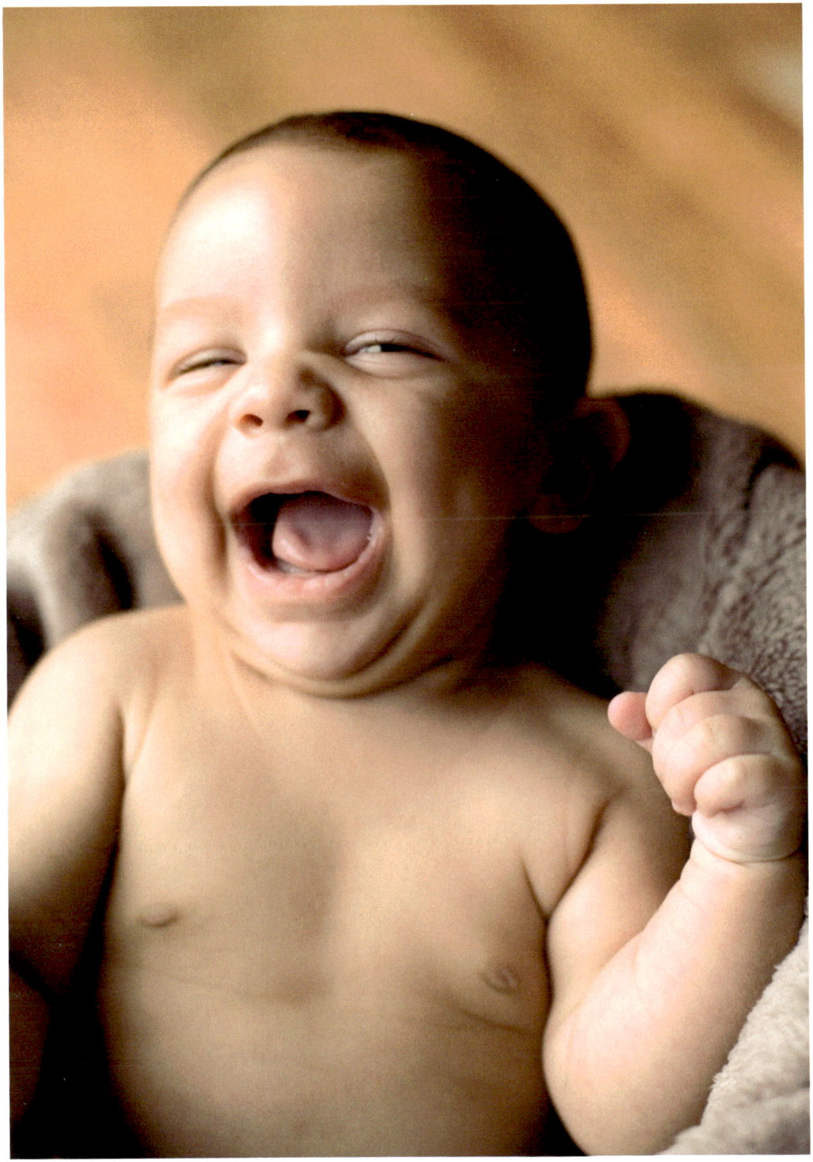

Kim Shapiro - Life Captured Photography

Long Island, NY

CapturedbyKim.com

Sara Welch Photography

Orange, TX

sarawelchphotography.com

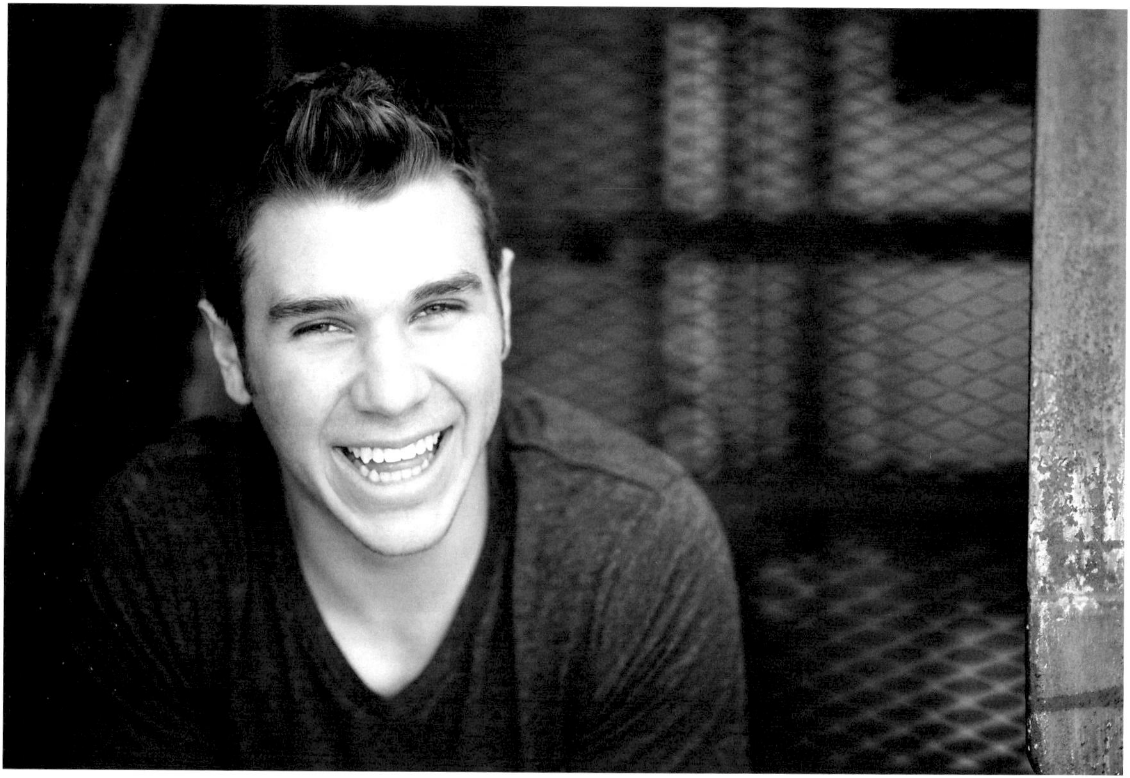

Tout Petit Pixel Photographie

Marseille, France

toutpetitpixel.com

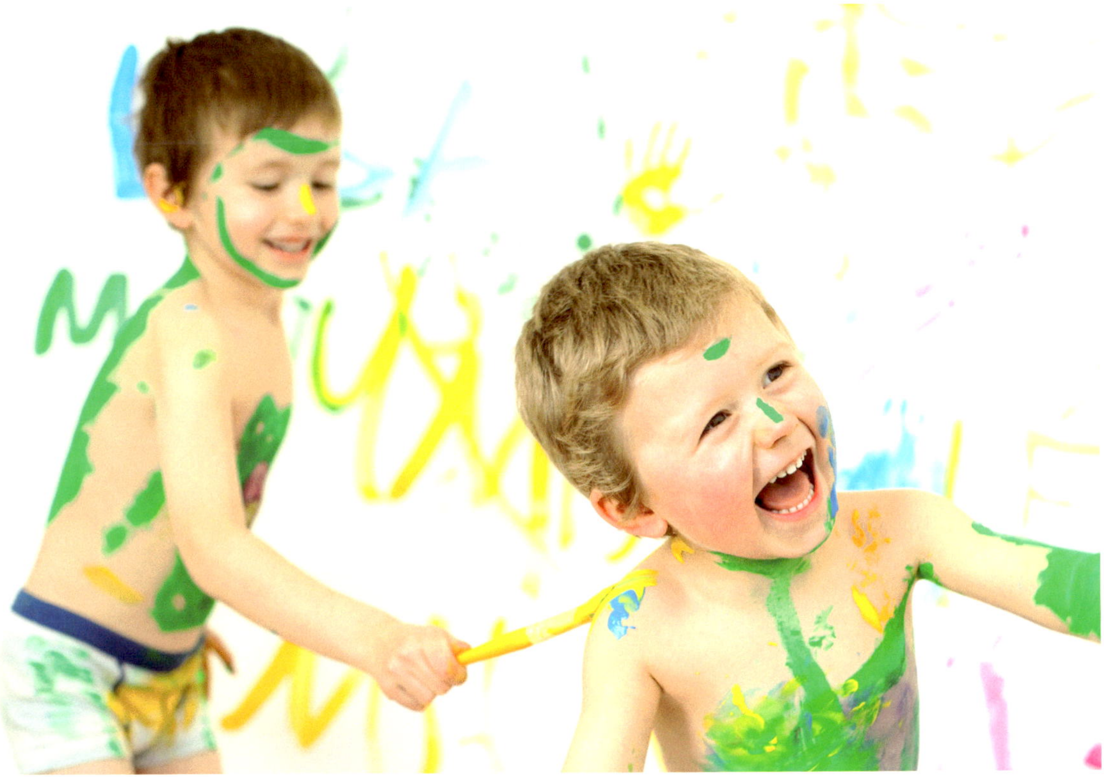

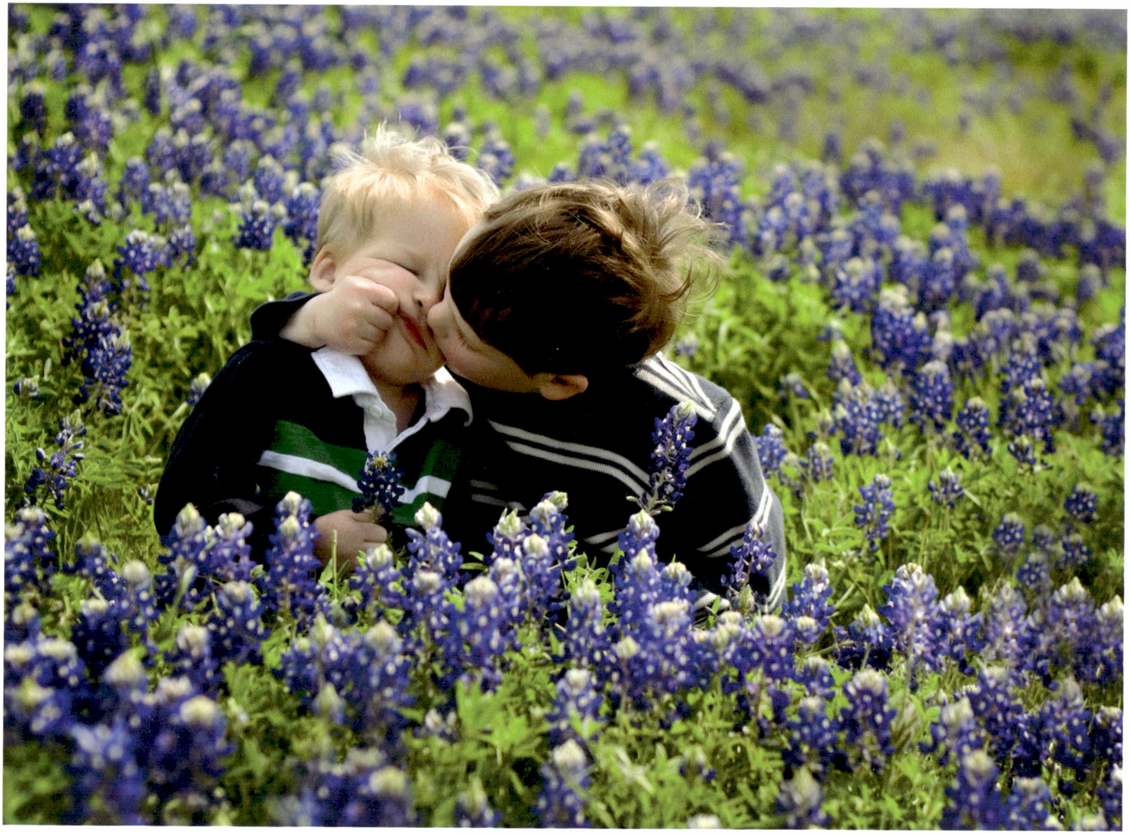

Jessica Starr Photography

Dallas, TX

jessicastarrphotography.com

Michelle Sheldon Photography

Waukesha, WI

michellesheldon.com

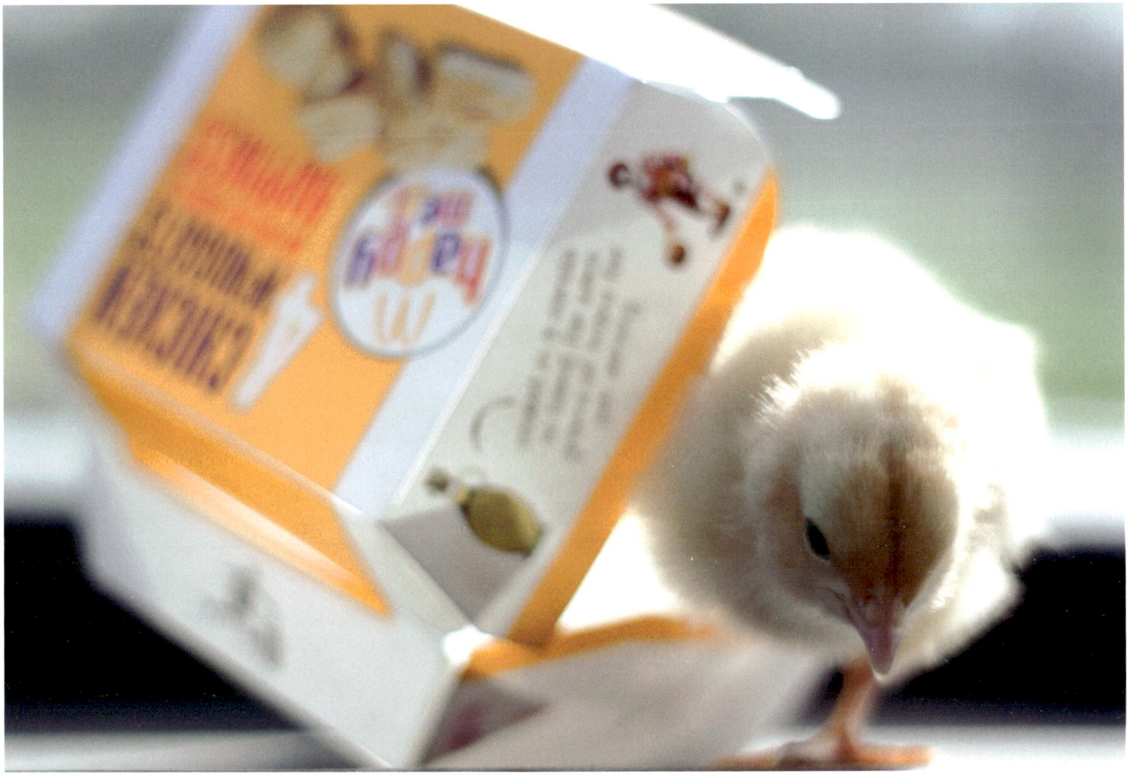

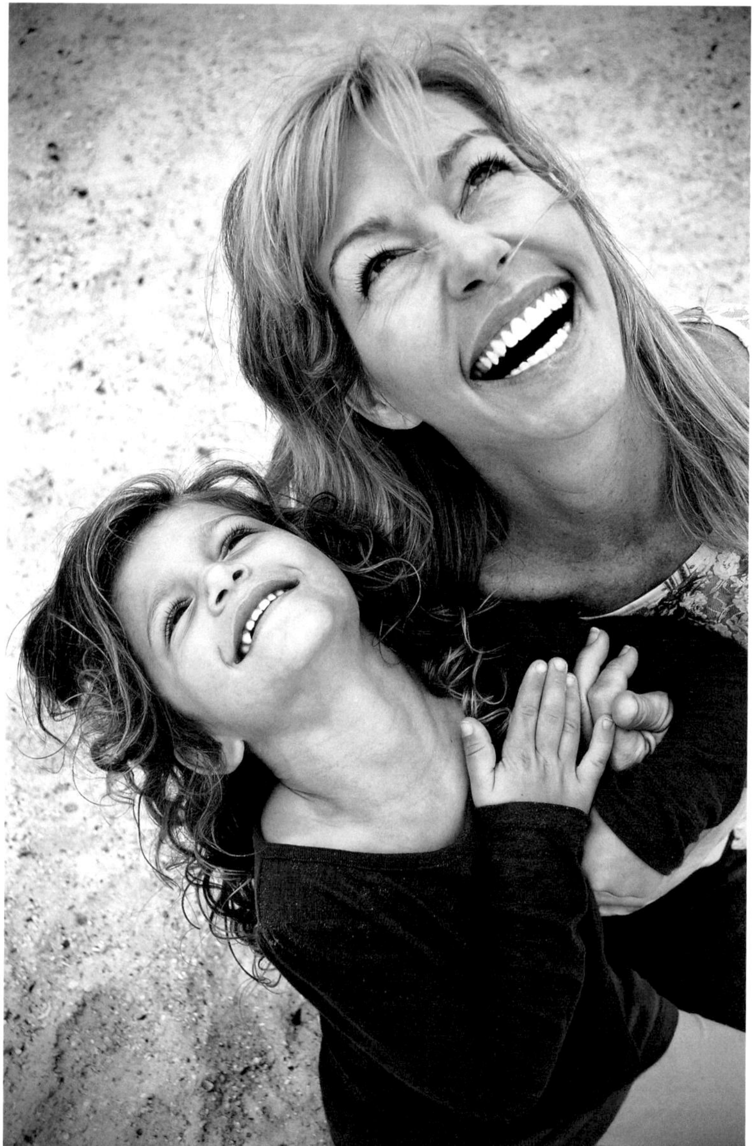

Cathleen Smith

Dunwoody, GA

pretty-in-pixels.com

Megan Squires Photography

Sacramento, CA

megansquires.com

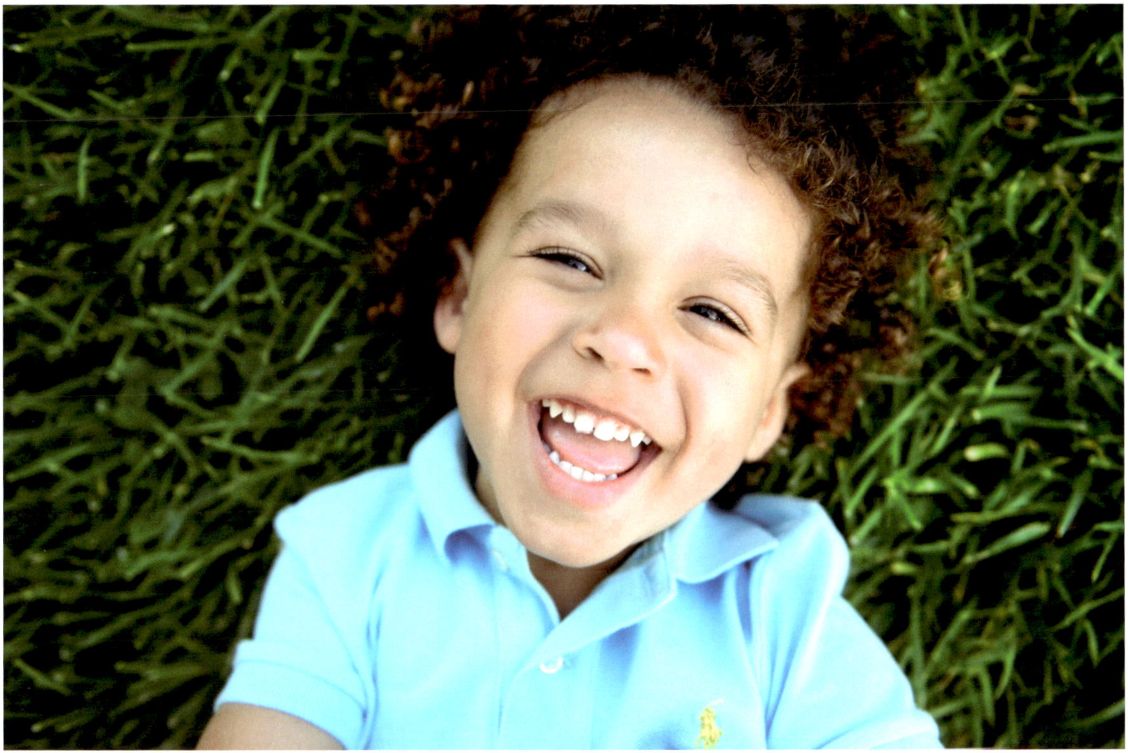

Marvett Smith

Utah

savoringthesimple.com

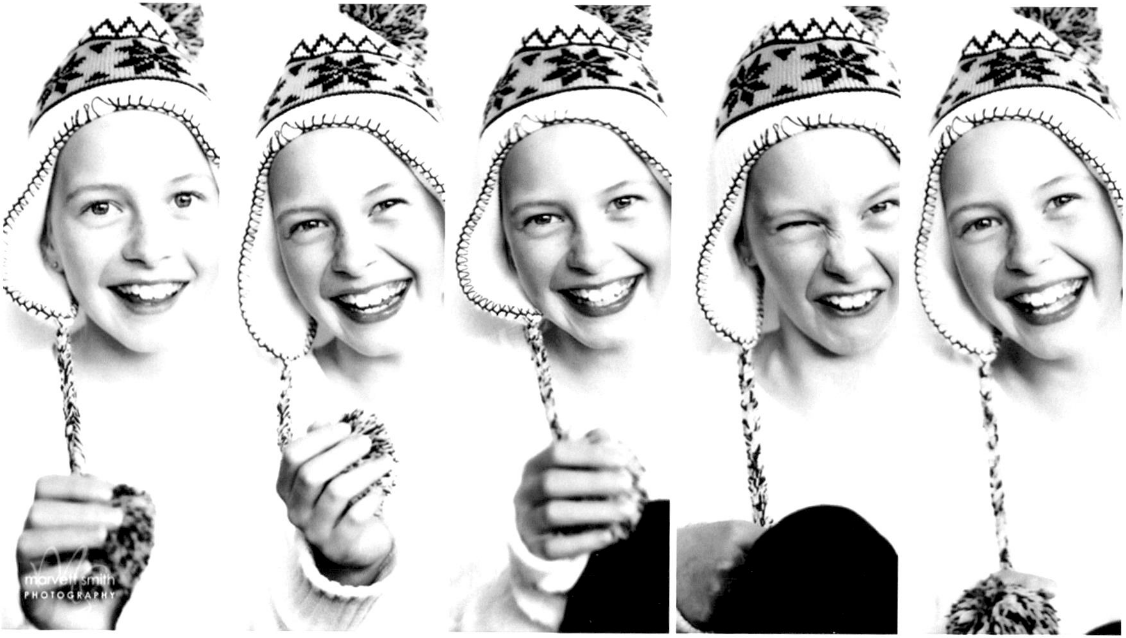

Andy & Jenna Photodesign

Bluffton, IN

andyandjenna.com

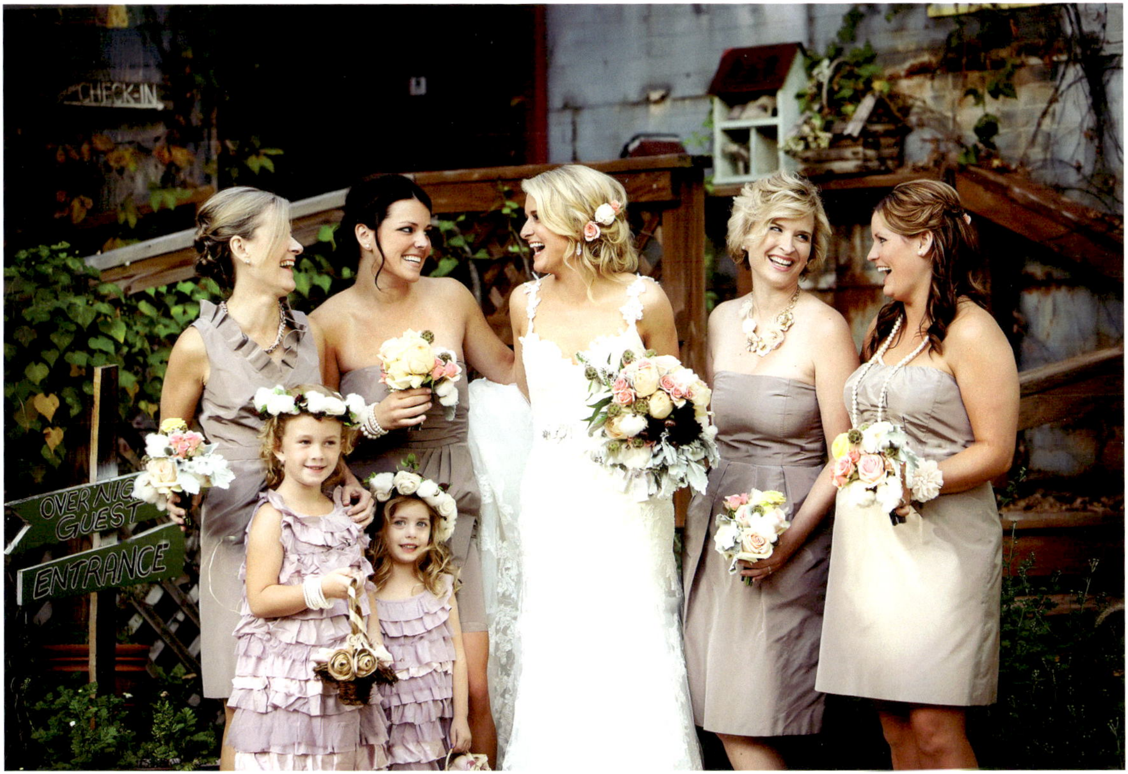

Holly Thompson

Austin, TX

hollyanissa.com

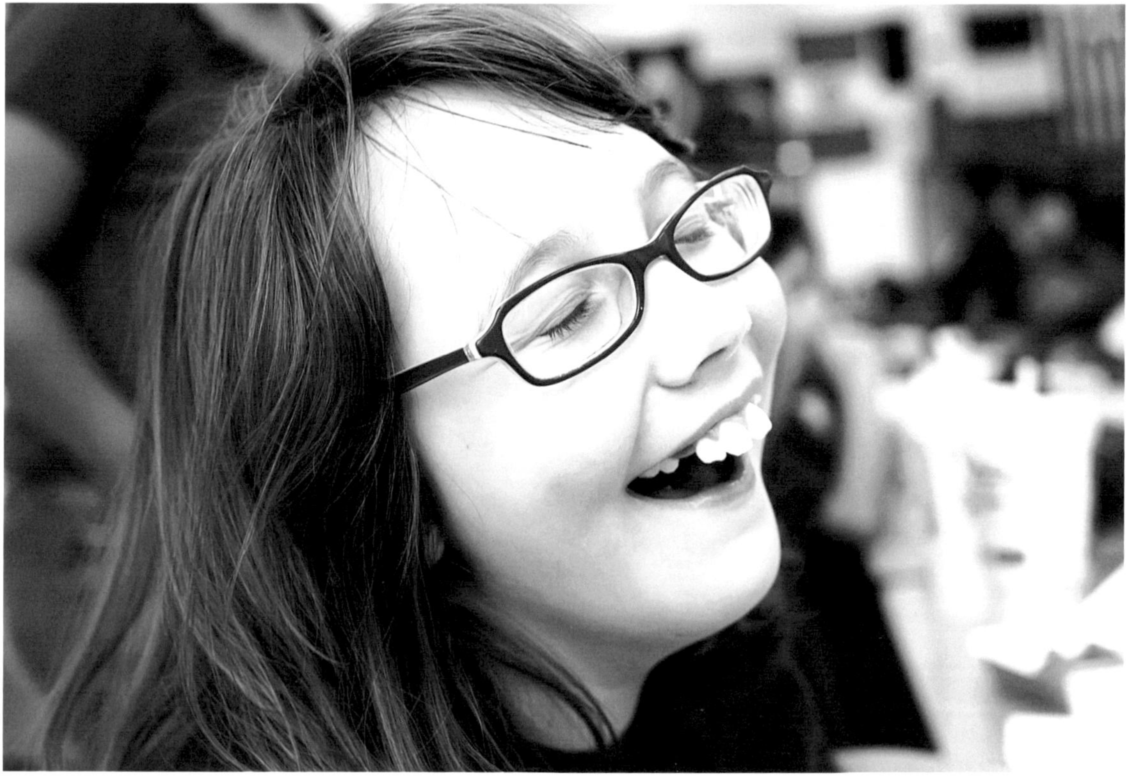

Jeanie Lapenna

Roseville, CA

jeaniemade.blogspot.com

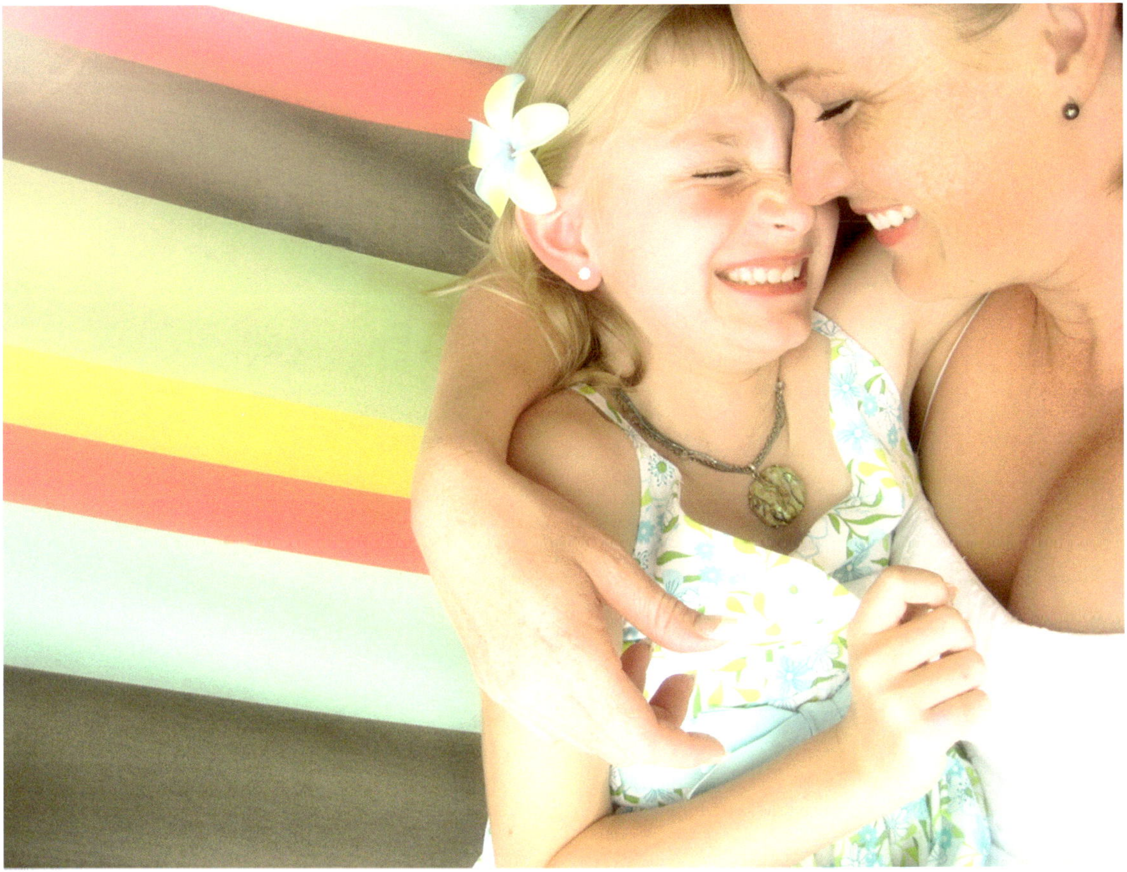

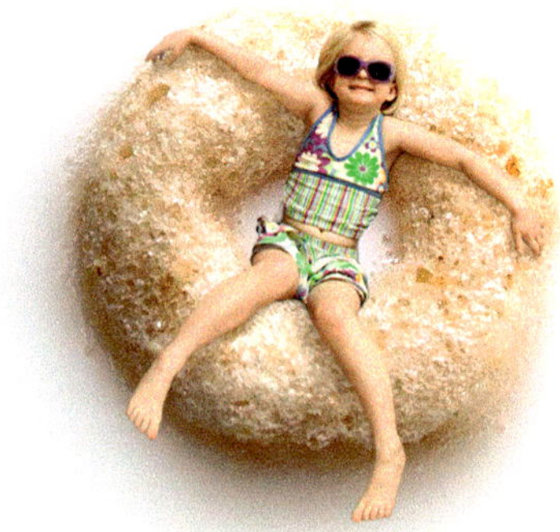

Erika Thornes

San Diego, CA

Bre Thurston Photography

Riverside, CA

brethurston.com

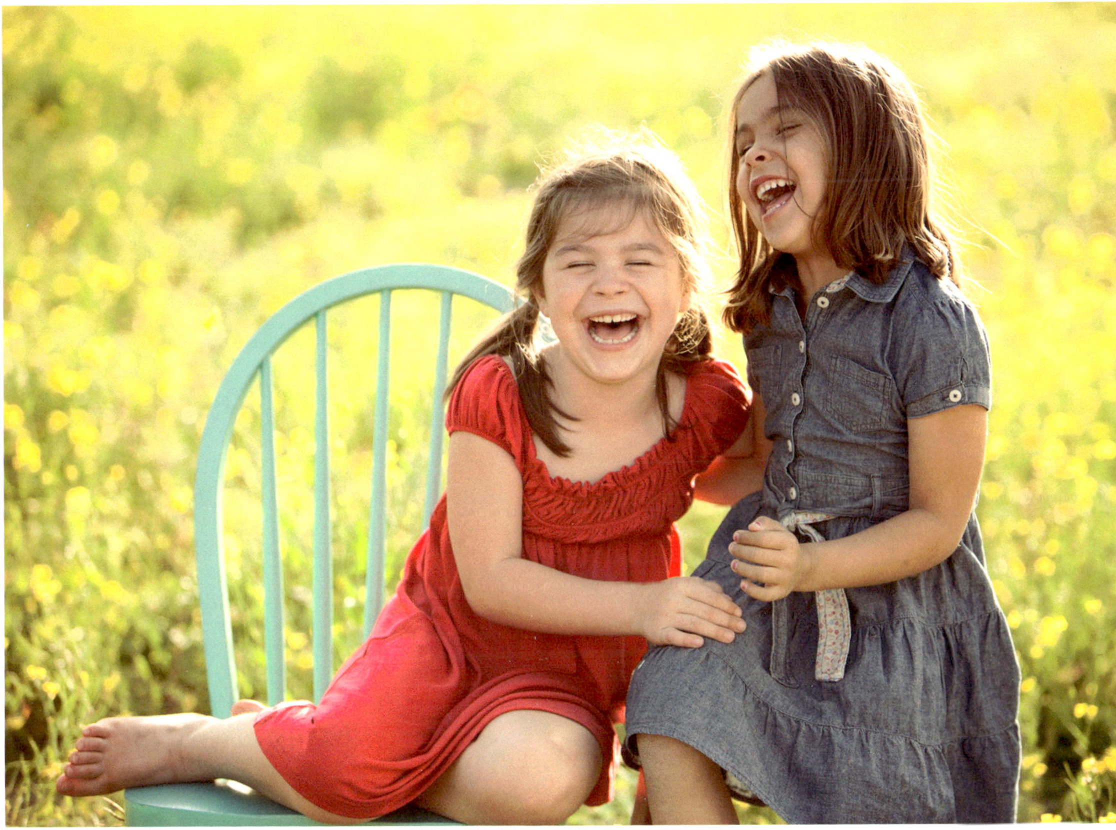

Tout Petit Pixel Photographie

Marseille, France

toutpetitpixel.com

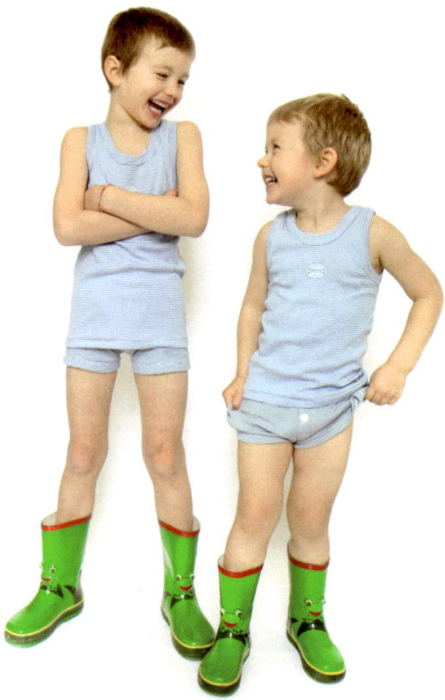

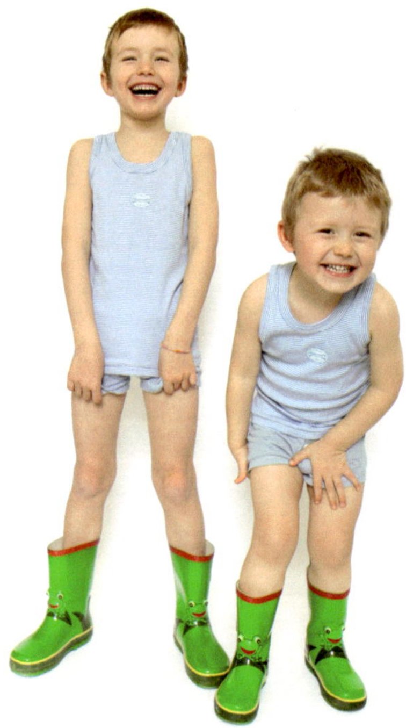

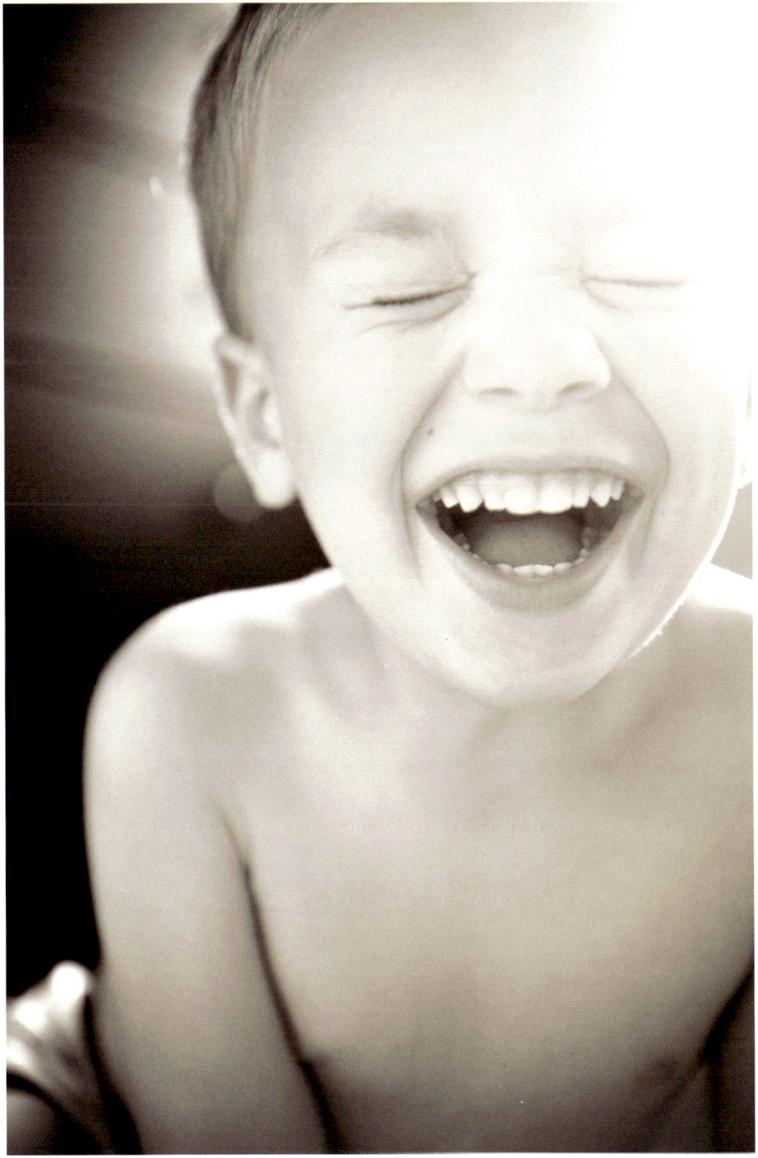

Megapixie

Chapel Hill, NC

megapixie.com

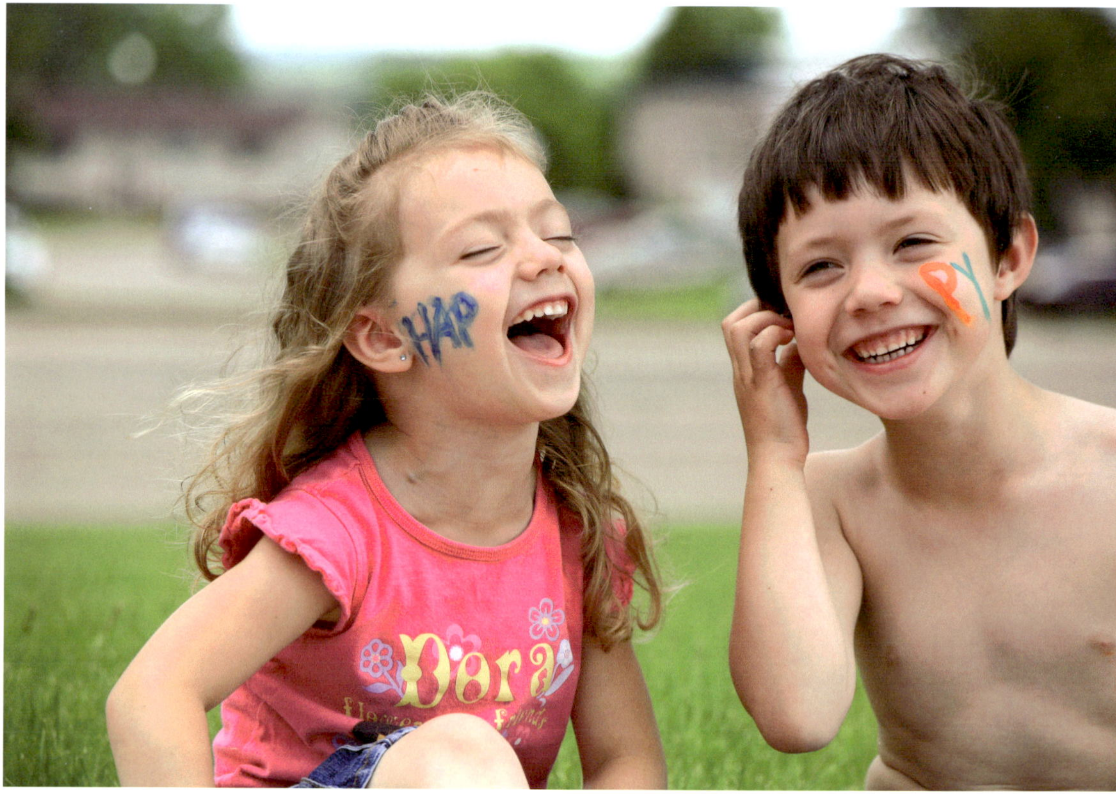

Erica McCauley

Minot, ND

littleorangebug.com

Linsey Wilt Photography

Bailey, CO

linseywiltphotography.com

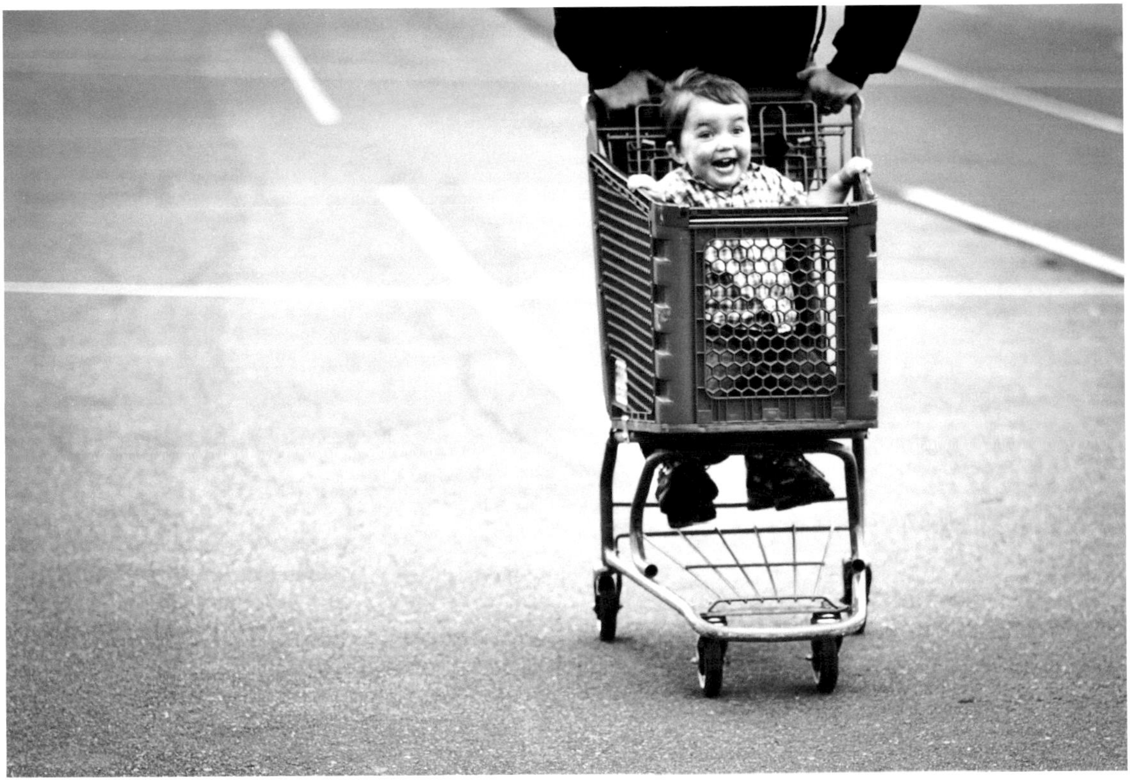

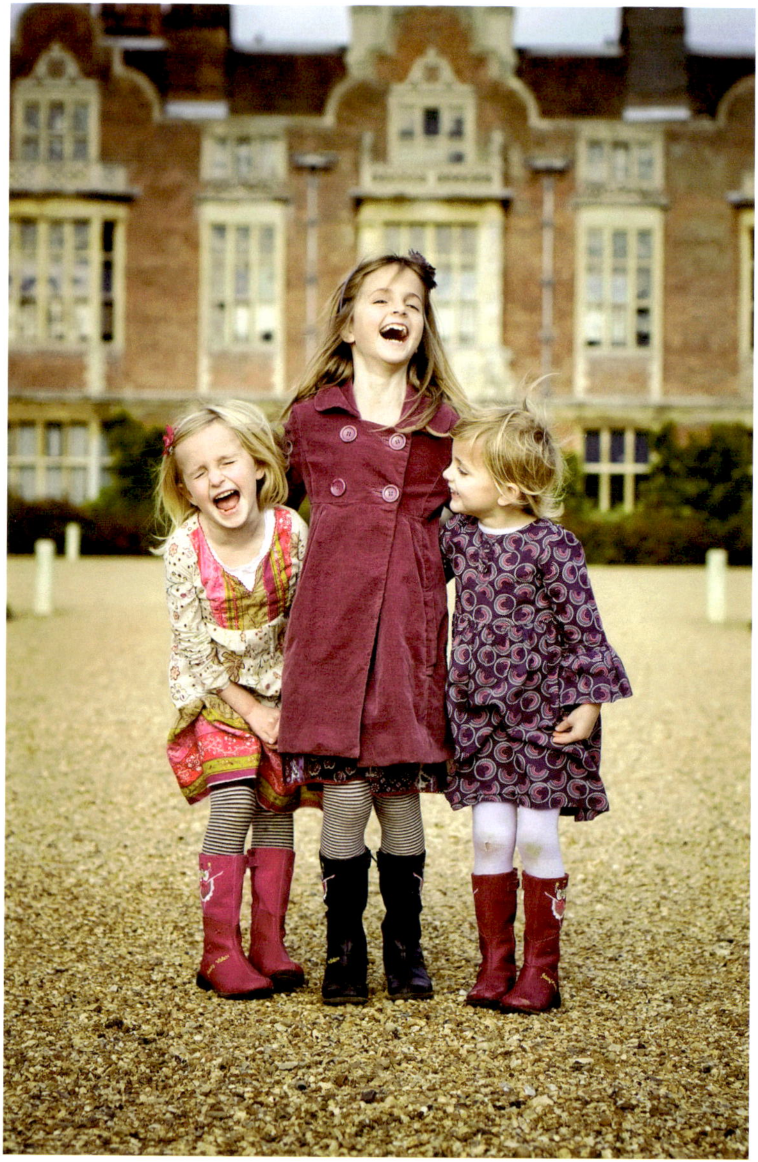

Vicki Utting

Norfolk, England

vickiutting.com

Megan Moore - Megan Jane Photography

Boston, MA

meganjanephotography.com

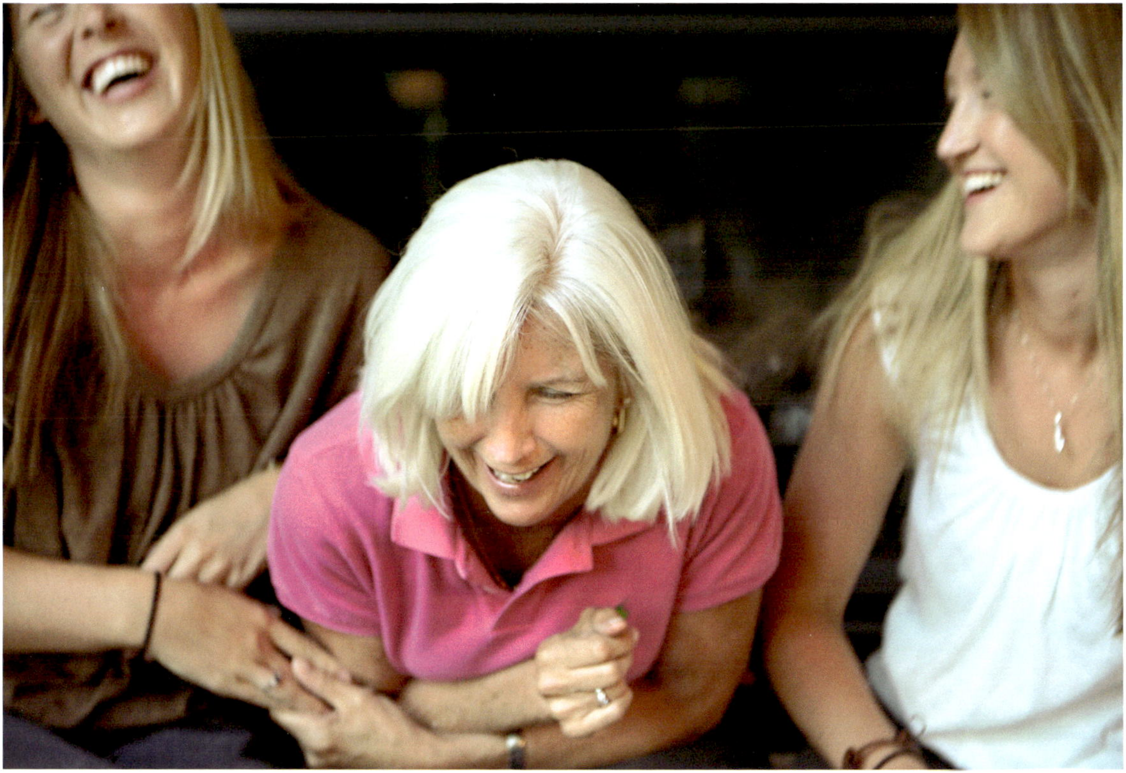

Ashley Spaulding

Shawnee, KS

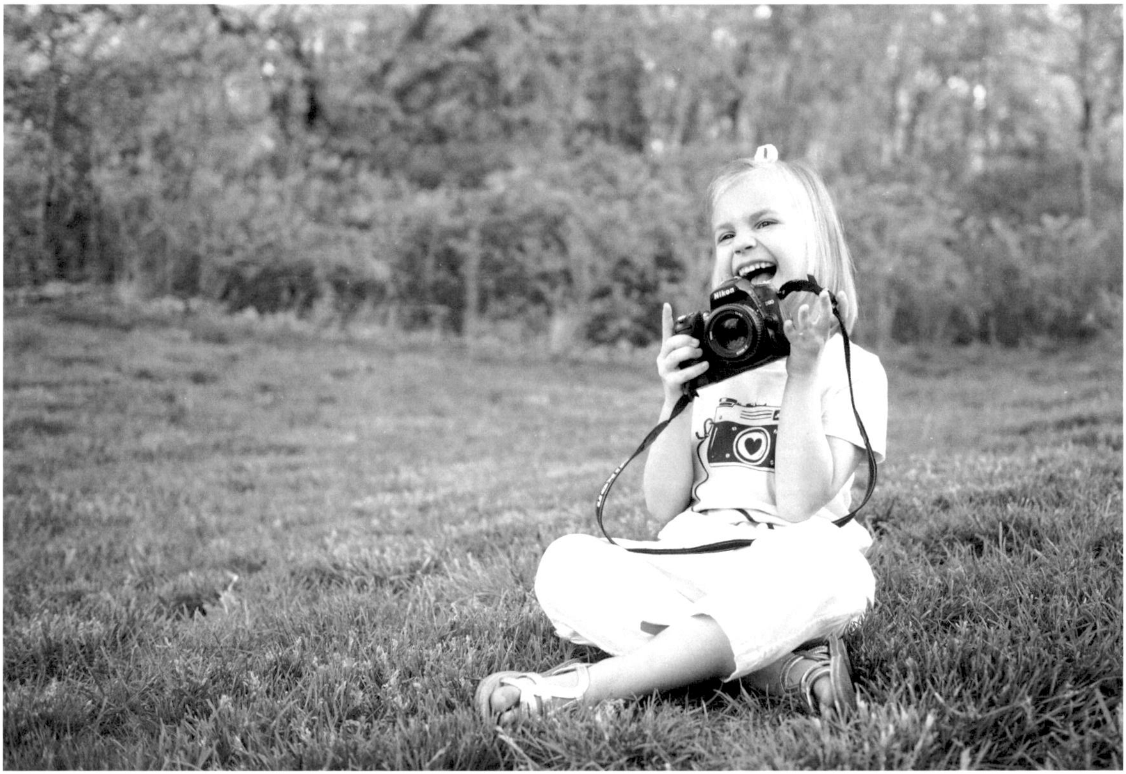

Sara Welch Photography

Orange, TX

sarawelchphotography.com

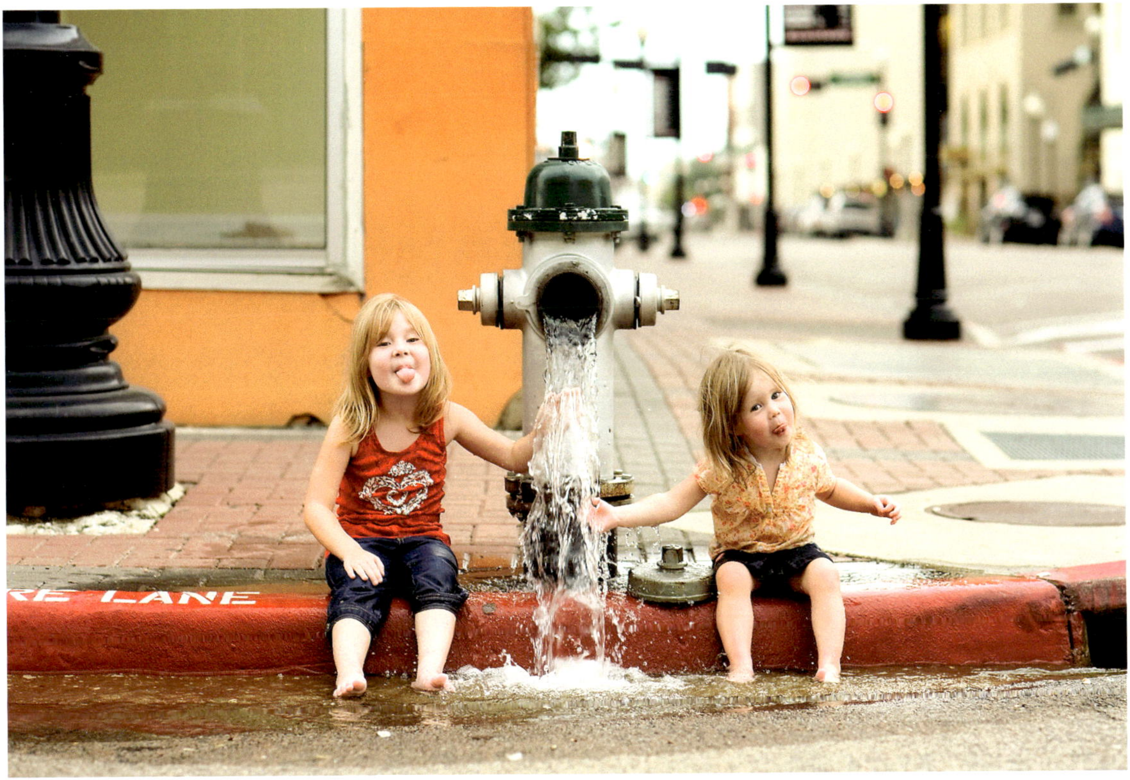

Monica Wilkinson Photography

Seattle, WA

monicawilkinson.com

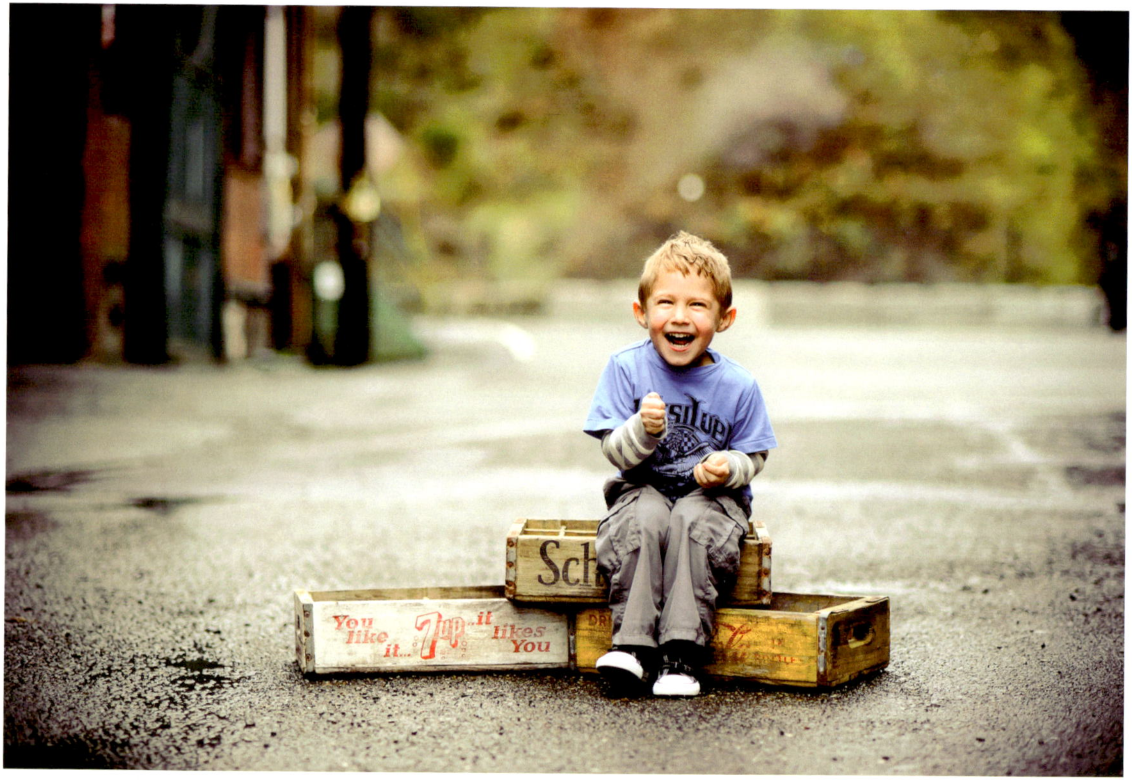

Wendy L White

Fort Smith, AR

wendylwhitephotography.com

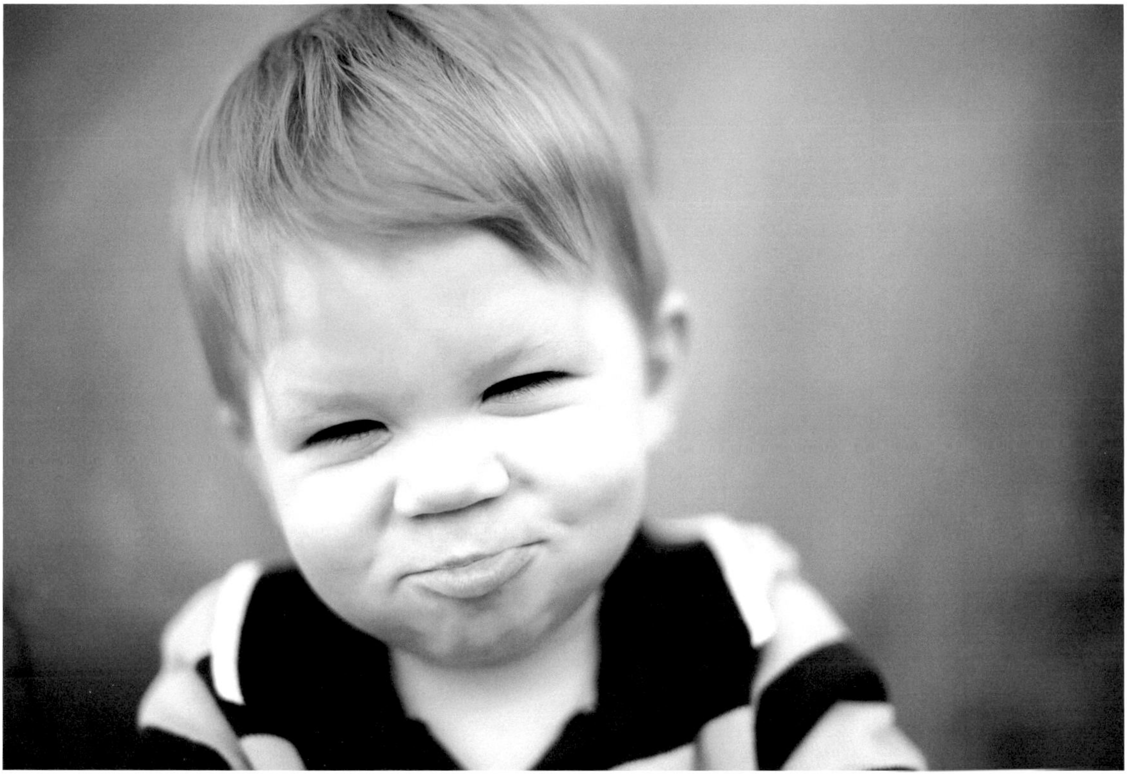

Kara Roberts Photography

Seattle, WA

kararoberts.com

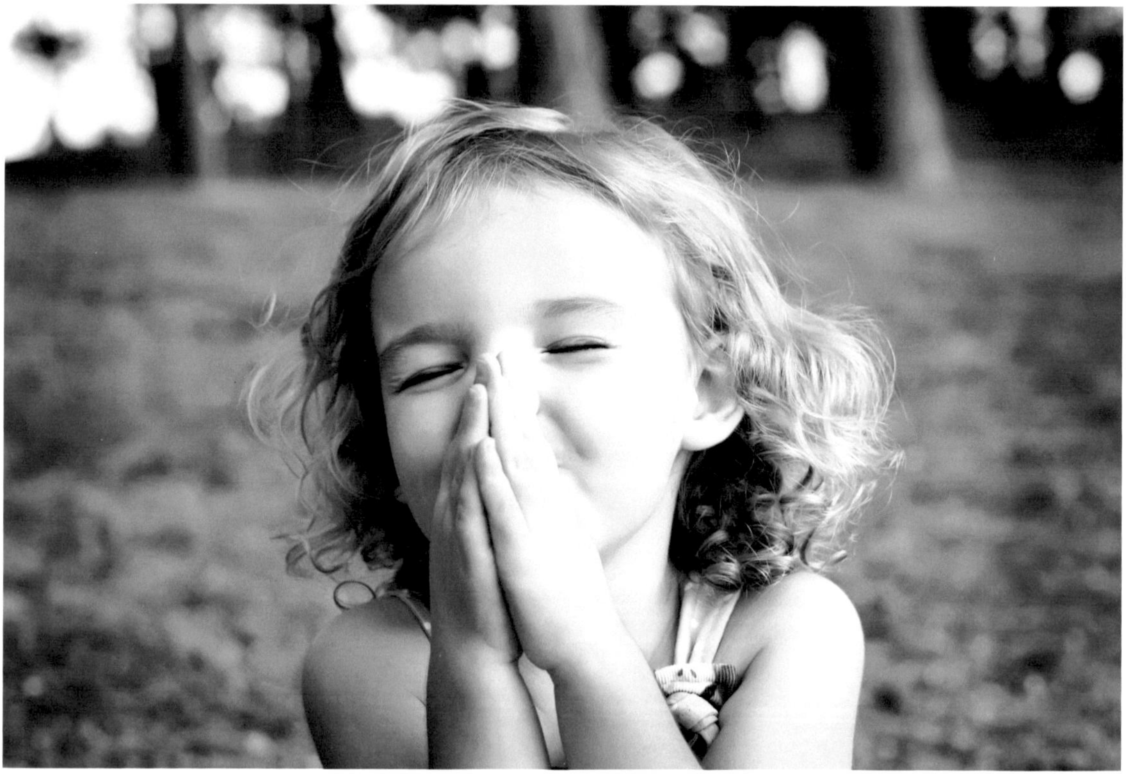

Jody McKitrick Photography

Washington, DC

jodymphotography.com

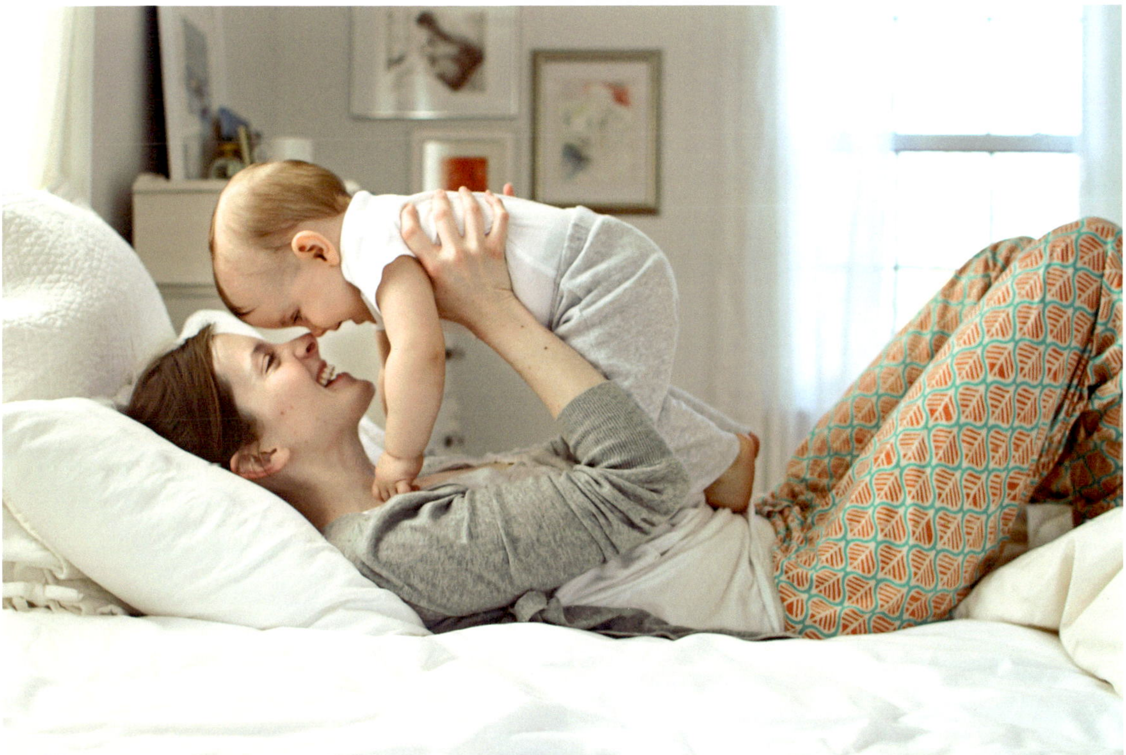

Kendra Watson Photography

Murrieta, CA

kendrawatsonphotography.com

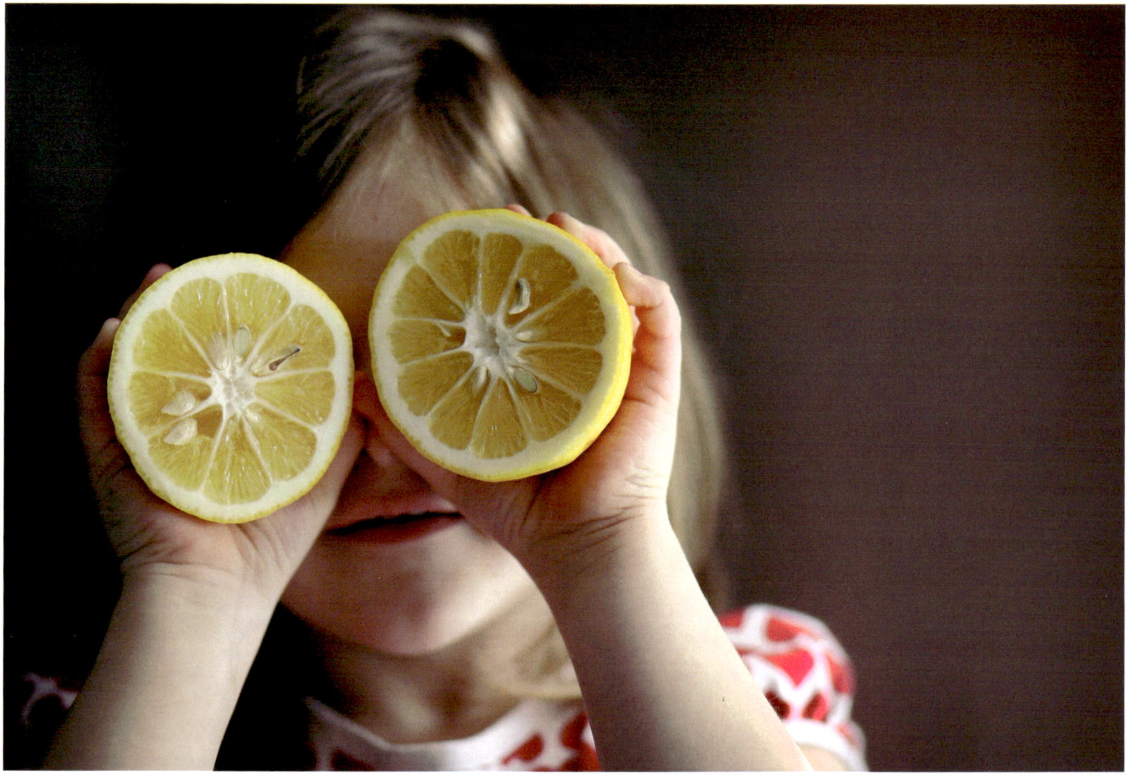

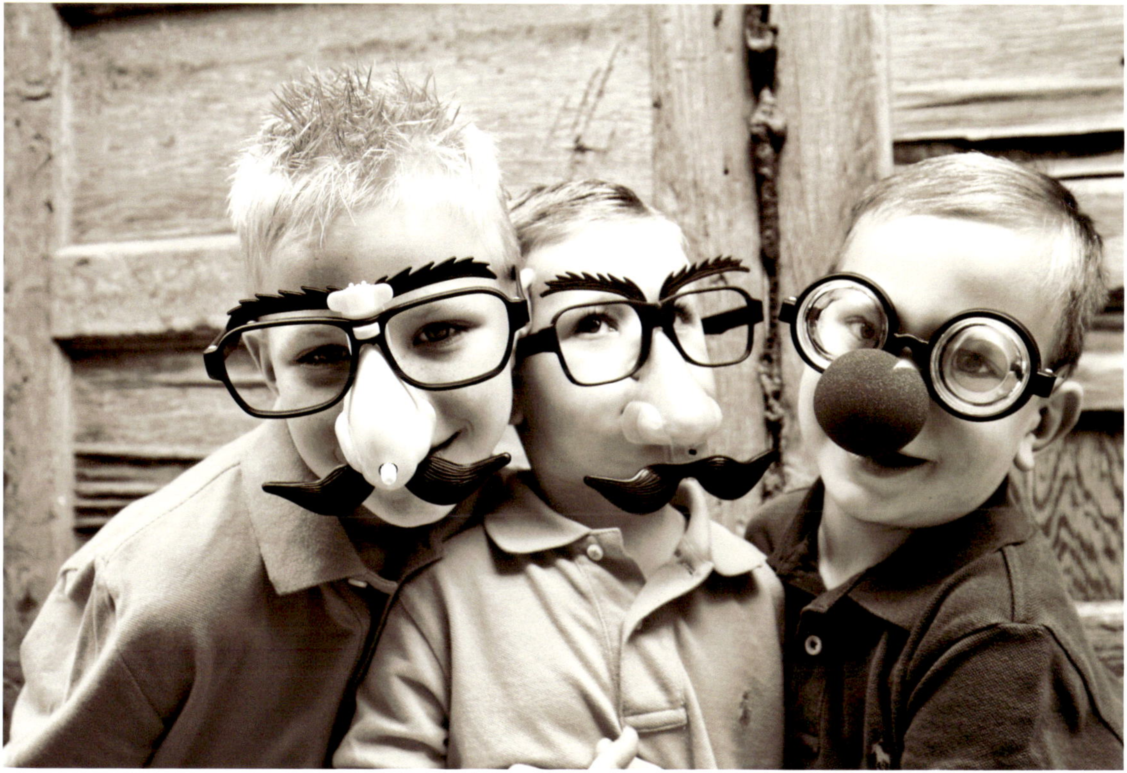

Stephanie Wilson Photography

Waxahachie, TX

stephaniewilsonphotography.blogspot.com

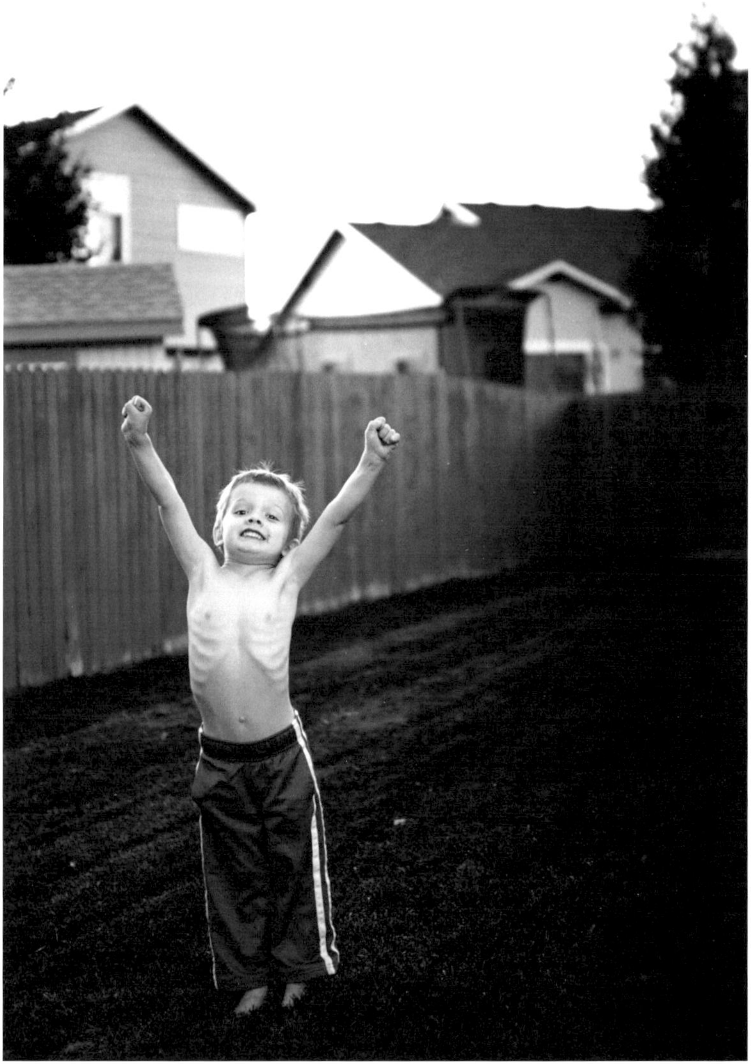

Sarah Wilkerson

Colorado Springs, CO

sarahwilkerson.com

Bre Thurston Photography

Riverside, CA

brethurston.com

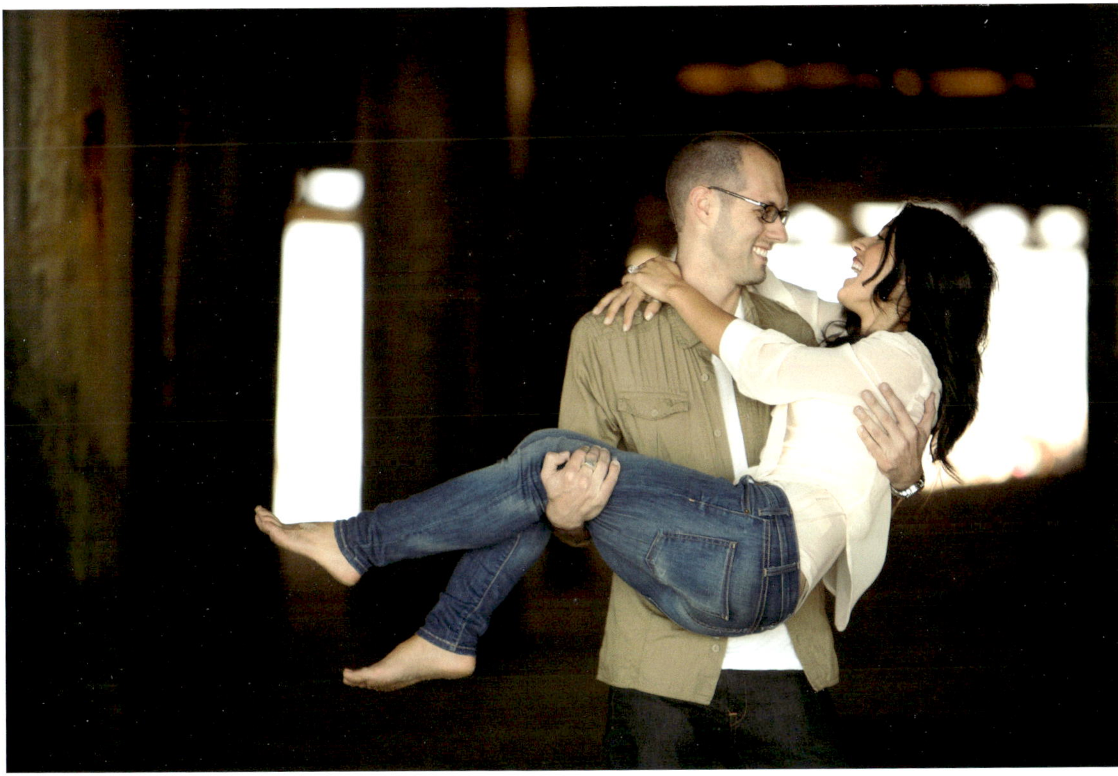

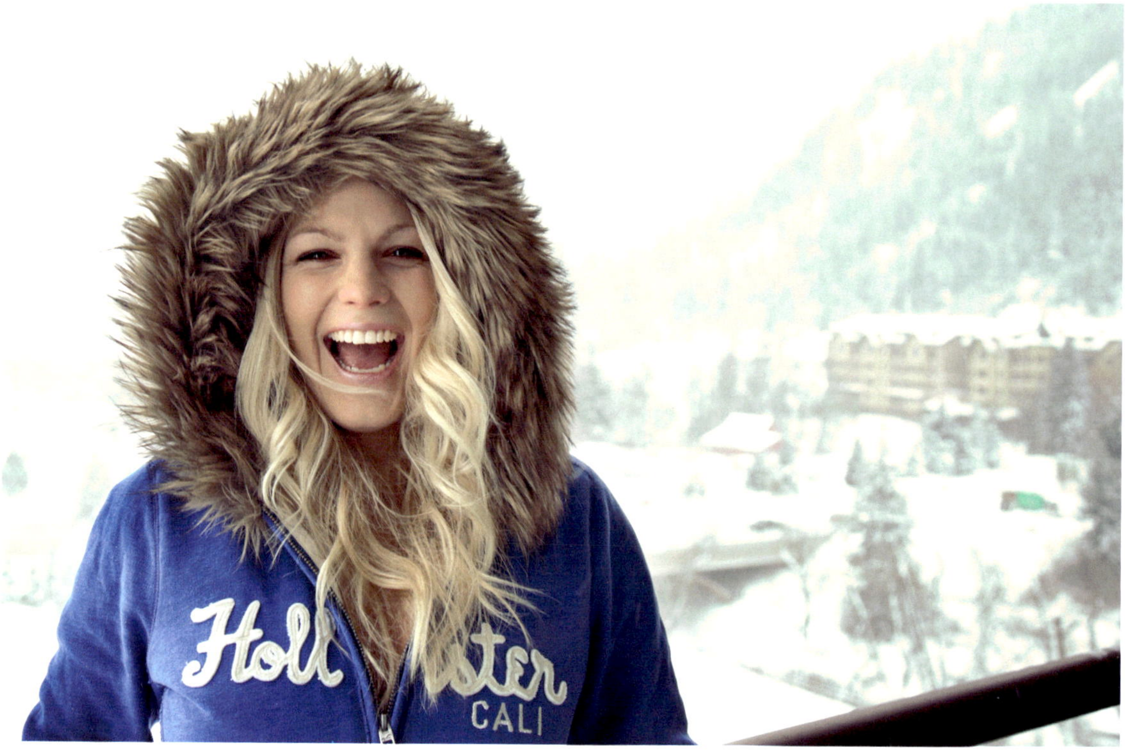

Romana Wyllie Photography

Prague, Czech Republic

romanawyllie.com

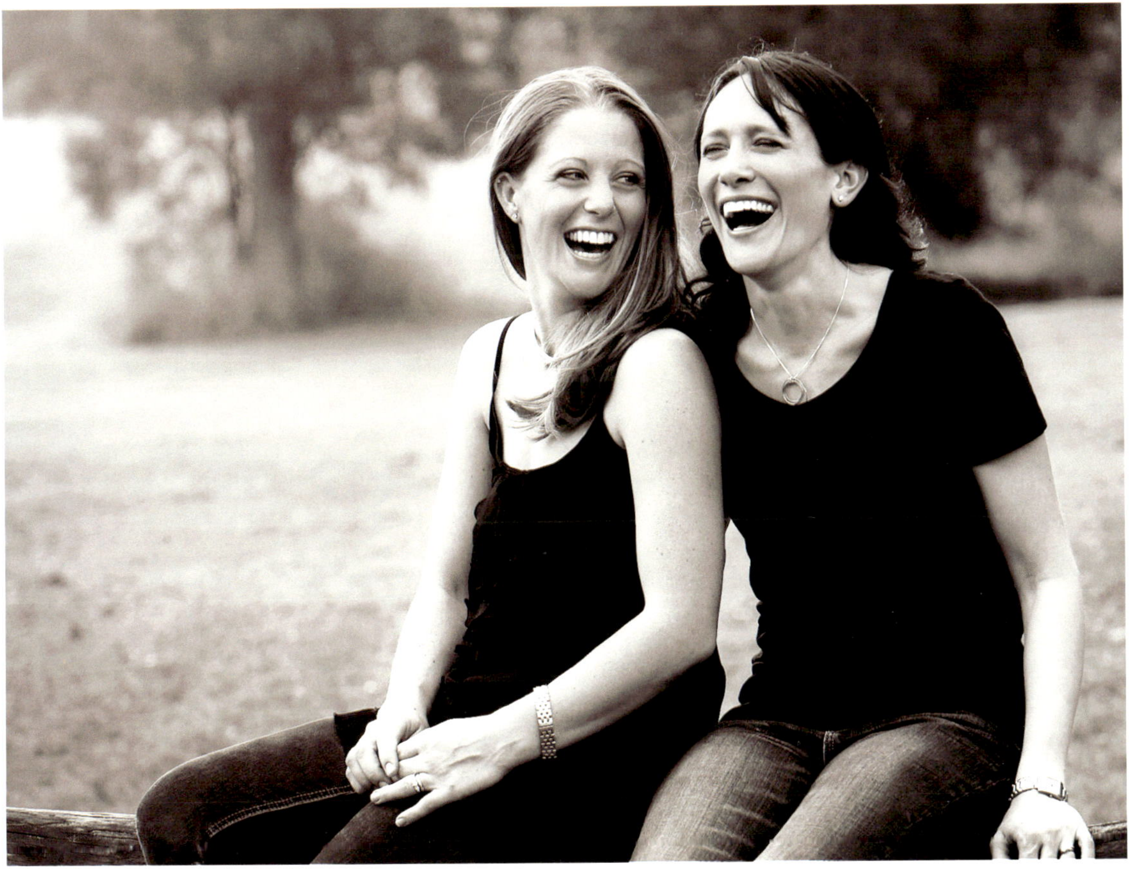

Emma Wood

9woods.blogspot.com

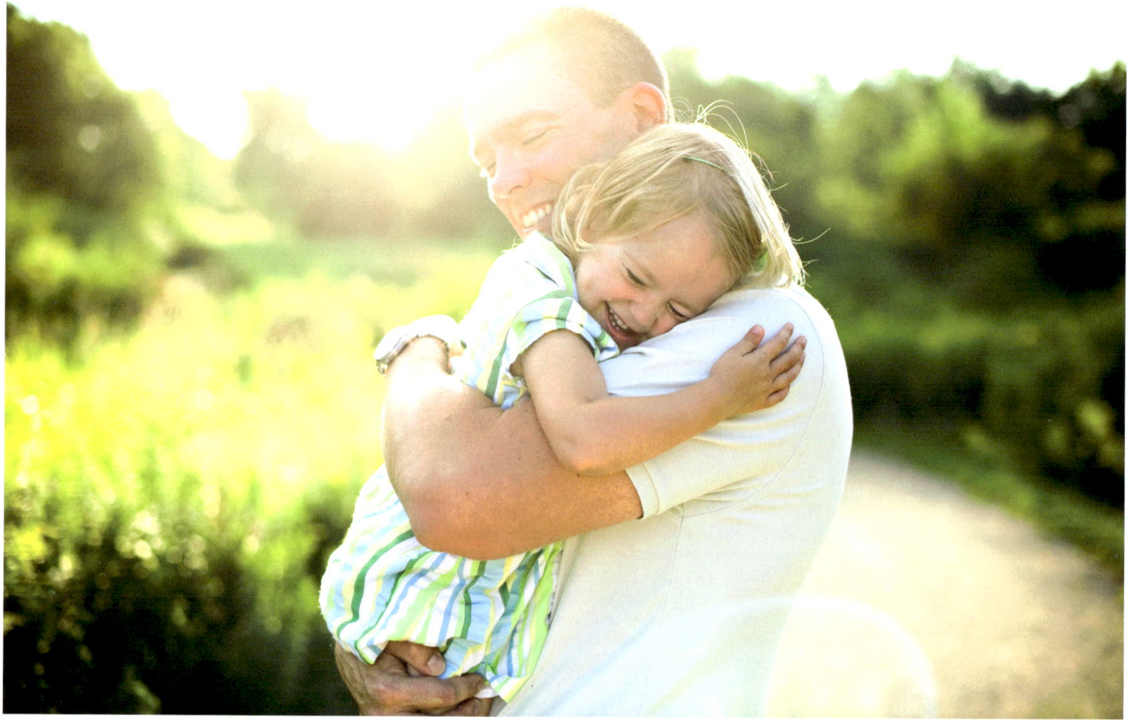

One for the Wall photography

Waterloo, ON Canada

onefor thewall.ca

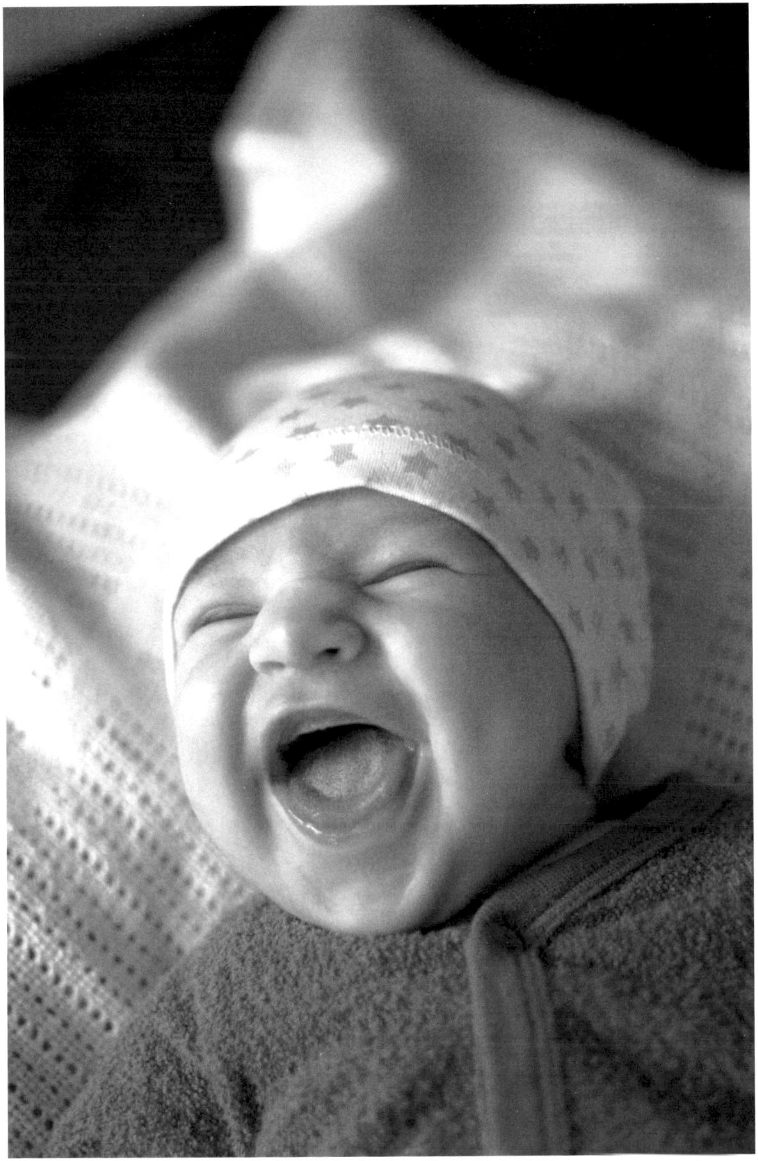

Sarah Jay Overland - Sarah Jay Inspired

Naracoorte, South Australia

sarahjayinspired.blogspot.com

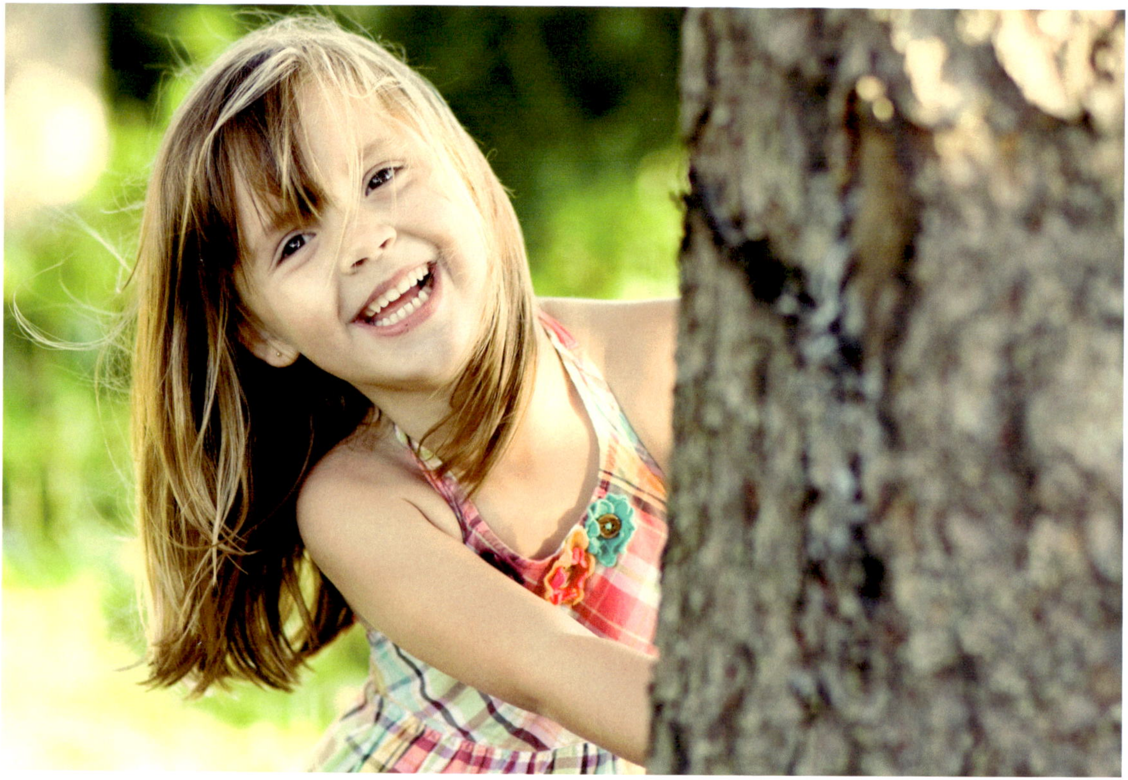

Liz Hayford - Windy Hill Photography

Mid Coast Maine

windyhillphotography.com

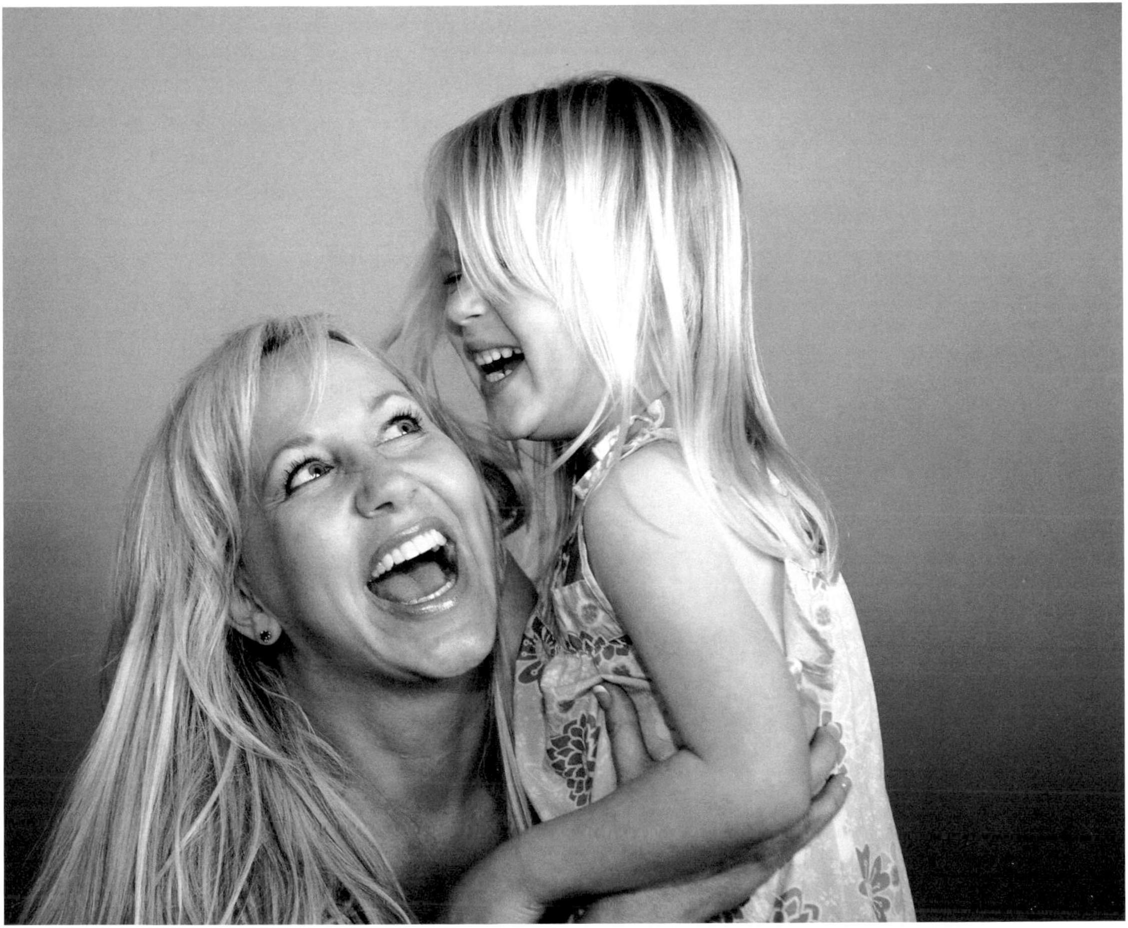

Jessica Cudzilo - 503 Photography

Cincinnati, OH

503photography.com

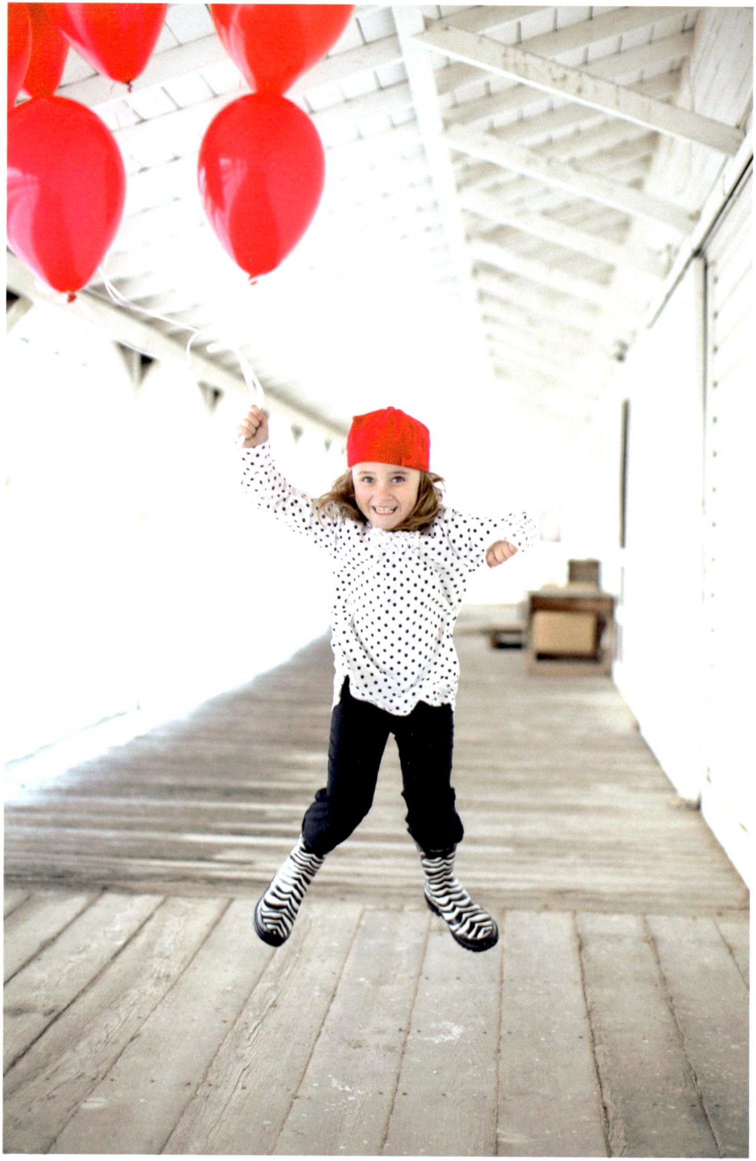

Tamara Kenyon Photography

Boise, ID

tk-foto.com

Summer Weeks Photography

Bahrain

summerweeks.com

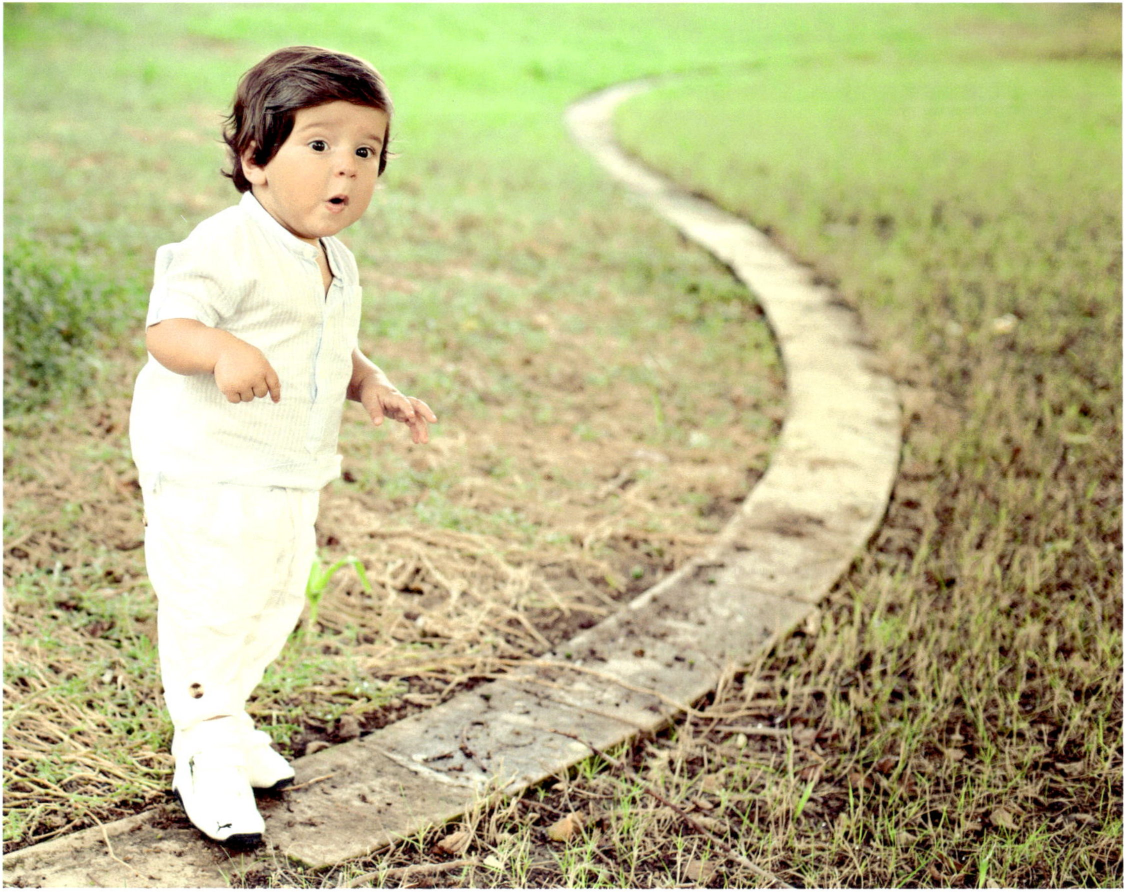

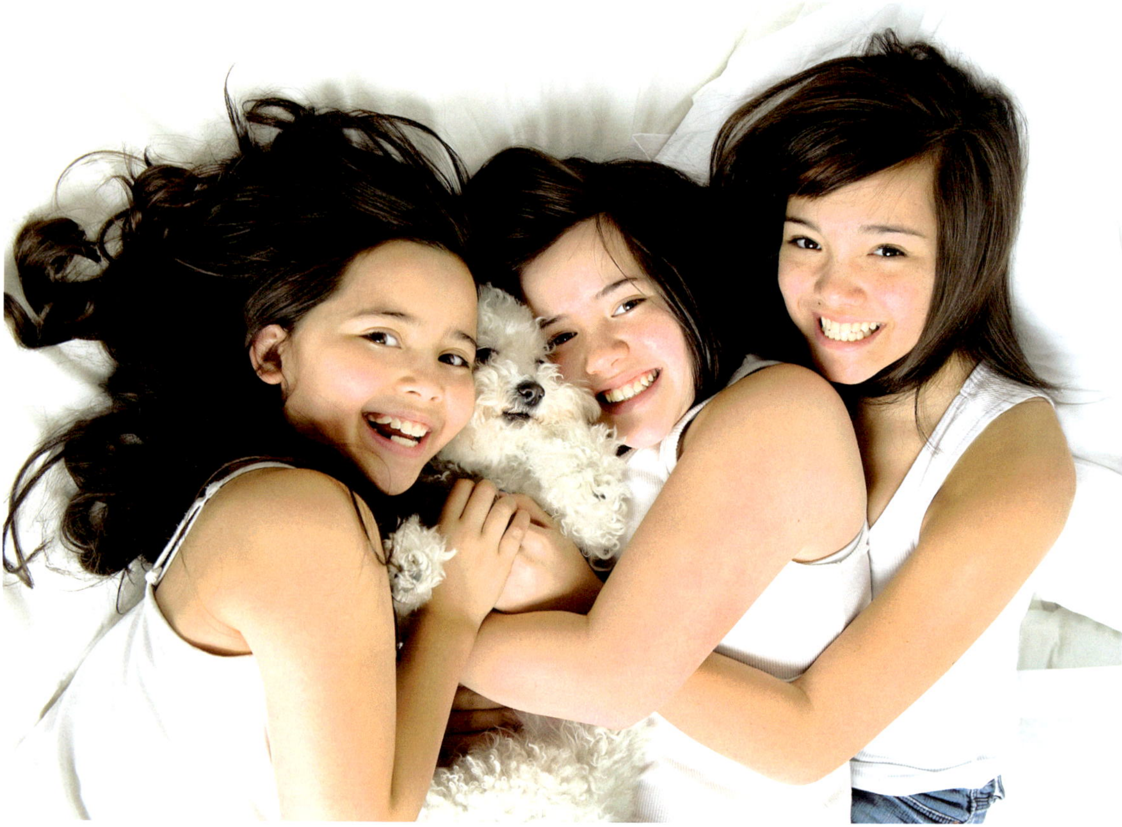

Lillybelle Rose Photography

Glen Ellyn, IL

lillybellerosephotography.com

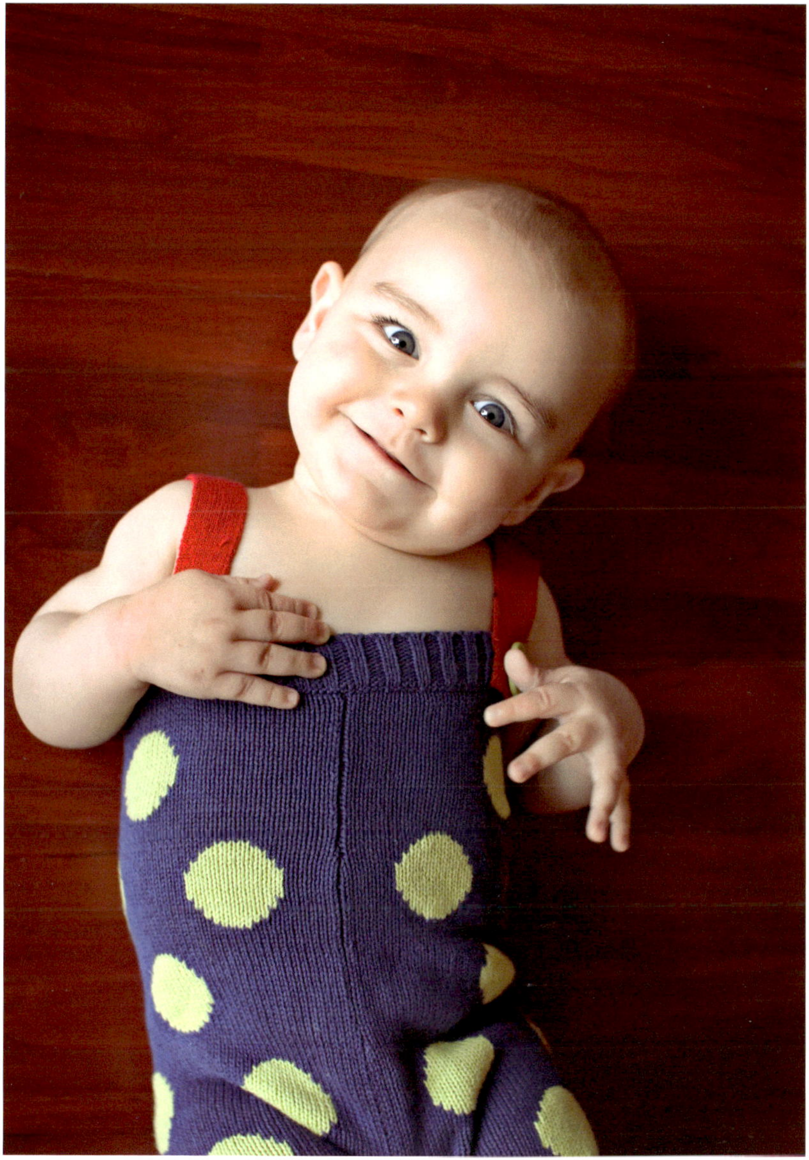

Becky Naffine

Adelaide, South Australia

beckynaffinephotography.com.au

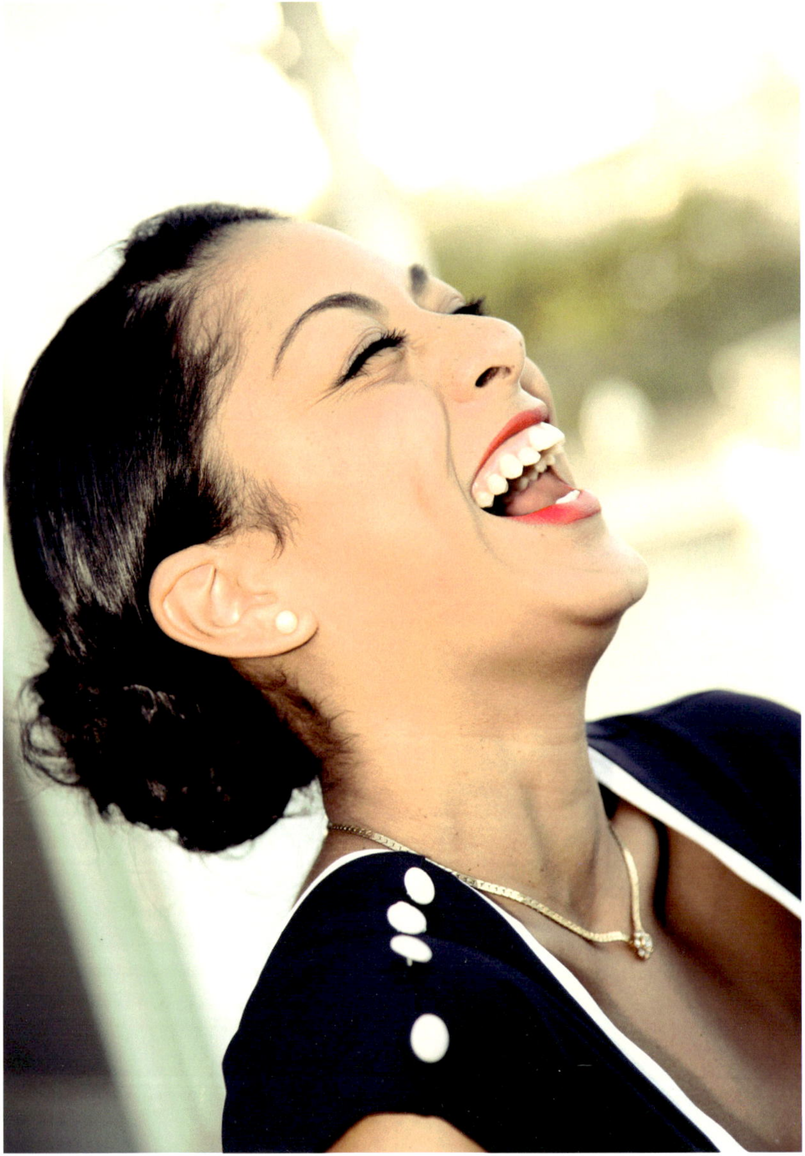

Amy Salessi Photography

Southern CA

amysalessiphotography.com

Marina Pershina

Moscow, Russia

pemavi.livejournal.com

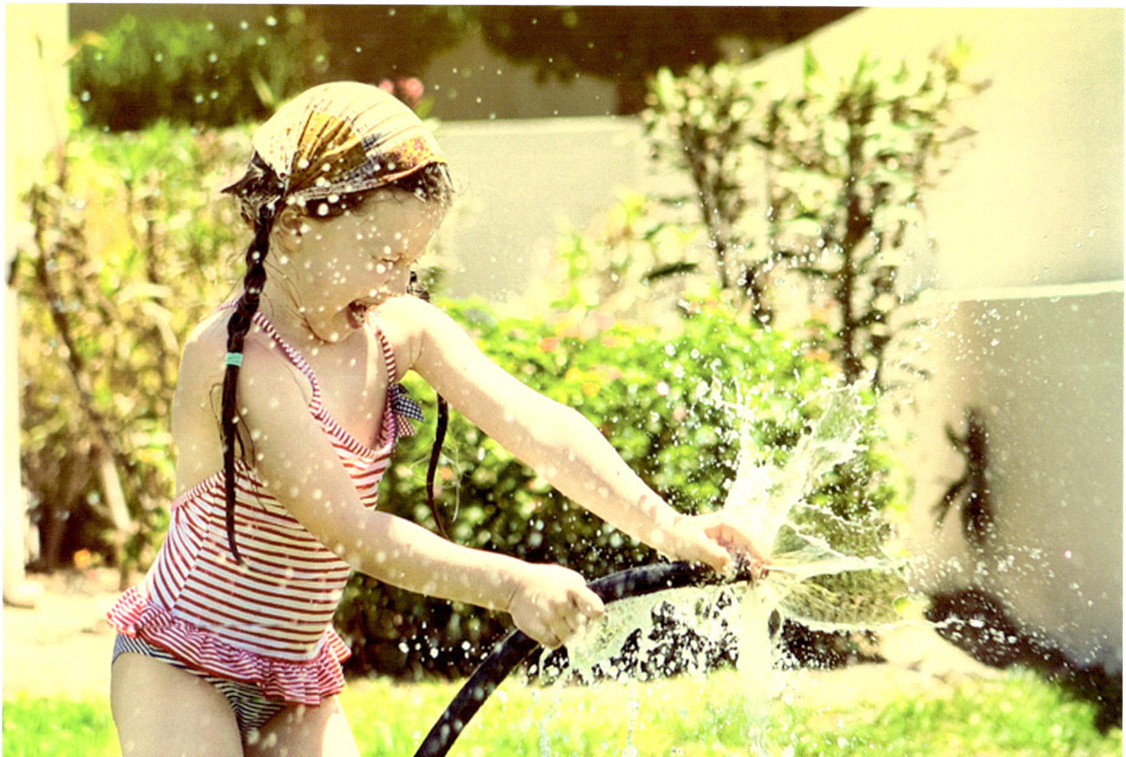

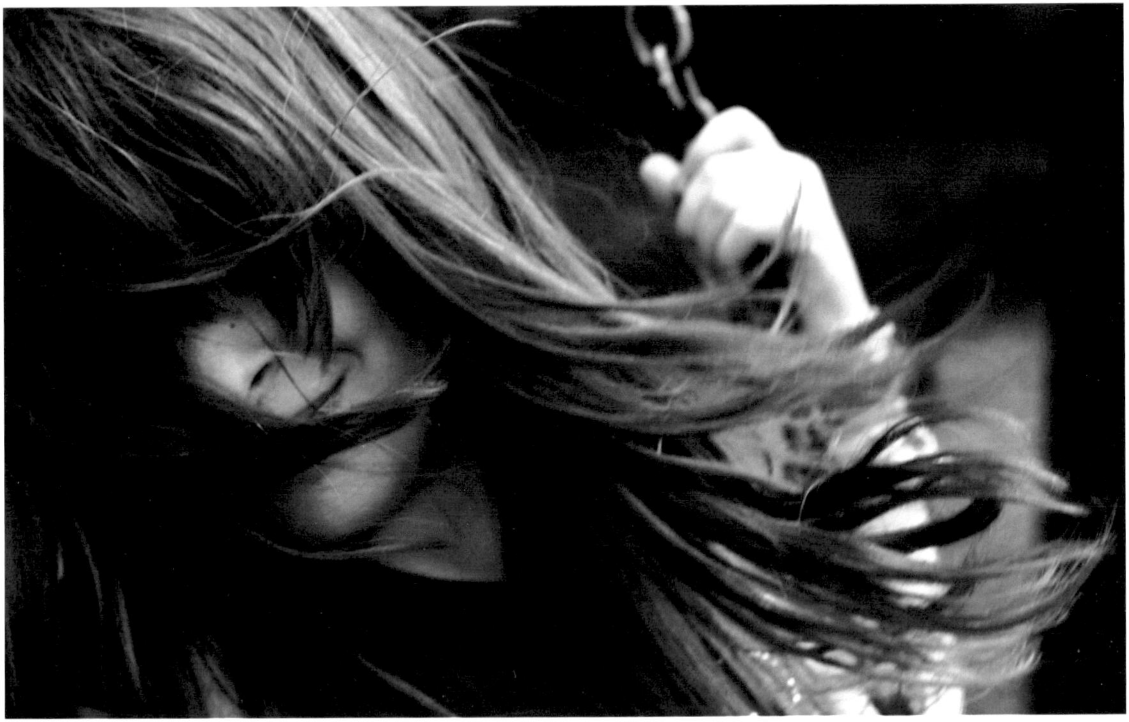

Meg Bitton Photography

Tenafly, NJ

megbitton.com